I DON'T HAVE ENOUGH FAITH TO BE AN ATHEIST

CURRICULUM

FRANK TUREK &
CHUCK WINTER

I Don't Have Enough Faith to Be an Atheist Curriculum

Published by
Apologia Press,
a division of Apologia Educational Ministries, Inc.
1106 Meridian Plaza, Suite 220
Anderson, Indiana 46016
apologia.com

Manufactured in the USA
First Printing: March 2012

ISBN: 978-1-935495-84-0

Cover and Layout: Doug Powell

Printed by Victor Graphics, Inc., Baltimore, MD

CONTENTS

This curriculum is dedicated to my friend Chuck Winter, who graduated to glory too early for those of us left behind. Chuck was the driving force behind this curriculum, having completed his draft a few months before the Lord welcomed him home. Though Chuck is gone, his wisdom remains. For the sake of the Lord and Chuck's wonderful wife, Buff, please learn the truths on these pages and then share them with others. Eternity is at stake.

Frank Turek

March 2012

HOW TO

USE THIS BOOK

The purpose of this study is to help you understand and remember the critical points about Christianity and other worldviews presented in the book *I Don't Have Enough Faith to Be an Atheist.* If you are going to "always be ready to give an answer" for the hope that you have (1 Peter 3:15), then it would be smart for you to understand and memorize the arguments and evidence presented in the book so that you can incorporate them into your daily interactions with others. It is also smart to thoroughly understand the evidence for Christianity—to know why you believe—so that you don't fall victim to the anti-biblical teachings prevalent in the world today.

This curriculum presents supplemental material, study questions, and activities designed to encourage personal reflection and discussion and build writing skills. The answers to most of the study questions can be found rather easily within the text, and sometimes page numbers are supplied to help you out. We recommend you take approximately two to three weeks to read each chapter and complete the accompanying study questions and assignments. You should be able to finish the course in less than nine months.

Each chapter in this study is organized to help you understand and remember the information presented in the book and make it real for your life. Every lesson begins with a heading titled *Before Starting This Chapter*, which lists the pages you'll need to read in *I Don't Have Enough Faith to Be an Atheist* before using the workbook. The *Key Topics* section provides an overview of what you can expect to learn in that chapter, while *Key Terms* lists important vocabulary words introduced in the chapter, with space for you to copy their definitions from the book. There's also a *Road Map* that shows which of "the twelve points that prove Christianity is true" will be covered in the chapter.

At various points in each workbook lesson, you will find profiles of important people or topics mentioned in the book to help you better understand the material.

The main content of each chapter in the workbook is presented in four sections:

HOOK

This section will remind you what the textbook chapter talked about and often includes a few questions to warm up your brain.

This section takes you deeper into the specific issues covered in each chapter, unpacking the topics and testing your knowledge and comprehension with questions from the textbook.

Don't just take the authors' word for it. Check out the information presented in the book for yourself. This section helps you build on your newfound knowledge with research assignments and other suggested activities. Work with your parent/teacher to determine which of these assignments you will undertake for your coursework.

This section summarizes the material and helps you apply the concepts you've studied to your life and witness for Jesus Christ.

I DON'T HAVE ENOUGH FAITH TO BE AN ATHEIST ON DVD

An optional DVD series featuring Frank Turek and based on the original book is also available. Watching these videos is not required for you to complete the course, though they can enhance your study of this material. For more information regarding these videos, visit www.impactapologetics.com.

WHERE CAN YOU FIND THE ANSWERS?

You can find the answers to every question in this study by downloading the answer key available on the Apologia website. This resource is free with the purchase of the *I Don't Have Enough Faith to Be an Atheist Curriculum*. Visit www.apologia.com/bookextras and enter the following password: apologetics. When you hit "enter," you will be taken to the course website.

CHAPTER TESTS

To help you evaluate your understanding of the material and chart your progress, a written test is available for each chapter in the book. These downloadable tests include fill-in-the-blank, multiple choice, true/false, and short answer questions designed to measure how much you've learned. The tests and solutions are free with the purchase of the *I Don't Have Enough Faith to Be an Atheist Curriculum*. Visit www.apologia.com/bookextras and enter the following password: apologetics. When you hit "enter," you will be taken to the course website.

INTRODUCTION

FINDING THE BOX TOP TO THE PUZZLE OF LIFE

BEFORE STARTING THIS CHAPTER

- Read the introduction of *I Don't Have Enough Faith to Be an Atheist* (IDHEF), pages 17–33.

KEY TOPICS

After completing this chapter, you should be able to:

- List the five most consequential questions in life and explain why they are so important.
- Discuss why it is important that God exists.
- Describe three reasons why the world claims that religion cannot answer life's big questions.
- Understand and explain the purpose for the "Twelve Points That Show Christianity Is True."
- Identify the biggest stumbling block that can keep a person from discovering the truth about the big questions of life.
- Explain what it means to be *open-minded* versus *empty-minded.*

KEY TERMS

Write the definitions for these words found in your reading:

Theist

Pantheist

Atheist

Agnostic

QUESTIONS THAT GRAB YOUR MIND

What is the meaning of life? Is there an ultimate purpose to our existence, or is life just a glorified *Monopoly* game in which the object is to get as much stuff as you can now because when the game is over it's all going back in the box?

One preacher put it like this: "One day, you are going to die. Then your family and friends are going to dress you up, put you in a box, lower you into a hole, throw dirt in your face, and then go back to the church and eat potato salad!" Is that it? After years of building a life and developing deep, loving relationships, does the consciousness that is you evaporate when you take your last breath? You simply return to dust?

Real, ultimate, unchanging meaning depends on a real, ultimate, unchanging *being*—God. If there is no God, then there is no ultimate purpose to life. We are just molecules in motion: We live for a short time and then cease to exist.

Even atheist Richard Dawkins admits there is no meaning to life without God. He writes, "Nature is not cruel, only pitilessly indifferent. This is one of the hardest lessons for humans to learn. We cannot admit that things might be neither good nor evil, neither cruel nor kind, but simply callous—indifferent to all suffering, lacking all purpose."

Is there a God? Is there a real purpose to life? Will we live on after we die or simply cease to exist? These are just a few of the questions we will explore during this study.

1. ***Based on the information you've read and seen so far, how would you define the meaning of life?***

2. ***Without God, does life have any ultimate meaning? Why or why not?***

SO WHAT?

One of the most relevant and important subjects you can ever investigate is eternity. Why? Because you're going to be dead a lot longer than you're going to be alive! If we exist forever on the other side of the grave, and if our choices on *this* side determine how we spend eternity, then it's vitally important for us to investigate these questions here on earth.

So how do we explore the question of eternity? Well, it begins with the question of truth. Some say there is no absolute truth, that everything is just a matter of opinion. As we will see in the next lesson, the assertion that there is no absolute truth logically contradicts itself. After all, if there is no truth, then not even atheism can be true.

I Don't Have Enough Faith to Be an Atheist begins with the basic question of whether truth exists and, using logic and evidence, arrives at the conclusion that the Bible is true. If this line of reasoning is correct (and be sure you examine the evidence for yourself—don't just take the authors' word for it), then the truth is that you will live for eternity. This gives everything you do today an eternal meaning. There can't be anything more important than that!

THE FIVE MOST CONSEQUENTIAL QUESTIONS IN LIFE

In college, Dr. Turek was exploring the question of whether God exists, but his university professor couldn't even give him a basic framework that could provide answers to life's biggest questions. That's what a worldview does: It's like the box top to a jigsaw puzzle; a worldview shows you how the pieces of life fit together. The true worldview shows you the true answers to life's biggest questions.

Unfortunately, the most important question to humanity—*Does God exist?*—didn't receive much serious thought at Dr. Turek's university. Since the default worldview of most university professors is atheism, classes are taught with the assumption that there is no God. But any worldview, including atheism, has to provide satisfactory answers for life's biggest questions.

3. ***Think about Dr. Turek's story about his religion professor. Have you ever been in a situation where someone mocked or questioned the veracity of the Bible? What did you say or do?***

4. ***What do you think is the best answer to each of these five questions?***

Where did we come from?

Who are we?

Why are we here?

CARL SAGAN

Born in 1934, Carl Sagan was a well-known astronomer and cosmologist. By the time he died in 1996, he had published more than six hundred scientific papers. But he was best known for writing best-selling books about science and for appearing on popular television programs to expound on the wonders of the universe.

As a child growing up in a Jewish home, Sagan was inquisitive. Although his mother believed in God and was active in synagogue, she taught him to be skeptical, to question and analyze the world around him. His father, on the other hand, was a quiet man who instilled in his son a sense of wonder, encouraging him to explore and discover new things. Young Carl enjoyed reading science fiction and spent as much time as he could at the library and museums, trying to figure out how the world worked.

Sagan attended the University of Chicago and earned several degrees, including a PhD in astronomy and astrophysics in 1960. He lectured and conducted research at Harvard before taking a position as a professor of astronomy at Cornell, where he served as associate director for the Center for Radio Physics and Space Research. From the time he was still in college, he worked as an advisor to NASA. Among his duties was briefing the Apollo astronauts and developing experiments they would conduct in outer space. He

Photo: NASA.

How should we live?

Where are we going?

later was active in the search for extraterrestrial life and promoted SETI—the Search for Extra-Terrestrial Intelligence—a scientific organization that listens to radio noise from space for signs of intelligent life.

Because of his passion for scientific discovery, Sagan wanted to popularize science so that many more people would become interested in the search for the truth about the universe. He wrote several books, including *Cosmos*, a companion to his thirteen-part television series for PBS. Both the book and the television series were huge successes. Cosmos became the best-selling science book ever published in English, and the 1980 television series has been seen by more than 500 million people around the world. Sagan also received a Pulitzer Prize for *The Dragons of Eden: Speculations on the Evolution of Human Intelligence*. His science fiction novel *Contact* was made into a movie starring Jodie Foster in 1997, a year after his death.

Religiously, Sagan believed that the notion of God as "an oversized white male with a flowing beard who sits in the sky and tallies the fall of every sparrow" was "ludicrous." Instead, he subscribed to the idea of God as "the set of physical laws that govern the universe." Sagan claimed to be an agnostic, saying, "An atheist has to know a lot more than I know. An atheist is someone who knows there is no god. By some definitions atheism is very stupid." Yet he implied atheism by declaring that, "The Cosmos is all that is or ever was or ever will be." Sagan was a strong promoter of skepticism, a method of reasoning that questions everything until proven conclusively by science and logic. One of his famous quotes, from the *Cosmos* television program, was that "extraordinary claims require extraordinary evidence." (Dr. Turek and Dr. Geisler discuss this concept in an upcoming chapter.)

Carl Sagan was an influential force in the scientific community during his lifetime, winning numerous scientific awards and contributing personally to the study of planetary atmospheres and exobiology, the study of the effects of extraterrestrial environments on living things. Yet his skeptical, naturalistic view of the world blinded him to the existence of a personal God.

BOOK

IS IT IMPORTANT THAT GOD EXISTS?

It's one thing to pose questions and state your own opinions. It's another thing entirely to answer them with verifiable truth. Where do you go to find answers to life's most important questions? On what sources do people most often rely as authoritative?

This is one of the key topics we will deal with as we proceed through this study. If God doesn't exist, then we'll have problems answering just the first question, about where we came from, let alone questions about our purpose on earth and our eternal destiny.

5. State three reasons why it is important that God exists (see IDHEF, page 20).

FACTS IN THIS CHAPTER

Throughout this study, you will be challenged to thoroughly learn the evidence and arguments for Christianity. The introduction to *I Don't Have Enough Faith to Be an Atheist* poses life's big questions and discusses how many people attempt to answer them. The introduction also introduces the major religious worldviews and defines what the authors mean by "faith." All worldviews, they say, including atheism, require a certain amount of faith.

Many people refuse to become Christians not because of a lack of evidence (intellectual reasons), but for emotional or volitional reasons. While evidence is critically important to many people, others simply don't want Christianity to be true and will reject it despite any evidence, no matter how strong. They simply don't want to give up their autonomy and submit to the lordship of Christ. Do you have friends or family members like that, people who wouldn't believe even if you could provide conclusive evidence to them?

Given the amount of evidence supporting Christianity in the book (if there wasn't so much hard evidence, the book would be a lot shorter!), for many people the decision to reject Christ is not a matter of the mind but of the will. In other words, there's a difference between proof and persuasion. You may be able to prove beyond a reasonable doubt that the Bible is true, but that doesn't mean someone is going to be persuaded by it. Evidence can only give a person reasons to believe that Christ is God. But it can't force anyone to accept the evidence and put his trust in Christ.

When the Bible talks about "faith," it usually refers to putting trust in something or someone based on evidence. However, in the title *I Don't Have Enough Faith to Be an Atheist*, the word "faith" is used in a modern sense, meaning belief without evidence or belief in spite of evidence. This modern definition is most often used by atheists to accuse Christians of blindly adhering to the Bible. Yet, as we shall see, the truth is, atheists are the ones who have an unsupported faith because they are ignoring the evidence!

Statue of C.S. Lewis: Ross Wilson. Photo: Genvessel (cc-by-2.0).

C.S. LEWIS

Born in Belfast, Ireland, in 1898, Clive Staples Lewis—who as a boy insisted his family call him Jack—grew up with a love of books. His family home was filled with books of all kinds, stacked wherever there was space. He read voraciously and even tried his hand at writing poetry and fiction as a boy.

But his idyllic childhood did not last, for Jack's mother died of cancer in 1908, and he was sent away to a series of boarding schools. At age fifteen, angry over the loss of his mother and influenced by secular teachers, Jack renounced the Protestant faith in which he had been raised and became an atheist. He later described his young self as being paradoxically "very angry with God for not existing."

This atheistic viewpoint was strengthened by his association with his private tutor, William T. Kirkpatrick, who exposed Lewis to a wide variety of classical literature. He even insisted that Lewis learn Greek so he could enjoy the classics in their original language. Kirkpatrick's tutelage sharpened young Jack's mind helping Lewis earn a scholarship to Oxford University in 1917.

Except for a year spent fighting in World War I, Lewis spent much of the rest of his life in Oxford. (Even in later years, when he was working in Cambridge as a professor of medieval and renaissance English, Lewis would always travel back home to Oxford on weekends.) He earned high honors as a student, and he went on to teach as a fellow at Magdalen College, Oxford, where he remained for nearly thirty years.

Over the next few years, Lewis came under the influence of a series of Christian thinkers, including his colleague and friend J. R. R. Tolkien. He slowly embraced Christianity, and in 1931, Lewis committed his life to Christ. This change of faith sparked a radical transformation. He began writing and lecturing as an apologist. With a sharp mind and keen grasp of logic, he proved a formidable advocate for Christianity. Lewis lectured throughout England and was often featured on radio broadcasts. Most notably, Lewis wrote a number of classic books, including *Mere Christianity, The Screwtape Letters*, and *The Chronicles of Narnia*. (If you're a Christian and have not read *Mere Christianity*, consider YOUR education incomplete!)

Near the end of his life, Lewis met Joy Gresham, an American divorcee with two teenage sons. Although at first attracted only to her intellect, Lewis soon fell in love, and they were married in 1956. Four happy years later, Joy died of cancer. Lewis followed her three years later, passing away on November 22, 1963, the same day President John F. Kennedy was assassinated.

Regarded as perhaps the most influential Christian apologist of his day, C. S. Lewis continues to impact skeptics and Christians alike.

Throughout this study, empirical, forensic, and philosophical evidence will be used to show that Christianity is the most reasonable worldview—the one that requires the least amount of faith. Studying that evidence should deepen your understanding of God, provide you with an even greater desire to trust Him, and equip you to represent Him to a lost and dying world.

6. ***Name three common reasons the world gives for its claim that religion does not hold the answers to life (see IDHEF, pages 20–22).***

7. ***Using the painter/painting analogy as it applies to God and creation, how would you describe what the following people believe about God's relationship to the world (see IDHEF, pages 22–23)?***

   Theist

   Pantheist

   Atheist

8. ***Name three kinds of objections that cause many people to doubt Christianity can be true (see IDHEF, pages 24–25).***

9. The "Twelve Points that Show Christianity is True" form the outline for this course. List these twelve points below (see IDHEF, pages 28).

YOU DO THE DIGGING

It's really quite sobering to realize we have the power to make our own decisions regarding our destiny, and this makes the big questions of life even more important. Without answers to the five most consequential questions, we can't have a clear picture about what is at stake in life. We must answer these questions in order to fully understand our purpose and destiny.

As you will see in this study, the answers to life's biggest questions are best explained by Christianity. Unlike other religions, the truth claims of Christianity can be evaluated through scientific and historical investigation.

Now it's time to for you to do some digging on your own. Choose at least one of the following assignments and complete it before moving on in the workbook:

Assignment 1: Interview two friends or relatives who are not Christians by asking them for their answers to the five most consequential questions in life. (Make sure you approach the discussion as an objective school project rather than as a religious debate.) Have them support their answers by asking questions like *How did you come to that conclusion?* and *What evidence do you have to support your answers?* Ask them, "If Christianity were true, would you become a Christian?" to find out whether their objections to Christianity are intellectual, emotional, or volitional. Record what you discover about their beliefs in a two-page report.

Assignment 2: Search newspapers, the Internet, magazines, and TV reports to collect current examples of people discussing any of the five most consequential questions. Do they believe truth can be known? What sources do they turn to as a foundation for their answers? What evidence do they have to back up their answers? Can you detect any holes in their reasoning? Pick one or two articles or reports and write a mock letter to each commentator, pointing out any faulty reasoning or incorrect assumptions. Be sure to keep a friendly tone, rather than being confrontational, so that you are speaking the truth "in love" (Ephesians 4:15).

Assignment 3: Find an online article by a current writer or philosopher who supports one of the three non-theistic religious views defined in the introduction—pantheism, atheism, or agnosticism. Write a two-page paper critiquing the arguments used by the author to support his beliefs.

WHAT DO I DO NOW?

Knowing the answers to life's biggest questions provides you a solid foundation for your entire life, influencing how you will think, act, speak, and make choices. Unfortunately, many people never take the time to think about these questions or search out the truth; they just piece together answers from what they have seen or heard from other people. Their worldview is actually very *impersonal*—just a collection of random opinions and ideas from others. They don't really know where their beliefs come from, what assumptions they are based on, or if they are in fact really true. It's as if they are at a spiritual buffet—they just pick out whatever looks good or feels right or allows them to live the way they want to.

Often a person's worldview is simply cobbled together from slogans heard in society, like *All truth is relative* or *Science disproves God* or *The Bible is full of errors.* If you ask people how they reached their conclusions about life's biggest questions, most of the time you'll get a blank stare or some appeal to authority rather than any real evidence. Many people can't give you concrete facts because they haven't thought their beliefs through.

So that means that you're already ahead of most people. You are taking the time to study *why* you believe what you believe and whether your beliefs are based on solid evidence. Get ready, though—many people will challenge you along the way. You'll also need to dig deep and study the scientific facts, historical evidence, and logical reasoning behind Christianity. We think you'll ultimately see that the Christian "Box Top" best shows how all the pieces of life fit together and that Christianity provides true answers to the critically important questions of life.

The best way to put these answers into practice is to talk with friends and family members about what you've learned. If you know the why behind your beliefs, not only will you be more confident in the truth of your worldview, but you will also be better equipped to answer the questions of others, helping them think through their worldviews, too.

THINKING ABOUT WHAT YOU LEARNED

Answer the following questions to sum up what you have learned in this chapter.

A. *In their discussion of the Twelve Points, do the authors expect you to just take their word for it that these points are true? Why or why not?*

B. *Why do the authors begin their line of reasoning by proving that truth exists and is knowable?*

C. *Why do the authors state that if the Bible is true, it proves other religions are false where they differ from the Bible? Isn't that an arrogant claim to make?*

D. Give several reasons why Christians should live their lives based on truth, and back up your reasons with Scripture verses.

E. Explain the difference between ***proving*** *a proposition and* ***persuading*** *someone to accept a proposition. Why is evidence not always enough to persuade someone?*

F. Humans have a tendency to adjust the truth to fit their desires rather than adjusting their desires to fit the truth. In Romans 1:18–32, Paul says we "suppress the truth" so we can practice unrighteousness. Give at least three real-life examples of people changing truth rather than changing their desires. These could be people you know (maybe even yourself) or someone you have heard or read about.

G. "Open-mindedness" is a popular sentiment in today's society, but it can easily be an excuse for "empty-mindedness." What is the difference between the two? Name three problems with this kind of thinking.

DON'T FORGET!

What we believe about God affects every area of our lives. It is the critical element to finding the Box Top to the puzzle of life, so that we can understand the true meaning of our time on earth. But not every human being will respond to God. And because God is love, He will not force people into heaven against their will. He has given everyone the freedom to choose his or her destiny. So while some will trust in Christ because you have given evidence that Christianity is true, others will still choose to reject the evidence and God Himself. (You can't bring everyone to Christ, but you can bring Christ to everyone.) Continue to love and pray for these people that in time their hearts will soften to the leading of the Holy Spirit and that they would accept the gospel—the "good news"! In the meantime, use the principles you learn in this study to strengthen your own relationship with Christ and influence the decisions you make every day.

BEFORE STARTING THIS CHAPTER

- Read chapter 1 of *I Don't Have Enough Faith to Be an Atheist* (IDHEF), pages 35–50.

ROAD MAP OF THE "TWELVE POINTS THAT PROVE CHRISTIANITY IS TRUE"

This chapter covers the following points:

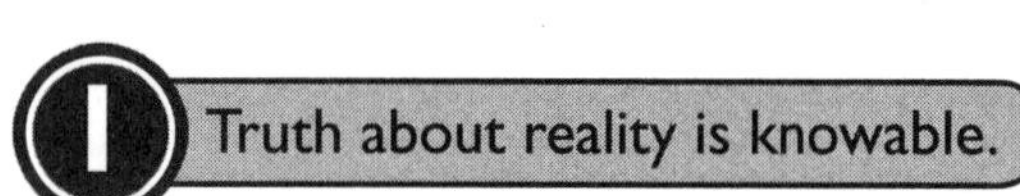

1
Truth about reality is knowable.

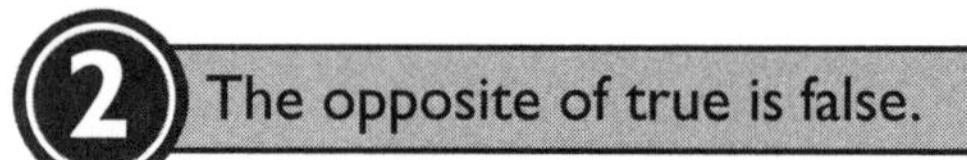

2
The opposite of true is false.

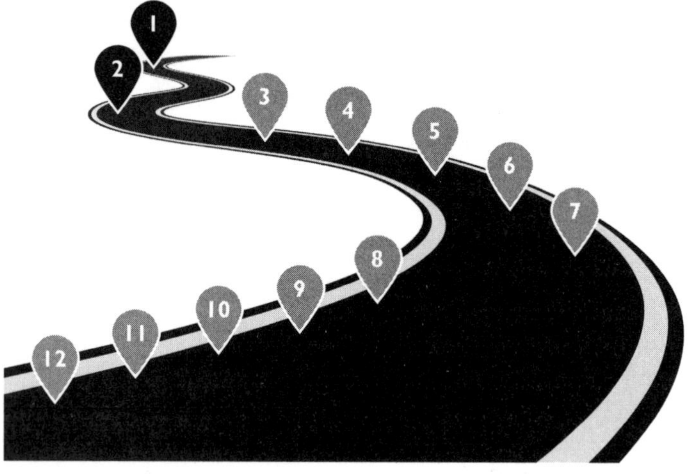

KEY TOPICS

After completing this chapter, you should be able to:

- Explain why knowing the truth is important.
- Define *truth*.
- List seven truths about truth.
- Recognize self-defeating statements.
- Describe the Road Runner tactic and explain how to expose self-defeating statements with it.
- Answer the question *Can all religions be true?* and defend your answer.

KEY TERMS

Write the definitions for these words found in your reading:

Absolute

Self-defeating statement

Skeptic

Pluralism

Tolerance (give both the original and modern definitions)

Truth (give all three definitions from pages 36–37)

QUESTIONS THAT GRAB YOUR MIND

Humans are truth seekers, but sometimes truth can be hard to find. People spend thousands of hours in courtrooms every year trying to uncover the truth. We listen to TV and radio advertisements, read articles on the Internet, and hear government leaders telling us that what they are saying is the truth. All too often we find out later that what we saw, heard, or read was not really the truth at all.

So why is truth so important to people? Why do we seek out mechanics and computer technicians we can trust? Why do we hate hearing lies from politicians? Why do we want our doctors to tell us the truth about our health, or our pharmacists to be truthful about the side effects of our medications? Why do we expect the bank to tell us the truth about our money? Why do we want our family and friends to be truthful with us? It's because knowing what is true and what is false impacts every area of our lives!

Unfortunately, while people say they want to know the truth about their health and money, they often deny or suppress the truth about morality and religion—issues that call them to change their behavior. Augustine said, "We love the truth when it enlightens us, but we hate it when it convicts us." The apostle Paul makes this point in Romans 1:18–32, especially when he writes "men suppress the truth by their wickedness." In other words, people suppress the truth so that they can feel free to do what they want.

So while people are truth seekers, we are often also truth suppressors as well. Are you a truth seeker or a truth suppressor? Do you *really* want to know the truth? Can you handle it?

1. Can you think of any areas in your life where you aren't as careful as you should be about discovering the truth? Explain.

2. Why is it dangerous to live your life based on half-truths or unverified assumptions?

SO WHAT?

Finding the answers to the biggest questions in life depends on knowing the truth: *Where did we come from? How did this universe and everything in it get here? What happens when our lives on earth are over?* If you have wrong ideas about truth, then you have wrong ideas about life too. If you live your life based on faulty ideas or assumptions, then you can seriously hurt yourself and others. That's because there really are moral standards and laws in the universe which, if broken, have harmful or even fatal consequences. Such truths are absolute—that is, unchanging throughout history—and knowable. These moral standards are not dependent on our opinions, feelings, or preferences.

So knowing the truth is important to us. However, some people are quick to say there is no real truth when it comes to areas of life such as morals or religion. We do this at our own peril.

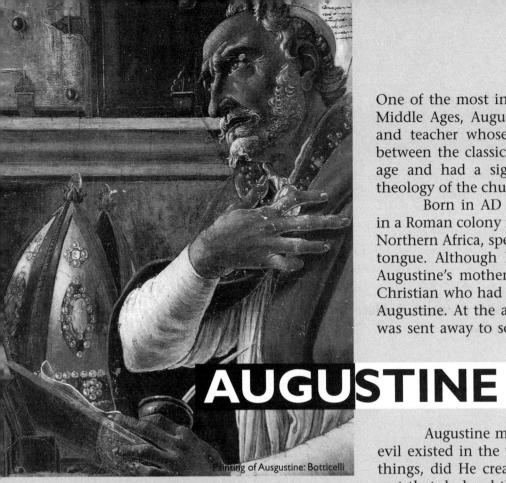

Painting of Ausgustine: Botticelli

AUGUSTINE

One of the most influential thinkers of the Middle Ages, Augustine was a philosopher and teacher whose ideas bridged the gap between the classical age and the medieval age and had a significant impact on the theology of the church.

Born in AD 354, Augustine grew up in a Roman colony in what is now Algeria in Northern Africa, speaking Latin as his native tongue. Although his father was a pagan, Augustine's mother, Monica, was a devout Christian who had a profound influence on Augustine. At the age of sixteen, Augustine was sent away to school in Carthage where he got his first taste of worldly life and was exposed to a wide variety of intellectual positions.

Augustine most wanted to learn why evil existed in the world. If God created all things, did He create evil too? Drawn to a sect that declared that evil was the result of an eternal battle between Light and Dark, Augustine eventually grew disenchanted with the sect's leaders, who were unable to answer his questions satisfactorily. He then became interested in skepticism, reasoning that maybe he couldn't find the answers because they simply didn't exist.

Augustine traveled to Rome to start a school of rhetoric, or philosophical reasoning, but was disappointed by his students' lack of desire to learn. At the age of thirty, he accepted the post of professor of philosophy in Milan, a highly prestigious position. Through the influence of the Bishop of Milan, with whom he became friends, Augustine began to see that only Christianity could truly answer his questions.

He officially converted to the Christian faith in AD 386 after reading a passage in Romans where Paul urges his listeners to stop paying attention to the things of the world and focus on Christ (Romans 13:13–14). Augustine gave up his prestigious post and returned home to Africa. He sold the majority of his possessions, keeping only his family home for use as a monastery. He was ordained a priest in AD 391 and four years later was named Bishop of Hippo.

For the next thirty-five years, Augustine studied, preached, and wrote about philosophy and theology. He ultimately recognized that although God created all things, He did not create evil because evil is not a thing—it is a lack or privation in a thing. In other words, evil exists only as a parasite to good. (To use a modern example, evil is like rust in a car—if you take all the rust out of the car, you have a better car. If you take all the car out of the rust, you are left with nothing.)

Now considered one of the greatest theologians of all time, Augustine made it his mission to counteract the teachings of heretical sects such as Pelagianism, which claimed that humans are born without a sin nature. He wrote numerous books, more than a hundred of which survive today, including the classics *The Confessions of St. Augustine* and *The City of God.*

3. Why is it important to know truth?

4. Why do many people demand absolute truth in every area of their lives except religion and morality?

BOOK

FACTS IN THIS CHAPTER

Every day, decisions are made in the courtroom, the government, and in our own lives, and these decisions rely on knowing what is true. Unfortunately, many people think truth is flexible, like rubber, able to be twisted into any definition they see fit so they can accomplish their personal goals. But truth is absolute, exclusive, and knowable—as hard to bend or wish away as a steel beam holding up a skyscraper. As we will see, to deny absolute truth is self-defeating. And our ability to function as individuals, businesses, or governments depends on knowing and acknowledging absolute truth.

In chapter 1 of the book, Geisler and Turek talked about how we can know truth, pointing out that truth is not dependent on our feelings or preferences, and that statements denying that truth can be known are self-defeating. Once you realize this, it is easy to expose self-defeating statements using what the authors call the Road Runner tactic. Just like the Road Runner would make the ground disappear from under

his nemesis, Wile E. Coyote, you can make the ground disappear from under the statements of relativists you talk with. As we'll see below, you can show them that many of their beliefs and statements are groundless because they are self-defeating and therefore cannot be true.

5. List seven truths about truth and explain why each is important (see IDHEF, pages 37–38).

6. What do the authors mean when they say, "Contrary beliefs are possible, but contrary truths are not possible"? (See IDHEF, page 38.)

7. Discuss one or two real-life situations where false ideas about truth can lead to false ideas about life.

Photo: Gustav-Adolf Schultze

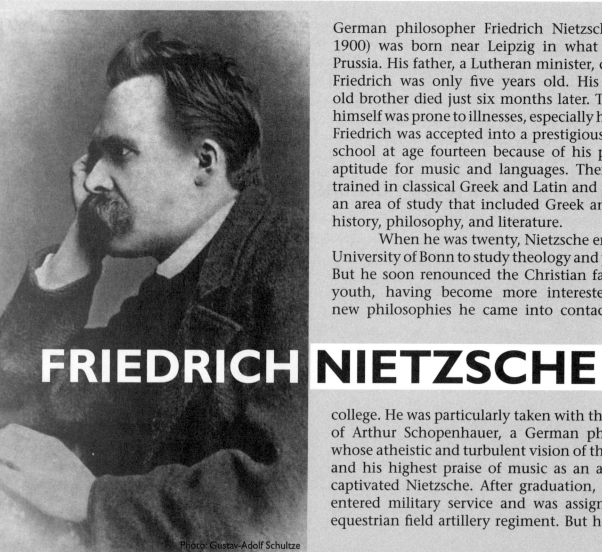

FRIEDRICH NIETZSCHE

German philosopher Friedrich Nietzsche (1844–1900) was born near Leipzig in what was then Prussia. His father, a Lutheran minister, died when Friedrich was only five years old. His two-year-old brother died just six months later. Though he himself was prone to illnesses, especially headaches, Friedrich was accepted into a prestigious boarding school at age fourteen because of his prodigious aptitude for music and languages. There he was trained in classical Greek and Latin and philology, an area of study that included Greek and Roman history, philosophy, and literature.

When he was twenty, Nietzsche entered the University of Bonn to study theology and philology. But he soon renounced the Christian faith of his youth, having become more interested in the new philosophies he came into contact with at college. He was particularly taken with the writings of Arthur Schopenhauer, a German philosopher whose atheistic and turbulent vision of the world—and his highest praise of music as an art form—captivated Nietzsche. After graduation, Nietzsche entered military service and was assigned to an equestrian field artillery regiment. But he suffered

TRUTH IS NOT RELATIVE: THE ROAD RUNNER TACTIC IN ACTION

All truths are absolute truths. Even truths about preferences—such as "John likes chocolate better than vanilla"—are absolutely true when referring to the person with the preference. It's absolutely true for all persons, at all times, in all places, that when referring to John, he prefers chocolate over vanilla right now. That's absolutely true.

To say that truth is relative is self-defeating. In other words, the statement doesn't meet its own standard. If all truth is relative, then that statement should be relative as well, but it is absolute instead—which contradicts the point the person making the statement is trying to make! Why should any thinking person take such statements seriously?

It's important that you know how to point out self-defeating statements like these, because often people don't even realize they're making the kinds of statements that contradict the rules of logical thought. The key is to apply every statement to itself to see if it meets its own standard. Those that don't are self-defeating and thus false. You can expose these false claims by turning the claim on itself. The authors call this the Road Runner tactic.

a serious chest injury while attempting to leap-mount into the saddle, and he was placed on sick leave. Nietzsche then accepted a position as professor of philology at the University of Basel where he would teach for ten years. During this time, he became close friends with composer Richard Wagner, who acted as a friend and father to Nietzsche.

In 1870, Nietzsche served for three months as a hospital attendant during the Franco-Prussian war. His experiences of war, coupled with his intellectual pessimism, led him to publish his first book, *The Birth of Tragedy*, in 1872. The book was not well received, but Nietzsche continued to write, publishing a series of four major essays critiquing German culture.

By 1879, his health had worsened, forcing Nietzsche to resign his post at the university. Seeking a climate that would improve his health, Nietzsche gave up his German citizenship and toured Europe, never residing in any place longer than several months at a time. Nietzsche found himself losing friends, including Wagner, and quarrelling with his family. Nevertheless, he was productive, completing ten books in almost as many years, including *Thus Spake Zarathustra* and *Beyond Good and Evil*, in which he advocated tearing down the Christian morality and biblical authority that supported so many European cultures. None of his titles sold particularly well, and Nietzsche found he couldn't return to teaching because most universities thought his ideas too subversive.

Nietzsche's rejection of Christianity seemed more volitional than rational. He once wrote, "If one were to prove this God of the Christians to us, we should believe Him all the less."

In January 1889, Nietzsche suffered a mental breakdown and spent the next few years in mental hospitals before returning to his childhood home under his mother's care. When his mother died a few years later, Nietzsche's sister Elisabeth became his nurse as well as his editor. Nietzsche died in August 1900. It was not until nearly a generation after his death that Nietzsche's ideas became popular with a society reeling from two world wars.

Today he is considered one of the nineteenth century's most influential philosophers. Ironically, Nietzsche predicted that the loss of belief in God would lead to lead to the twentieth century's being the bloodiest in history. He was right.

Claim: There is no truth!
RR tactic: Is that true?

Claim: All truth is relative!
RR tactic: Is that a relative truth?

Once you know the Road Runner tactic, you can refute many false claims against Christianity. For example, a skeptic might say, "That's true for you but not for me." A Christian using the Road Runner tactic might answer, "Is that statement true for everyone?" The Christian could also use real-life examples to show why the claim is absurd. "If you went to withdraw $5,000 from your bank account, knowing you only had $50 in it, would the teller hand over the five grand if you told her that the $50 balance was only true for her but not for you?"

8. What makes a statement self-defeating?

9. List some of the self-defeating statements used as examples in chapter 1 of the book. How would you respond to them?

WHY CAN'T ALL RELIGIONS BE TRUE?

When it comes to identifying and applying truth, one of the areas where people are most sensitive is religion. We all take our personal beliefs very seriously, even if we don't have any evidence to back them up!

It's common in today's culture for people to claim that "all religions are true." This is sometimes called "pluralism." You may have even heard someone say, "It doesn't matter what you believe, just as long as you believe." Unfortunately, most people don't realize that world religions contradict one another's beliefs more often than they profess similar ones. Even those religions that share basic moral concepts disagree on other major issues such as the nature of God, the nature of man, sin, salvation, heaven, hell and creation. Because of these mutually exclusive beliefs, it is impossible for all religions to be true.

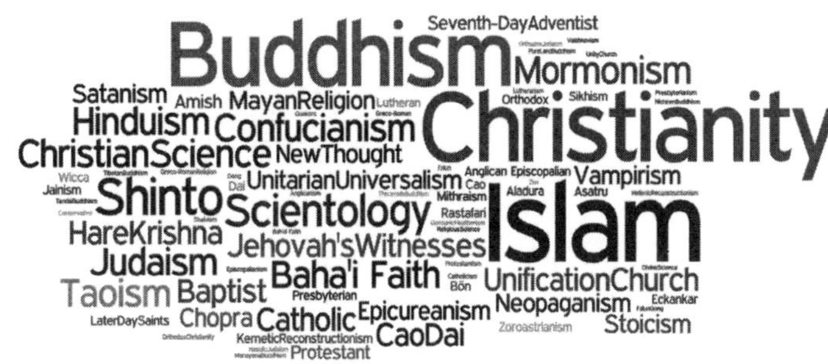

10. Explain what you would say to someone who claimed:

a. "All religions teach basically the same things."

b. "You shouldn't judge me."

c. *"You shouldn't force your beliefs on other people."*

YOU DO THE DIGGING

Even though relativism is popular in our culture, truth remains absolute. Take mathematics, for example. Mathematical truths are the same no matter what country or culture you live in. Some people perceive truth differently, just as some people get their math sums wrong, but the truth remains the same. Contrary *beliefs* are possible (since believing something doesn't make it true or false), but contrary *truths* are not. And if something is true, then anything that contradicts it must be false.

Truth is the correspondence between belief and reality. If merely believing in something made it true, then the pluralists would be right and Christians would have to accept the views of atheists, Muslims, Mormons, Jehovah's Witnesses, and other belief systems as true, too. But sincerity is not the same as truth. Mormons, for example, are sincere in their belief that the *Book of Mormon* is another testament of Jesus Christ. But they cannot produce anywhere near the same level of historical authentication that exists proving the reliability of the New Testament. (Upcoming chapters will talk about the historical proof for the New Testament.) The reality is that the New Testament is the only true testament of Jesus Christ. Just because a Mormon believes with all his heart that the *Book of Mormon* was given to them by God doesn't mean that it was.

As we have seen in this chapter, not all religions can be true. Although pluralists claim that all religions are true, the fact is that since mutually exclusive principles cannot all be true, so it doesn't make any sense to pretend that all religions teach the same things. Contrary to popular opinion, all truth claims are absolute, exclusive, and knowable, even those about religion.

Now it's time to for you to do some digging on your own. Pick at least one of the following assignments and complete it before moving on in the workbook.

Assignment 1: Give at least two examples of people who have chosen not to believe the truth in order to accomplish their personal goals or pursue their desires.

Assignment 2: Look for self-defeating statements in the media or on the Internet. Choose at least three examples and write a report on each using the following parameters:

- Describe the situation or circumstance the person used to justify his or her self-defeating viewpoint.
- Quote the statement (or describe the action) used.
- Describe the reaction to the statement. Did anyone point out a problem, or did listeners just nod and accept the self-defeating statement as truth?
- Briefly explain how the Road Runner tactic could have been applied in this situation and how it might have changed the person's argument.

Assignment 3: Conduct a brief study about the differences between the three major theistic religions—Christianity, Islam, and Judaism—then write a one-page report on each religion and its beliefs. Use the chart on the next page to compare their teachings on the following topics:

- Jesus (Who was He?)
- Sin (What defines sin?)
- Salvation (How can we be saved?)
- Heaven (What happens when we die?)
- Hell (What is the punishment for sin?)
- Creation (How did the universe come to be?)

	CHRISTIANITY	ISLAM	JUDAISM
JESUS			
SIN			
SALVATION			
HEAVEN			
HELL			
CREATION			

WHAT DO I DO NOW?

This chapter is extremely important because the material will help you to establish a critical baseline not only for how you live, but also for how well you will understand and absorb the principles covered in the rest of this course. Without a foundation of truth, there is nothing to talk about—if nothing can be discovered, nothing can be decided.

Getting people thinking about truth—if it exists, if it is understandable, if it applies to all people everywhere—opens them up to new possibilities concerning God, what He expects from us, and how we should live our lives.

THINKING ABOUT WHAT YOU LEARNED

Answer the following questions to sum up what you have learned in this chapter.

A. Why can it be dangerous to pretend that all religious beliefs are true?

B. Why are pluralists just as exclusive as those they accuse of being narrow-minded?

C. People often say, "All religions teach basically the same things." Explain why that is not true.

D. What is the Elephant Parable and how can you answer it?

E. Would most pluralists agree that all religious beliefs are equal, even those that support violence or harm children? Why or why not?

DON'T FORGET!

As you challenge people to really think about the truth behind their morals, personal beliefs, and values, you will get mixed responses. People want to do what they want to do, and they often view truth as a restriction stopping them from having fun. Sometimes you will need to challenge people gently. Other times you may have to be more direct, though always speaking the truth in love. Jesus boldly confronted the religious and political leaders of His day (see Matthew 23). Using the right approach for each situation and person can greatly increase your success and may open doors for future opportunities to speak with them.

Pluralism is all around us. It permeates television, movies, newspapers, and the Internet. You will need to be ready to recognize pluralism and relativism and defend the truth. People who have been bombarded with "untruth" tend to accept and believe what they hear without thinking it through. You are God's ambassador. Your job is to be equipped with good answers and to guide people to Jesus Christ, the only truth that can set them free from their bondage to sin and death.

CHAPTER 2
WHY SHOULD ANYONE
BELIEVE
ANYTHING
AT ALL?

BEFORE STARTING THIS CHAPTER

- Read chapter 2 of *I Don't Have Enough Faith to Be an Atheist* (IDHEF), pages 51–69.

ROAD MAP OF THE "TWELVE POINTS THAT PROVE CHRISTIANITY IS TRUE"

This chapter covers the following points:

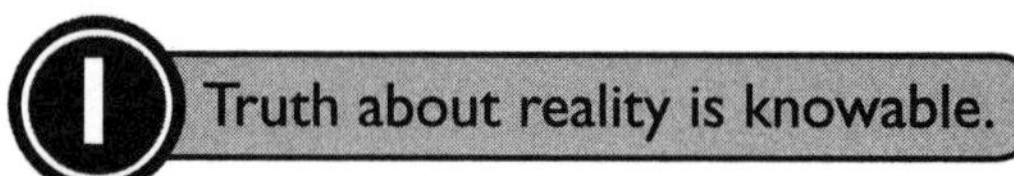

1
Truth about reality is knowable.

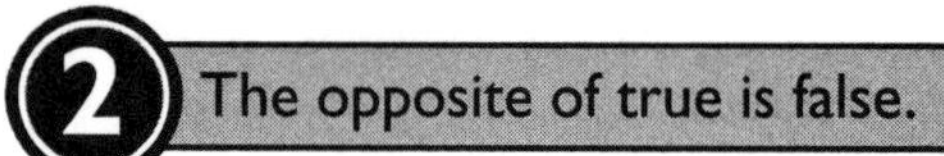

2
The opposite of true is false.

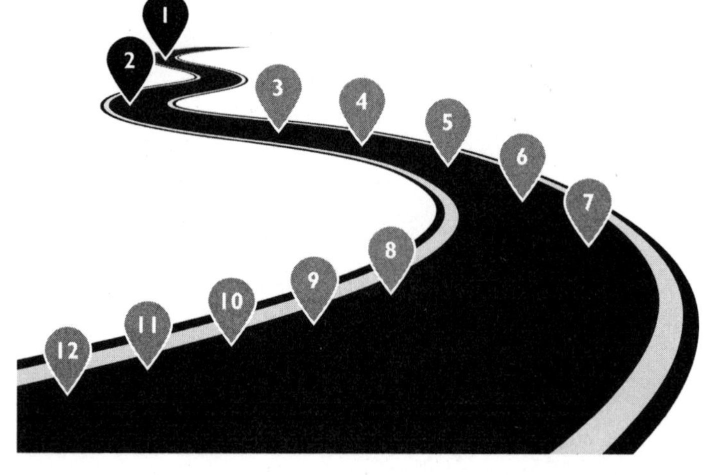

KEY TOPICS

After completing this chapter, you should be able to:

- Describe what *apologetics* is and what its goals are.
- Explain the importance of using logic to discover truth.
- Describe how the Road Runner tactic is based on the Law of Noncontradiction.
- Explain Hume's empiricism and why it fails.
- Explain Kant's agnosticism and why it fails.
- List and explain two major self-evident laws of logic ("first principles").
- Demonstrate how deductive and inductive reasoning help us discover truth about God.
- Explain why people should care about the truth.

KEY TERMS

Write the definitions for these words found in your reading:

Apologist

Law of Noncontradiction

Empiricism

Empirical Verifiability

Induction

Deduction

QUESTIONS THAT GRAB YOUR MIND

You might have heard someone say, "It doesn't really matter *what* you believe, as long as you believe *something*." While many people think this is true about religious beliefs (following the logic that all religions pretty much end up at the same place), they would never apply this same reasoning to medicine or money. How would your friends react if you told them "It doesn't really matter what medicine you take, as long as you believe it will help you" or "It doesn't really matter what investment you make as long as you believe it will grow"? Beliefs don't trump facts in the real world, so why should people think they do when it comes to religion?

Many people arrive at their beliefs not on the basis of proof, but on the basis of what they find attractive. In other words, many build their religious belief system on what they *hope* to be true without checking to see if their beliefs actually *are* true. But doesn't it make sense to verify what you believe to be true, especially if the truth has eternal consequences? Of course! That's why the Bible commands us to search out the truth about Christianity.

1. Read 1 Peter 3:15. What does it tell Christians to do?

SO WHAT?

Many people are either ignorant of the truth or simply don't care. They may say that morality is relative or that it doesn't matter what you believe. But those same people *do* believe morality matters when they are treated badly. If you lied, cheated, or stole from them, they would be the first ones to shout, "That's not right! That's not fair!"

Some people say religion doesn't matter. But if the Bible is true, then someone who chooses not to become reconciled to God through salvation will spend eternity separated from Him. That's one reason why apologetics is so important—what we believe can have eternal consequences.

Apologetics has been defined as the science and art of defending the faith. In the Greek, it means to present an *apology*, or defense. It doesn't mean to apologize for doing something wrong, it means to defend your beliefs by providing evidence for them. For Christians, this means being prepared to answer questions like "Why do you believe that Jesus is God?" or "Why do you believe the Bible is true?" The Christian apologist reveals the truth about the truths of Christianity, God, and the Bible and supports his or her position with facts. This study is intended to help you do just that.

2. Why is it vital to know the difference between truth and falsehood?

TRUTH AND THE LAW

A courtroom is supposed to be a place where truth matters—truth about what actually happened and why. It is the job of the people involved in a trial to discover that truth.

There is a prosecuting attorney, who tries to prove that the person on trial broke the law and should be punished. There is also a defense attorney, who is trying to demonstrate the innocence of the client (or at least provide reasonable doubt as to the client's guilt). A judge keeps order in the court and makes sure both sides follow procedure, while the members of a jury try to listen objectively to all the facts and make a ruling about the guilt or innocence of the person on trial. Witnesses are also brought to the courtroom to testify about circumstances they witnessed or about facts pertaining to the crime or the character of the defendant.

The entire process in a court of law is based on three things: 1) the law, or the standard against which the behavior of the person on trial is compared; 2) the truth, which exists but must be discovered; and 3) the evidence, which reveals the truth with facts about what happened or the way the world works.

In a courtroom, a prosecuting attorney presents evidence that will help the judge and jury *discover* the truth. We use the word "discover" rather than "determine" because technically we don't determine or create truth—we discover what is already there. This principle applies to religious questions as well. If God truly exists, then we should be able to discover this fact through evidence.

A good prosecuting attorney will try to present scientific and eyewitness testimony, using sound reasoning, in order to demonstrate that the person on trial is guilty beyond a reasonable doubt. If the attorney is fair, he or she will also try to avoid building the case on personal preferences or unsupported claims. Likewise, the jury must set aside personal considerations and make their decision about the truth of the case based on logical reasoning, ruling out anything that isn't supported by evidence.

3. ***Why is it important to rely on objective standards (logic) rather than subjective ones (emotion) when trying to discover the truth?***

FACTS IN THIS CHAPTER

Now that you've had a chance to think about why logic is such a vital tool in your search for truth, we are going to challenge you to answer the question "Why should anyone believe anything at all?" Of course, you could just say you believe because you believe. But that wouldn't be solid foundation to build on! You wouldn't build your house on a foundation without verifying that the foundation was sound. Likewise, you should verify your beliefs because they will affect your life here and in eternity.

Chapter 2 of *I Don't Have Enough Faith to Be an Atheist* opened with a question by author and speaker James Sire: *Why do people believe what they believe?* Sire gave four categories of reasons why people choose their beliefs:

1. ***Sociological reasons***—sharing the beliefs of family, friends, or society
2. ***Psychological reasons***—beliefs that give us hope, purpose, or peace of mind
3. ***Religious reasons***—what we were taught in Sunday school or church or by some other religious source
4. ***Philosophical reasons***—beliefs that are logically consistent and match reality as we know it

Sire shows that the first three groups often offer only subjective reasons for why they believe something. Individuals, parents, friends, and cultures do not necessarily test their beliefs to discover if they are really true. The only way to test what is correct is to use sound reason and evidence (philosophical reasons).

4. Why are philosophical reasons the best way to discover the truth?

THE LAW OF NONCONTRADICTION

An important step in discovering truth is identifying what is false. Many times you will hear people make a truth claim that sounds fine on the surface, but is actually self-defeating. This is where the Road Runner tactic is essential to your work as an apologist and someone who seeks truth. The Road Runner tactic utilizes the Law of Noncontradiction, which helps us recognize arguments that are self-defeating and therefore false.

The Law of Noncontradiction is one of the most fundamental laws of thought. As with the other laws of logic, the Law of Noncontradiction is self-evident—it can't be discovered by reasoning from other principles. You can't prove it; you just know it. The laws of logic are tools of thought that allow you to learn everything else. In fact, we couldn't think or reason without the Law of Noncontradiction. It is to thinking what your eyes are to seeing. You can't see without eyes, and you can't think without the Law of Noncontradiction.

5. Briefly describe what the Law of Noncontradiction states (see IDHEF, pages 56–57). How does this law form the foundation for the Road Runner tactic?

6. ***What would you say to someone who said he didn't believe in the Law of Noncontradiction?***

DAVID HUME AND EMPIRICISM

David Hume's ideas about skepticism and empiricism have had a tremendous impact on modern society. Hume believed that all meaningful ideas could only be true by definition or based on experience gained through the senses. If this is true, it means that anything that cannot be verified by reason or experience isn't meaningful. Philosopher A. J. Ayer eventually turned these assertions from Hume into something called "the principle of empirical verifiability," which helped lay the foundation for skepticism, a philosophical belief that accepts as truth only what has been proven empirically. But the problem with this principle is that it doesn't live up to its own standards.

7. ***Give an example of something that is true by definition.***

8. ***How can you use the Road Runner tactic to defeat Hume's empiricism (later known as the Principle of Empirical Verifiability)? (See IDHEF, pages 57–59.)***

Painting: Allan Ramsay

DAVID HUME

Scottish philosopher and historian David Hume (1711–1776) is considered one of the most influential thinkers in Western culture. He was a proponent of empiricism, the theory that knowledge can only be reliably obtained through observation and experience. He believed that ethics and morality were based on feelings, and that desire—rather than reason—was the driving force behind most human behavior. Hume was perhaps the only true atheist of the so-called Enlightenment period.

Born in the lowlands of Scotland, David was an unusually precocious boy. After his father's death when he was two years old, David's mother devoted her time to raising him and his brother and sister. When his brother was ready to attend the University of Edinburgh, their mother allowed David to go along, though he was only twelve. His family wanted him to study law, but David decided to pursue philosophy instead.

After three years of intense study and reflection, David Hume found himself on the verge of a nervous breakdown. He spent some time in London recovering, and then made his way to France to resume his studies. For the next few years, Hume lived in the sleepy village of La Flèche, living as cheaply as possible and reading and writing for hours every day. At the age of twenty-six, Hume published what would be one of his greatest works, *A Treatise of Human Nature*. In this three-volume work, Hume laid out his thoughts on how ideas are formed and what they are made of, how morality is determined, and how it affects society and government.

Even after he edited out some of the more controversial passages so the publisher would agree to release it, the book did not prove successful. Hume later decided that the problem was with the style, not the content, and he reworked several sections to release as essays. The most famous of these are "Enquiry Concerning Human Understanding" and "Enquiry Concerning the Principles of Morals," which Hume believed represented his best work.

After working abroad for a time as secretary to his cousin, a lieutenant general in the Scottish army, Hume took a job as a librarian at the University of Edinburgh. Although the pay was meager, the job gave him access to research materials for a comprehensive history of England. The six-volume set was a best-seller, earning Hume a lasting reputation and making him financially independent.

In 1763, he accepted a position as private secretary to England's ambassador to France. Hume lived in Paris for several years, during which he gained popularity in the Parisian salons, enjoying the conversation and company of French nobles and intellectuals. Then, at the age of fifty-eight, Hume retired to Edinburgh where he spent his later years quietly and comfortably, dining and conversing with friends and revising his writings.

Diagnosed with cancer in 1776, David spent the final months of his life working on his book *Dialogues Concerning Natural Religion*, which was published three years after his death. Although many of Hume's contemporaries denounced his writings as works of skepticism and atheism, David Hume's ideas influenced agnostic and atheistic minds such as Immanuel Kant, Arthur Schopenhauer, Jeremy Bentham, and Charles Darwin, and contributed greatly to the skepticism movement.

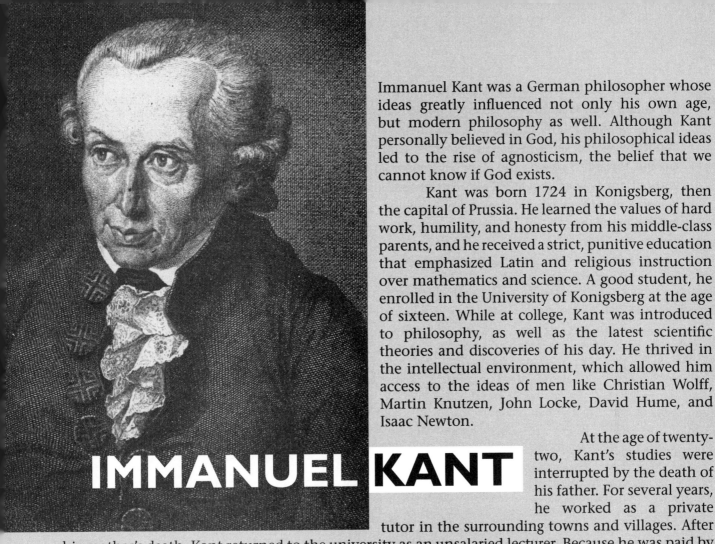

IMMANUEL KANT

Immanuel Kant was a German philosopher whose ideas greatly influenced not only his own age, but modern philosophy as well. Although Kant personally believed in God, his philosophical ideas led to the rise of agnosticism, the belief that we cannot know if God exists.

Kant was born 1724 in Konigsberg, then the capital of Prussia. He learned the values of hard work, humility, and honesty from his middle-class parents, and he received a strict, punitive education that emphasized Latin and religious instruction over mathematics and science. A good student, he enrolled in the University of Konigsberg at the age of sixteen. While at college, Kant was introduced to philosophy, as well as the latest scientific theories and discoveries of his day. He thrived in the intellectual environment, which allowed him access to the ideas of men like Christian Wolff, Martin Knutzen, John Locke, David Hume, and Isaac Newton.

At the age of twenty-two, Kant's studies were interrupted by the death of his father. For several years, he worked as a private tutor in the surrounding towns and villages. After his mother's death, Kant returned to the university as an unsalaried lecturer. Because he was paid by his students rather than the university, he was required to lecture on a wide variety of subjects and take on many students in order to earn a living. His lecture topics ranged from logic, metaphysics, and ethics to mathematics, physics, and even geography, and he soon became a popular instructor.

During this time, Kant also wrote books and essays on philosophy and science, one of which postulated that the solar system had formed from a nebula, now called the Nebula Theory of the origin of the universe. Then in 1770, Kant was awarded the Chair of Logic and Metaphysics at the university, and the promotion gave him more time to devote to his writing. For the next decade, he worked on his magnum opus, *A Critique of Pure Reason*. Lengthy and intellectually challenging, the book did not receive much notice upon its release. Yet he continued writing, producing several more works over the next few years, including a thorough revision of his *Critique* that streamlined the concepts.

By the late 1780s, Kant's reputation had grown. A new generation of European philosophers was talking about his ideas, popularized in large part by a series of open letters written by Austrian philosopher Karl Reinhold that promoted Kant's views of knowledge and morality. When Kant retired from teaching at the age of seventy-six, he was one of the foremost names in European thought.

After his retirement, Kant continued to write but began experiencing mental problems. He died in 1804, just a few weeks short of his eightieth birthday. In his entire life, he never traveled more than ten miles from Konigsberg, yet his ideas about epistemology (how we know what we know) and metaphysics (how we explain the nature of the world around us) shaped the future of philosophy for the next few centuries.

IMMANUEL KANT AND AGNOSTICISM

Immanuel Kant is another philosopher who made a significant impact on modern thought. Moving beyond Hume's skepticism, Kant believed that there was no real way to know anything about the world, since we are forced to rely on our senses. It's as if we are all pilots locked in a plane, forced to rely on the plane's instruments for information about the world around us without any way of knowing if the instruments are correctly calibrated. Because of this, Kant believed that there was no way to know anything at all about the world. This philosophy is called agnosticism.

9. ***How can you use the Road Runner tactic to defeat Kant's agnosticism? (See IDHEF, pages 59–61.)***

10. ***On pages 60–61, the authors describe the "nothing but" fallacy. How is Kant's agnosticism an example of that fallacy?***

THE LAW OF THE EXCLUDED MIDDLE

Truth can be discovered using the self-evident laws of logic, which are also known as first principles of thought. These principles are not proved by other principles; they are simply inherent in the nature of reality. Self-evident principles are the tools we use to help us discover truth. You know these principles, even though you might not know that you know them or how to apply them consistently. (A course in logic can help you think better and more consistently.) We've already looked at the Law of Noncontradiction. So let's examine another first principle: the Law of the Excluded Middle.

The Law of the Excluded Middle states that something either is or it is not—there isn't a third option. For example, either God exists, or God doesn't exist. There aren't any other choices. Because it makes perfect sense and doesn't need other principles to prove that it's true, it is considered self-evident.

Let's return to the courtroom so we can look at it another way. The prosecuting attorney says that the defendant *did* commit the crime; the defense attorney says that the defendant *didn't* commit the crime. Although the jury would need to see and weigh the evidence to discover which attorney is correct, everyone knows that both sides cannot be right. Either the defendant will be found guilty or not guilty—there is no middle alternative.

The same can be said about questions related to Christianity. For example, either the Bible tells us the truth about Jesus' resurrection from the dead, or it does not. He either rose or He didn't—there is no middle alternative. (We'll investigate the evidence about the Resurrection and other questions central to Christianity in an upcoming chapter.)

11. Based on the Law of the Excluded Middle, list all the possible answers to the following questions:

a. Does God exist?

b. Did Jesus rise from the dead?

c. Did Paul write the letter in the Bible to the Romans?

DEDUCTIVE AND INDUCTIVE REASONING

To discover the truth about Christianity we must use both induction and deduction. Induction is the method of drawing general conclusions from specific observations. This is often called the scientific method. While induction allows us to establish premises that are most likely true (beyond a reasonable doubt), it can't prove most things beyond all doubt, because it relies on the observations of finite human beings.

For example, you can reach an inductive conclusion about gravity, because every unsupported object you have observed has fallen to the ground. In other words, through your specific observation of falling objects, you can draw a general conclusion that gravity exists. Do you know that it exists everywhere? No, because you haven't been everywhere. So the most we can state is that it is most probably true.

Deduction involves lining up premises in a logically sound way to make an argument—you may have derived the premises from induction, but you form those premises into an argument by using deduction. Technically speaking, deduction can only tell you whether an argument is logically sound or unsound; it can't prove whether the argument is true or false. But if the form of your argument is sound and your premises are true, then the conclusion necessarily follows and must be true.

A deductive argument looks like this:

Premise 1: If Jesus rose from the dead, then Jesus is God.
Premise 2: Jesus rose from the dead.
Conclusion: Therefore, Jesus is God.

If premises 1 and 2 are true, then the conclusion must also be true (though we would to use induction to determine the validity of the premises). In the case of this example, we would need to do some historical investigation to determine if there is enough evidence to prove that Jesus rose from the dead. Stay tuned. We'll investigate this in an upcoming chapter.

12. Induction is often called the "scientific method." Give an example of how inductive reasoning can prove that something is true.

13. Give an example of a deductive argument that is logically sound but not true.

YOU DO THE DIGGING

In this chapter, you have learned about some of the first principles of logic. You've also learned how inductive and deductive reasoning can be used to answer questions about Christianity and refute many of the key philosophies being taught in today's colleges and universities. Now it's time for you to do some digging on your own. Pick at least one of the following assignments and complete it before moving on in the workbook.

Assignment 1: Write a page about why you believe what you do about Christianity. Talk about the reasons and people that have influenced your thinking.

Assignment 2: Search newspapers and magazines for an example of someone reaching a conclusion. (It doesn't matter what the conclusion is—how to make your garden grow better, how to improve your looks, etc.) Then explain how the conclusion was reached. Did the author rely on preference or evidence and logic?

Assignment 3: Research an influential figure in today's society to find out what he or she believes. What are his moral values? How do her ideas impact the way she lives? What does he believe constitutes truth? Write a one-page essay documenting your findings, concluding with a paragraph on what you think his or her beliefs and practices will do—today, tomorrow, and ultimately, after death.

WHAT DO I DO NOW?

The first two chapters have concentrated on how we know what we know and have provided you with some tools to discover truth and expose self-defeating arguments. Now it's time to apply what you have learned to the world around you.

TOOK

THINKING ABOUT WHAT YOU LEARNED

Answer the following questions to sum up what you have learned in this chapter.

A. *Explain why "either-or" logic forms the foundation for all logical thought and argument at all times and in all places.*

B. *What is the fatal flaw in the principle of empirical verifiability? How can it be easily counteracted?*

C. *What is the fatal flaw in Immanuel Kant's agnostic philosophy? How can it be easily counteracted?*

D. We can't see gravity and we can't see God. So how do we know either exists?

E. Why does it matter whether your beliefs are true or false? How does truth affect your decisions and outcomes in life?

WHAT YOU DON'T KNOW *CAN* HURT YOU!

Too many people simply believe what they want to believe without bothering to learn if their beliefs are really true. There's an old saying that goes "What you don't know can't hurt you." Unfortunately, this is often false. If you don't know the bridge is out on the road ahead of you, you're going to get hurt!

Emotions or sincerity aren't tests for truth. You can sincerely believe something is true when it really isn't. Emotions may make life fun, but reasoning makes life safe. Since your life is important, so is truth.

The tools and reasoning methods we've discussed here are intended to help you discover truth and then make the right decisions. If Christianity is true, then what you decide about Christ is the most important decision you will ever make.

CHAPTER 3

IN THE BEGINNING THERE WAS A GREAT SURGE

BEFORE STARTING THIS CHAPTER

- Read chapter 3 of *I Don't Have Enough Faith to Be an Atheist* (IDHEF), pages 73–94.

ROAD MAP OF THE "TWELVE POINTS THAT PROVE CHRISTIANITY IS TRUE"

This chapter covers the following points:

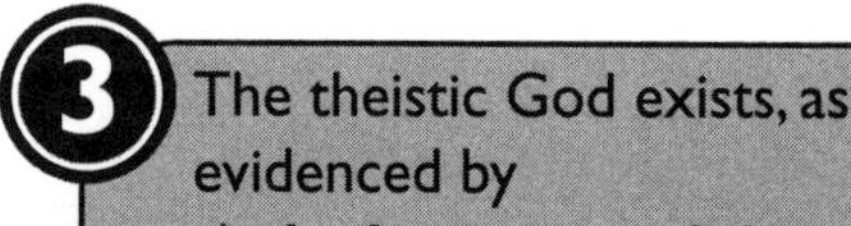

3 The theistic God exists, as evidenced by
a) ***the beginning of the universe,***
b) the design of the universe,
c) the design of life, and
d) moral law.

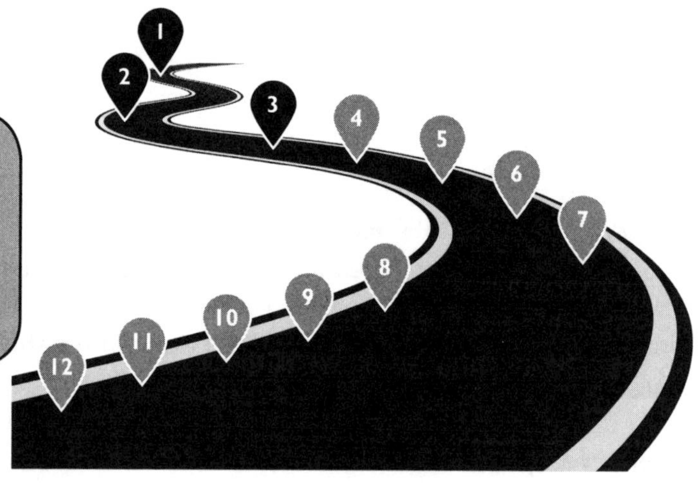

KEY TOPICS

After completing this chapter, you should be able to:

- Explain the cosmological argument for the beginning of the universe.
- Show that the universe had a beginning by citing the SURGE evidence:
    - a) The **S**econd Law of Thermodynamics
    - b) The expansion of the **U**niverse
    - c) Cosmic background **R**adiation
    - d) Great **G**alaxy seeds
    - e) **E**instein's theory of general relativity
- Describe two opposing theories atheists use to argue against a beginning for the universe.
- Describe how the Kalam Cosmological Argument proves time had a beginning.
- Explain how the universe's beginning supports the argument for a theistic God.

KEY TERMS

Write the definitions for these words found in your reading:

Cosmological Argument

Law of Causality

Second Law of Thermodynamics

First Law of Thermodynamics

Law of Entropy

Cosmic background radiation

Kalam Cosmological Argument

QUESTIONS THAT GRAB YOUR MIND

People have probably asked you where you came from, especially if you were meeting them for the first time. Most likely you answered that you were from Texas or California, New York or Florida—wherever you were born or raised. But have you ever thought about this question in terms of the origin of all mankind? Where did the *human race* come from? And even more intriguing, where did the universe come from?

As you learned in the last chapter, we have several tools available to help us discover truth, such as logic, science, and historical evidence. As we search for the answer to the question of the origin of the universe, you are going to use all three of these. The answer you discover will likely impact how you think about your life and your future.

1. ***Why is it important to know all we can about the origin of the universe? How will knowing how the universe came about change the way you live right now?***

SO WHAT?

Either God created us, or we created God. If we created God, then there is no ultimate meaning or purpose to life. There is no objective right or wrong, and in the end it doesn't matter how we live because we're all just going to return to dust anyway. If there is no God, then we are completely on our own. But if God created us, then there is an ultimate meaning and purpose to life. The Creator has put us here for a reason.

So how do we know whether or not there was a creation? How do we know if the universe had a beginning, and how do we know if God caused it? That's what we'll cover in this chapter.

THE COSMOLOGICAL ARGUMENT

To answer the question of whether the universe had a beginning, we need to use the Cosmological Argument. The word *cosmological* from the Greek word *cosmos*, meaning "having to do with the universe."

The last chapter taught us that for an argument to be true, it has to be logically sound (that is, determined by deductive reasoning) and its premises must be true (determined by inductive reasoning). There are two key premises that make up the Cosmological Argument:

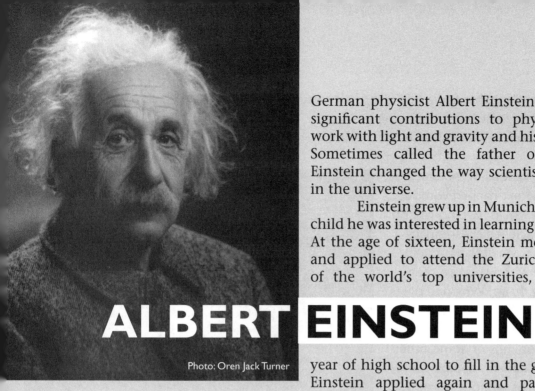

ALBERT EINSTEIN

Photo: Oren Jack Turner

German physicist Albert Einstein was known for his significant contributions to physics, including his work with light and gravity and his theory of relativity. Sometimes called the father of modern physics, Einstein changed the way scientists look at our place in the universe.

Einstein grew up in Munich, Germany. Even as a child he was interested in learning how things worked. At the age of sixteen, Einstein moved to Switzerland and applied to attend the Zurich Polytechnic, one of the world's top universities, but he failed the non-scientific portions of the entrance exam. After another year of high school to fill in the gaps in his learning, Einstein applied again and passed, entering the physics teaching program. In order to avoid military service in Germany, which would have interrupted his schooling, Albert also renounced his German citizenship.

Albert graduated at the age of twenty-one and began looking for a teaching position. In the meantime, he took a job at the Swiss patent office. Although mundane, the job gave Einstein time to work on his own scientific theories and pursue a doctorate. Based on his research into electromagnetism and gravity, he didn't believe that the old Newtonian explanations of how the world worked were sufficient to explain the universe as a whole. He therefore worked on a new explanation that would account for recent scientific discoveries.

In 1905, later called his "miracle year," Einstein received his PhD in physics and published four ground-breaking scientific papers dealing with his theories of light, mass (his famous $E=mc^2$ formula), and relativity. These established his reputation in the scientific community, and soon he had more job offers than he knew what to do with. He accepted a position as a physics professor at the University of Zurich in 1909. Two years later he moved to Prague to become a professor at Karl-Ferdinand University, then in 1914 was appointed director of the Kaiser Wilhelm Institute for Physics in Berlin.

At the age of forty-two, Einstein was awarded the Nobel Prize for Physics for his theories about light. This brought Einstein international fame, and he spent the next two years touring Europe, Asia, and America. His face became so well known that he would be stopped on the street by people wanting him to explain his theories. Einstein would often reply, "Pardon me. Always I am mistaken for Professor Einstein."

In 1919, observations made during a solar eclipse showed that gravity bends light, confirming Einstein's theory of General Relativity. One implication of General Relativity is that space-time and matter are co-relative—that they came into existence together. This points to an absolute beginning of the universe, something Einstein tried to avoid until he personally observed the expanding universe from Hubble's telescope in 1931. While Einstein never publically expressed belief in a personal God, his well-confirmed theory provides evidence for a spaceless, timeless, immaterial, personal First Cause.

In 1933, with the Nazis gaining power in Germany, Einstein chose to immigrate to the United States with his wife, Elsa. Seven years later they became U.S. citizens. For the next thirty years, he worked at the Institute for Advanced Study in Princeton, New Jersey, and a letter he wrote to Franklin D. Roosevelt (and later regretted) helped kick-start America's atomic research program. Einstein died in 1955, leaving behind a world forever changed.

Premise 1: Everything that had a beginning had a cause.
Premise 2: The universe had a beginning.
Conclusion: Therefore, the universe had a cause.

Photo: NASA

From our observations of the universe, we can see that things don't happen without a cause. If they did, we would have no reason to do science, because science is essentially a search for causes. Moreover, if things could just pop into existence without cause, then why doesn't everything do so? Why don't snakes, lions, and thousand-dollar bills just appear out of nowhere? We never worry, for example, that a hippopotamus or some other wild animal is going to suddenly appear out of nowhere and devour us without warning. We all understand that everything that has a beginning has a cause. Therefore, it makes sense to conclude that if the universe had a beginning, then the universe must have had a cause.

Since the first premise is true, we need only to worry about the evidence for the second premise—that the universe itself had a beginning. But how do we obtain the evidence we need to tell us about the origin of the universe? Consider again the courtroom example. The purpose of a trial is to discover the truth about a crime. The judge and jury must discover the cause of the crime from the evidence found at the crime scene. Scientists also look at evidence at the scene—in this case, space and stars and planets—to discover if the universe had a beginning and, therefore, a cause.

From observing evidence about our universe, we can discover if it had a beginning and then draw some conclusions about the nature of the cause. For example, if space, time, and matter all had a beginning, then it is reasonable to conclude that the universe's cause must be spaceless, timeless, and immaterial. That's because if space, time, and matter were created at that beginning, their cause must have existed apart from these things.

If we can discover *who* started the universe, we might be able to understand *why* it was started. And if we can find out *why* it was started, then we can better understand why *we* are here and what we are supposed to do with our lives and resources. (We'll see later why the cause of the universe must be a personal *who* and not an impersonal *what.*)

2. *Why is premise 2 the only one that really needs to be proven?*

FACTS IN THIS CHAPTER

If the universe had a beginning, then the obvious next question is "Who did the creating?" If God created the universe, then we need to find out why, what His plans and purposes for the universe are, and how we fit into them. Looking at it that way, understanding the beginning of the universe becomes very important, because the answer could change the way we live and make decisions on a daily basis.

But first things first. This chapter focuses on how we can show there was a beginning using the tools of logic, science, and historical evidence.

THE *SURGE* OF THE UNIVERSE

In examining the Cosmological Argument, we can see there are at least five lines of scientific evidence leading to the conclusion that the universe did indeed have a beginning. They help disprove the idea that the universe has always existed, something scientists believed for many years.

3. ***Geisler and Turek use the acronym SURGE to represent five lines of scientific evidence that the universe was created. Summarize below the evidence each letter represents.***

THE SECOND LAW OF THERMODYNAMICS

The Second Law of Thermodynamics states that the universe is running out of usable energy. With each passing moment energy is being used up, just like gasoline in a car or batteries in a flashlight. Like a flashlight with only a finite amount of energy in its batteries, the universe runs on a finite amount of energy that isn't being replenished. If a flashlight were on from eternity, it would be out of energy by now. Likewise, due to the Second Law, if the universe were eternal, it would be out of energy by now. Since we still have usable energy right now, the universe must have had a beginning.

Sometimes called the Law of Entropy, the Second Law of Thermodynamics also states that the universe is moving toward disorder rather than order. (Just take a good look at your room to prove this one.) Entropy ensures that nature will eventually turn a building into a pile of bricks, but it will never turn a pile of bricks into a building.

Both of these aspects of the Second Law of Thermodynamics show that the universe had to have a beginning. Without a beginning, by now the universe would be in complete disarray with no usable energy remaining. But as the stars are still burning and the universe remains in motion, it must have had a beginning. And if the universe had a beginning, then it must also have had a beginner.

4. ***Why does the fact that the universe is running out of usable energy mean that it can't have existed eternally?***

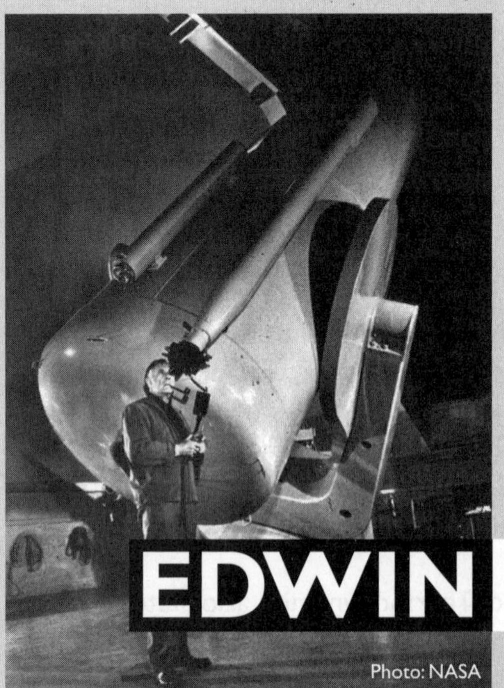

Photo: NASA

EDWIN HUBBLE

American astronomer Edwin Hubble is considered the founder of modern cosmology—the study of the nature of the universe. Born in 1889, young Edwin was more interested in athletics than schoolwork. He ran track and field in high school (even setting a high jump record), and he loved basketball and amateur boxing. But he had a keen mind as well. He received a scholarship to the University of Chicago and, in 1910, graduated with a degree in math and astronomy.

On the strengths of his academic and athletic abilities, Hubble earned a Rhodes Scholarship to study at the University of Oxford in England. His father believed that as a career path law was more stable than astronomy, so Hubble dutifully studied the law. While in England, the young man reinvented himself, taking on an English accent and mannerisms that stayed with him all his life.

In 1913, his father died, and Hubble returned to the United States to care for his mother and siblings, teaching Spanish, math, and physics at a high school in Indiana. But he couldn't stay away from his first love, astronomy. The following year he returned to the University of Chicago and graduated in 1917 with a PhD in astronomy.

THE EXPANDING UNIVERSE

In 1929, astronomer Edwin Hubble observed that the other galaxies in the universe are moving away from us. He knew this because the light from the galaxies had shifted toward the red end of the spectrum. (A shift toward blue would have indicated motion toward Earth, while a red-shift indicated movement away.)

From this, Hubble correctly deduced that if the galaxies are currently moving apart, then previously they must have been closer together. The ultimate extrapolation of this idea is that all of the matter in the universe originated from a single point. (It is important to understand that this beginning point was not a dense point of matter, like some kind of extremely compacted pellet, but was literally nothing—there was no space, no time, no matter.) This discovery aligned nicely with Albert Einstein's theory of General Relativity.

So if all the galaxies in the universe are moving away from us, does that mean that our galaxy, the Milky Way, is at the center of the universe? No. Picture a black balloon with white dots on it. When you blow up the balloon, the dots move away from one another, whether they are near the center or not. In fact, the dots on opposite sides of the balloon (those farthest away from one another) separate more quickly than those next to one another. This is exactly what we observe happening in the universe. Hubble discovered that there is a mathematically linear relationship between distance and speed, showing that a galaxy twice as far from us moves away from us at twice the speed of a closer galaxy. This became known as Hubble's Law.

Hubble was offered a position at the Mount Wilson Observatory in Pasadena, California. But since the United States was on the brink of entering World War I, he refused the position and enlisted in the army. He served overseas for two years, earning the rank of major. After the war, Hubble moved to California and was given the job he had turned down earlier.

In 1923, using mathematical formulas recently developed by fellow astronomers, Hubble measured the distance between the Earth and stars in the Andromeda cluster. What he found changed our understanding of the cosmos forever. Up to that time, it was commonly believed that the entire universe was contained in the Milky Way galaxy. But Hubble discovered that the stars he was measuring were located far beyond the boundaries of our galaxy.

Other astounding discoveries followed. In 1929, Edwin proved that the light from the distant galaxies had red-shifted, meaning that galaxies weren't static in their position, but were rapidly moving away from Earth. This was something that Einstein's theory of General Relativity had predicted, but few had accepted. In 1931, Einstein traveled to the observatory to meet with Hubble and see the expanding universe for himself. This led Einstein to finally admit that the universe did have a beginning and to famously say later, "I want to know [God's] thoughts . . . the rest are details."

The expanding universe and other contributions catapulted Hubble into the international limelight. Today, one of the world's most powerful telescopes bears his name—the Hubble Space Telescope, launched in 1990. You can examine a collection of stunning images produced by the Hubble telescope at www.spacetelescope.org.

5. ***How does the expansion of the universe prove that the universe couldn't have existed eternally?***

COSMIC BACKGROUND RADIATION

Good scientific theories often predict future discoveries. On account of the expanding universe, scientists predicted as early as 1948 that the universe began in a great explosion, derisively called "The Big Bang" by atheist Fred Hoyle. Scientists theorized there would be remnant heat from that explosion still out there. But no one bothered to look for it until two scientists discovered it by accident in 1965.

The remnant heat is actually *cosmic background radiation.* If you've ever watched an older TV in the dark, you have probably seen the glow that remains for a moment after you turn off the TV. That's remnant heat coming off the TV. That's what cosmic background radiation is like—it's remnant heat coming off the universe from the initial Big Bang explosion.

While working at Bell Labs in Holmdel, New Jersey, scientists Arno Penzias and Robert Wilson accidently discovered this radiation, which is only a couple of degrees above absolute zero. Its wavelength patterns were consistent with the heat and light that would result from a great cosmic explosion. Quite literally the "smoking gun" of the Big Bang, this cosmic background radiation put to rest any lingering thoughts that the universe was eternal.

6. ***How does cosmic background radiation disprove the Steady State theory, which states that the universe is eternal and continues as it always has?***

GREAT GALAXY SEEDS

In further investigating the radiation discovered by Penzias and Wilson, other scientists believed there should be slight variations in the temperature of that radiation, like ripples in a pond. They believed that if the radiation were uniform throughout the universe, there would have been no way for matter to collect and form the seeds of galaxies.

This theory was confirmed in 1992 by data gathered by the NASA satellite COBE (Cosmic Background Explorer). The pictures COBE sent back showed precise temperature variations in radiation, allowing just enough matter to congregate to form galaxies, but not so much as to cause the universe to collapse back in on itself.

The ripples in the radiation show that the beginning of the universe was extremely precise—accurate to one part in 100,000. Had it been even slightly different, galaxies would not have formed, leaving no place for life to have begun. Therefore, the Big Bang was not a chaotic, random explosion but seems to have been a purposeful, controlled event. It was a highly fine-tuned explosion, as if someone was guiding it along.

This discovery means that any talk of biological evolution dispensing the need for God is foolish. Even if macroevolution were true (it's not as we'll see later), that wouldn't mean God is out of a job. The discovery of these extremely precise temperature variations shows that a designer was needed to start the universe!

7. ***How were scientists able to measure the temperature variations in the cosmic background radiation of the universe?***

8. ***What did the project leader say when he announced the data COBE sent back? (See IDHEF, page 82.)***

EINSTEIN'S THEORY OF GENERAL RELATIVITY

In 1916, Albert Einstein developed the theory of General Relativity. The theory of General Relativity demands an absolute beginning for time, space, and matter and proves that all three are interdependent—you can't have one without the others.

General Relativity is congruent with the other lines of evidence making up our SURGE acrostic. Scientists predicted and then found the expanding universe, the radiation afterglow, and the great galaxy seeds that allowed our universe to form. These discoveries—added to the Second Law of Thermodynamics—tell us that the universe must have had a definite beginning.

In 1931, Edwin Hubble invited Einstein to the observatory in Pasadena, California, to observe the expanding universe for himself. Up to that time, Einstein assumed the universe to be static and eternal and had even put a fudge factor into his relativity equations to keep the universe static and eternal. But when Einstein saw the galaxies' red-shifted light through the observatory telescope (then the most powerful telescope on earth), he abandoned his fudge factor, returned to his original equations, and admitted that the universe had a beginning.

The SURGE evidence shows that space-time and matter came into existence together. In other words, the universe exploded into being out of nothing. Scientists call this the Big Bang, and theologians call creation out of nothing *ex nihilo*.

Photo: NASA/ESA/Hubble Heritage Team (STScI/AURA)

9. Where in the Bible is ex nihilo creation taught or implied?

OPPOSING THEORIES

Unhappy with the implications of the second law of thermodynamics and general relativity, atheists have tried to provide their own naturalistic theories about how the universe began. Let's take a quick look at two prominent ones.

The Cosmic Rebound Theory. Unable to avoid the evidence that the universe is expanding, some scientists have suggested that this is because the universe has been expanding and contracting forever. Although this approach sidesteps a definite beginning, the theory has a number of problems, the least of which is the lack of evidence for multiple "bangs."

One fatal flaw with this theory of eternal expansion and contraction is that there does not appear to be enough matter in the universe to pull everything back together in preparation for the next "bang." The latest data show that the universe will continue to expand indefinitely. Based on readings sent back from a recent space probe, Charles Bennett of NASA's Goddard Space Flight Center declared, "The universe will expand forever. It will not turn back on itself and collapse in a great crunch."

Another flaw with this theory is that the Second Law of Thermodynamics precludes perpetual explosions and expansions. Because there is a finite amount of energy in the universe, it would eventually run out and collapse after enough "bangs." Since the universe still exists today, we may conclude that the universe must have had a beginning.

Quantum Uncertainty. In an effort to avoid the fact of a beginning for the universe, some have questioned the truth of the first premise of the Cosmological Argument—the Law of Causality. They claim that since we cannot know both the precise location and speed of subatomic particles (known as the Heisenberg Uncertainty Principle), these particles aren't dependent on causality and therefore may have come into existence without a cause. There are several problems with these assertions:

- The quantum vacuum is not absolutely nothing. It is not non-being. It needs a cause itself! Similarly, the creation of space-time and matter out of nothing (non-being) requires a cause.
- This quantum uncertainty theory confuses causality with predictability. We may not be able to predict the movement of a subatomic particle (an event), but that doesn't mean that the existence of the particle itself is uncaused.
- The assertion that subatomic particles pop into existence without a cause has not been proven. There are several interpretations of causality at the quantum level. Some are determinate (requiring cause and effect), and others are indeterminate. No one knows which is correct. In fact, much of the speculative science of quantum mechanics consists of mathematical equations that have not even been worked out yet.
- To cast doubt on the Law of Causality is to cast doubt on all of science because science is a search for causes. And if subatomic particles can pop into existence without a cause, why doesn't everything do so?

Other atheistic theories have been put forth, but all have failed. (Check out the book *Reasonable Faith* by Dr. William Lane Craig for an in-depth refutation of these theories.) In the end there is no atheistic theory that adequately refutes the Cosmological Argument. The universe had a beginning, and therefore had a Cause that exists outside of time, space, and matter.

THE KALAM COSMOLOGICAL ARGUMENT

There's one last argument supporting a beginning for the universe that you should consider. The Kalam Cosmological Argument is not a scientific argument but a philosophical one. It shows that the universe had a beginning because time itself cannot be infinite.

Think of it this way: If there were an infinite number of days before today, how could this day have ever arrived? It couldn't. In other words, if the universe is eternal, then this day we are in right now would be forever in the future because more past days would have to pass before this one arrived. In an eternal universe, there are an infinite number of days, which means there would always be more days to pass before this one arrived. But since today is here, the universe must have had a beginning. This means that history cannot be infinite. Time had a beginning just as the Bible declares.

10. Why is this philosophical argument an important addition to the evidence that the universe must have had a beginning?

WHO MADE GOD? AND OTHER OBJECTIONS

The atheist may ask, "If the universe needs a cause, then God needs a cause. So who made God?" Although this may sound convincing on the surface, this question misapplies causality. The Law of Causality does not say that everything requires a cause. Rather, it says that everything that comes to be requires a cause. The universe came to be, so the universe needs a cause. But God does not.

If time was created (and the evidence we've just examined shows that it was), then the cause of time must exist outside of time. If something is timeless, it had no beginning and therefore needs no cause. Because God is eternal and exists outside of time, space, and matter, He did not need someone to create Him. Even the ancient Greek philosophers knew that there had to be an uncaused First Cause—an eternal, self-existing cause that got everything else started. The evidence shows that the cause of the universe has the same attributes as the being theists call God.

Atheists also tend to bring up the "God of the Gaps" objection, which charges you with plugging God into a gap in your knowledge. "You don't know the cause, so you're just going to say God did it!" they say, claiming that one day we will find a natural cause for the creation of the universe. But this objection doesn't work either.

We are not using God to plug holes in our knowledge, but rather, we are simply following the positive evidence for a supernatural cause where it leads. We don't simply lack a natural cause for the universe, but we have *positive* evidence for a supernatural cause. Since nature had a beginning, its cause must be *supernatural*, or "beyond nature." And since space, time and matter had a beginning, their cause must transcend all three—it must be spaceless, timeless, and immaterial. It must also be as personal because it made a decision to create.

The atheists tell us that science will find a natural cause for the creation of the universe. Notice that this is a faith position! Moreover, it is a blind faith position because they will never find a natural cause for all of creation. Nature itself was the effect, so nature cannot be the cause. It's like saying that if we look long enough, one day we will discover that we gave birth to our own parents!

11. How would you answer a friend who asks you, "Who made God?"

THE COSMOLOGICAL ARGUMENT AND THE AGE OF THE UNIVERSE

Some Christians don't believe in the Big Bang because they think it contradicts the teachings of the Bible. The authors think it fits. In fact, they believe in the Big Bang—but they know who caused it!

The Bible summarizes the creation event in the first verse: "In the beginning God created the heavens and the earth" (Genesis 1:1). Indeed, all the available evidence points to a beginning caused by our Creator. Although the authors don't believe in the naturalistic theory called the Big Bang— that the universe exploded into existence from an infinitesimally small, hot, dense concentration of energy—they do believe that the evidence for the beginning of the universe (including the evidence supporting the idea of a Big Bang) proves that our universe had a beginning. The authors also believe that the evidence irrefutably points to a personal Creator who transcends the universe.

So how does this relate to the age of the universe? Some people claim that the Bible and some scientific evidence indicate that the universe is very young, only thousands of years old rather than billions. Other Christians say the biblical and scientific data point to an older universe.

The age of the universe wasn't much of a controversy in the early church. In fact, Augustine wrote that the Bible did not tell us how old the universe is. The greater controversy that eventually arose 400 years ago was whether or not the earth moved. At first glance, the Bible seems to make it clear that the earth is stationary. The Bible says that the sun rises and sets (Ecclesiastes 1:5), that the "world is established" and "cannot be moved" (1 Chronicles 16:30), and that "the foundations of the earth are the Lord's" and "upon them he has set the world" (1 Samuel 2:8).

But we soon came to realize that our interpretation of the Bible was incorrect. With the invention of the telescope, we learned through observing the heavens that the earth is not the immovable center of the universe and that the sun does not literally rise and set. This fact is no longer controversial. We don't accuse people of turning their backs on the Bible for believing that the planets revolve around the sun. Instead, we recognize correctly that the Bible often uses observational or phenomenological language as we do ourselves. Even modern-day weather forecasters say, "Sunrise will be at 6:15 tomorrow morning." They do not say, "The earth's rotation will become apparent at 6:15 tomorrow morning"!

Turek and Geisler think the current debate over the age of the universe, like the old debate over heliocentricism, is not about the *inspiration* of scripture but, rather, the *interpretation* of scripture. God has written two books—the book of Scripture and the book of nature. The Bible itself teaches that God reveals Himself in nature (see Psalm 19:1, Romans 1:18–20, Romans 2:12–15), which is also called "General Revelation." While some of our interpretations of the Bible and nature may contradict one another, the two books do not (and cannot) contradict one another because God is the author of both.

Since both interpretations about the age of the universe require assumptions that cannot be proven, there is room for disagreement on this issue. While most scientists think the universe is billions of years old, they were not standing there when the universe began. Therefore, they have to make assumptions in order to arrive at an age, such as assuming that the speed of light hasn't changed (which makes the universe appear to be about 13.7 billion years old). But what if that assumption is wrong? If the speed of light was different in the past, then the light from the stars can't show us how old the universe is now.

We also have to make assumptions when interpreting the length of creation described in the book of Genesis. For example, how is the word "day" used, and can we use those "days" to discover the age of the universe? There appear to be at least four possible ways the word "day" may be used in the opening chapters of Genesis:

- Twenty-four hours
- Twelve hours, as in Genesis 1:5, which calls the light "day" and the darkness "night"
- A longer period of time or era, as in Genesis 2:4, which uses "day" to refer to the entire creation period. (We use the word "day" in this sense when we say "Eli Manning was one

of the best quarterbacks in his day."). This sense could also be the case with day three and day six, which chronicle events—the growth of fruit-bearing plants and the naming of the animals—that would seem to require longer than twenty-four hours.

- An indefinite period of time, as in the seventh day, which according to Hebrews 4:3–5, hasn't ended yet (God is still at rest from creating). In other words, the seventh day is certainly longer than twenty-four hours.

Yet even if the days of Genesis 1 are all twenty-four hours in length, the creation of the heavens and the earth takes place *before* the first day *begins*. The creation of the heavens and earth is declared in verses 1–2, but the first "day" begins in verse 3 with the phrase that begins all seven days: "And God said . . ." How long before the first "day" did all this take place? The text doesn't say. Therefore, regardless of the length of the days in Genesis 1, one could make a good case that the Bible leaves the age of the universe and the age of the earth indeterminate.

However, this ambiguity does not impact the fundamental foundation of our faith. When you die, God isn't going to determine your eternal destination based on how old you believed the universe to be. He's going to base it on your acceptance or rejection of His one and only Son, Jesus Christ (Romans 10:9)!

In fact, being dogmatic on the age of the universe may prove counterproductive. Most scientists believe the evidence for an older universe is much stronger than that for a younger universe. If people think you are asking them to swallow something that, in their minds, is demonstrably false, this could turn many of them away from Christianity as a whole. The fact *that* God created the universe is more important and certain than *when*.

Some will tell you that there is no possibility that the universe is old because there could not have been animal death before the Fall. But Romans 5:12 says that death came to all *men*, not all life. Moreover, Satan's fall preceded man's fall and may have impacted animal life. Yet even if the fall of mankind is responsible for animal death, it may have been so before Adam actually sinned. Just as the effects of salvation were in place before Christ went to the cross—the Old Testament saints were covered by the blood of Christ—the effects of the Fall on the rest of creation may have been in place before Adam actually sinned. This is implied by the very fact of a "garden." Why did God create and portion off a garden for Adam and Eve if the entire world was a paradise?

In any case, even if the earth is "old" it doesn't mean evolution is a fact, as we'll see in chapter 5. Nor do those who believe in an old earth necessarily believe in theistic evolution instead of a literal Adam and Eve. Indeed, there are reasonable scientific and biblical grounds to believe in an old universe and a recent literal Adam and Eve.

The truth is, the universe could be old or it could be young. The evidence is not definitive either way. Therefore, Christians need to focus on defeating the arguments for naturalism—not on the arguments of other Christians who agree that God created the universe and Adam and Eve but may disagree on *when* those events occurred. The foe is liberalism, not different stripes of conservatism.

If you would like to study this debate further, check out these resources. For a young-earth perspective from intelligent and sincere Christians, visit www.icr.org. For an old-earth perspective from intelligent and sincere Christians, visit www.reasons.org. Also, check out the book *Seven Days that Divide the World: The Beginning According to Genesis and Science* by Dr. John Lennox. This is a compact and very readable treatment of the subject.

12. Why is it impossible to know for certain how old the universe is?

13. How would it impact Christianity if the Big Bang were eventually proven wrong?

YOU DO THE DIGGING

All of the evidence we've examined in this chapter points to the fact that the universe had a beginning and thus was caused. From the Cosmological Argument, we can deduce that this cause must be spaceless, timeless, and immaterial, because this cause created space, time, and matter. The cause must also be personal, because only a personal being can choose to create. That personal being must also be immensely powerful, because he created the universe out of nothing. Finally, the cause must be intelligent, because our universe was created with extreme precision.

So using only the Cosmological Argument, we can see that the First Cause is spaceless, timeless, immaterial, personal, powerful, and intelligent. These are the attributes of a theistic God, all of them identified without referencing the Bible. Although this alone cannot prove that Christianity is true, it is strong evidence that points to the existence of a theistic God.

Now it's time to for you to do some digging on your own. Pick at least one of the following assignments and complete it before moving on in the workbook.

Assignment 1: Find an article on the Internet or in a scientific magazine that either rejects the idea that the universe had a beginning or says the beginning was not caused by God. Write a one-page report documenting at least three facts the article uses to support its position and how you would respond to each.

Assignment 2: Using your Bible, find five verses that show that God was either present at the beginning of the universe or was directly involved in creation. Write a paragraph for each verse stating what that passage tells us about the character of God.

Assignment 3: Find a copy of *God and the Astronomers* by Robert Jastrow. Read the first chapter and write a two-page report about Jastrow and what he had to say in that chapter about the beginning of the universe.

Assignment 4: Interview a non-Christian friend about what he or she believes about the origin of the universe, and then write a two- to three-page mock letter responding to his/her objections. Explain the evidence that convinces you that a theistic God is responsible for the beginning of the universe. (If you feel it is appropriate, use this letter to open a dialogue with your friend about his/her beliefs.)

TOOK

WHAT DO I DO NOW?

You have seen in this chapter that there is ample proof for the premise that the universe must have had a beginning. You've also seen that anything with a beginning must have a cause, and that the cause for the universe has attributes congruent with a theistic God. Now it is time to apply what you have learned to the world you live in.

THINKING ABOUT WHAT YOU LEARNED

Answer the following questions to sum up what you have learned in this chapter.

A. *Look again at the five most consequential questions in life as discussed in the Introduction. Does any of the information in this chapter help you answer these vital questions? How?*

B. Most scientists now admit the Big Bang occurred, but many seem reluctant to admit that God caused it. In fact, many of them react emotionally to the idea. According to astronomer Robert Jastrow, why is that so? (See IDHEF, pages 88–89.)

C. In Romans 1, the apostle Paul gives another reason why people reject the truth. What is it?

D. Based on the evidence for the beginning of the universe, we can determine several attributes of the First Cause. Explain how each of the following attributes can be derived from the SURGE evidence (see IDHEF, page 93).

Spaceless

Timeless

Immaterial

Personal

Powerful

Intelligent

E. *Read at least one of the following passages: Psalm 8, 19, 33, 65:5–8, 104, or 145. Which attributes of the First Cause are mentioned? Who does the Bible apply those attributes to?*

ASK FOR THE EVIDENCE!

The next time you hear someone say the universe has always been here or there is no God, ask him how he came to that conclusion. Remember, when someone makes a statement like that, it's not your job to refute it—it's his job to support it. So ask for the evidence!

Once he's answered, depending on the strength of his evidence and logic, you can continue the conversation by providing him with some of the evidence you've just studied supporting the beginning of the universe. Whip out your SURGE points or explain why the Kalam Cosmological Argument proves that time had a beginning. Then see where you can go from there!

CHAPTER 4

DIVINE DESIGN

BEFORE STARTING THIS CHAPTER

- Read chapter 4 of *I Don't Have Enough Faith to Be an Atheist* (IDHEF), pages 95–112.

ROAD MAP OF THE "TWELVE POINTS THAT PROVE CHRISTIANITY IS TRUE"

This chapter covers the following points:

3 The theistic God exists, as evidenced by
a) the beginning of the universe,
b) ***the design of the universe***
c) the design of life, and
d) moral law.

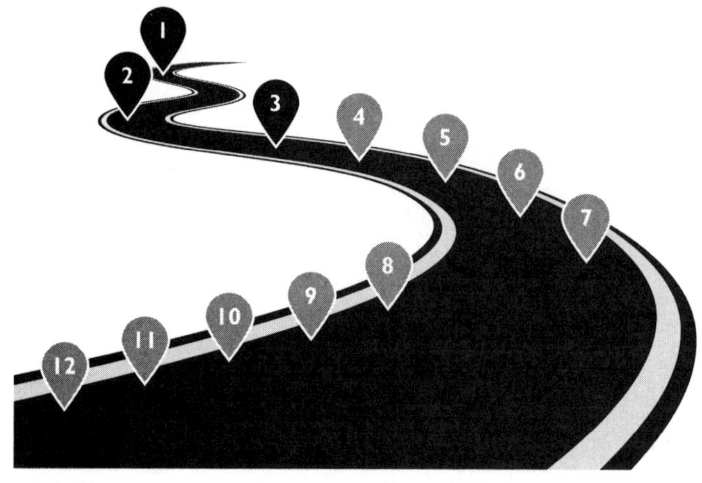

KEY TOPICS

After completing this chapter, you should be able to:

- Explain the Teleological Argument.
- Define the Anthropic Principle.
- Use the five Anthropic Constants discussed in this chapter to support the idea that the universe was divinely designed.
- Describe the problems with the Multiple Universe Theory.
- Explain how Psalm 19 and Isaiah 40:25–26 support the Teleological Argument.

KEY TERMS

Write the definitions for these words found in your reading:

Teleological Argument

Anthropic Principle

Anthropic Constants

QUESTIONS THAT GRAB YOUR MIND

When you go on a trip, you probably don't think too much about who designed and built the airplane you're flying in. You trust that it was designed and built to exacting specifications, taking into consideration aerodynamics and engineering. If the design or any of the parts that make up the airplane are even slightly flawed, your trip could end in tragedy.

If it takes that much planning, preparation, and precision to get an airplane off the ground safely, how much more does it take to create and maintain the universe at large? Without exactly the right amount of oxygen and nitrogen in Earth's atmosphere, the optimal distance from the sun, and several other important factors, life as we know it would cease to exist. So did that precise mix of environmental factors just happen, or was there design and forethought behind them?

As we'll see, even the slightest change in any of a number of environmental constants that make up the world we enjoy would result in catastrophe on a global scale. If a highly specialized machine like an airplane requires a designer, doesn't a complex universe require one as well?

1. Why is it important to follow a plan or design when building something?

2. If there is a "design" for the universe around us, how would knowing the designer impact you?

SO WHAT?

Many atheists claim that if Darwinism is true, there's no need for God. We'll see in the next two chapters that Darwinism does not appear to be true. But even if it were true, that would not put God out of a job. As we're about to see, the universe requires a designer—not just to explain new life forms, but also to explain the existence and design of the universe itself!

The universe was created with extreme precision and has been operating like a fine-tuned machine ever since. This requires the existence of an extremely intelligent being to have engineered it and to maintain its precise operation from the very beginning of the universe to this very moment. This means that there is purpose to our universe and, therefore, purpose to your life.

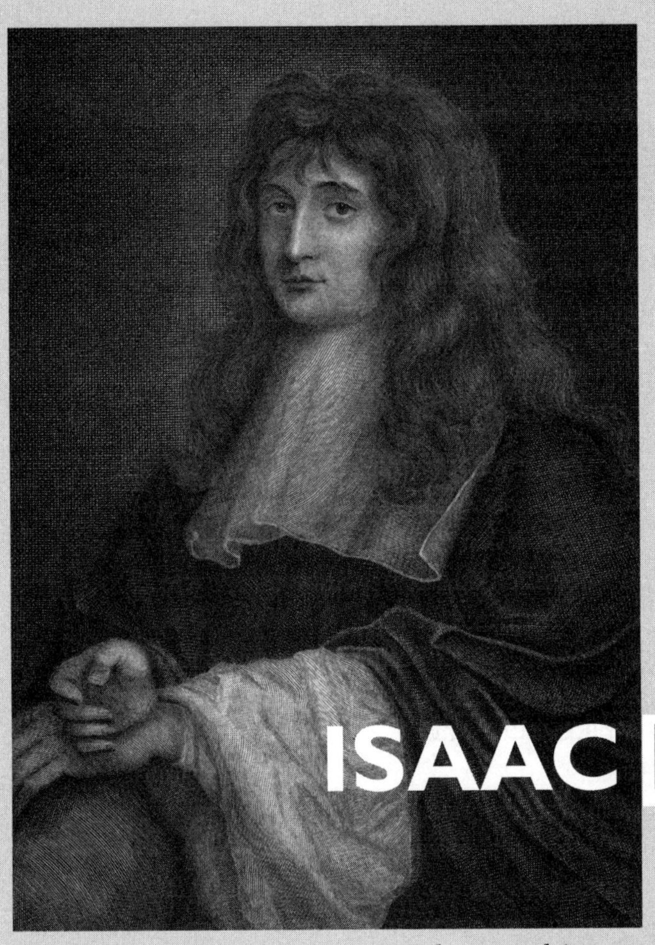

Considering that he is known today as one of history's foremost scientific minds, Sir Isaac Newton's life started rather inauspiciously. Born prematurely in England in 1643, he arrived three months after the death of his father. His mother soon remarried and left three-year-old Isaac to be raised by his grandmother. Struggling with feelings of abandonment, school became his consolation.

At the age of eighteen, Newton entered Trinity College in Cambridge. Although he didn't earn high marks in the classroom, Isaac reveled in the study of mathematics, physics, and chemistry on his own in the libraries of Cambridge. He graduated shortly before the university was temporarily closed because of the Great Plague. Newton continued his studies at home, and it was during this time that the legendary apple incident is said to have occurred.

ISAAC NEWTON

Although the incident is thought by some to be apocryphal, Newton himself often told the story that he was inspired to formulate his theory of gravitation by watching an apple fall from a tree. He wondered why the apple should always descend perpendicularly to the ground. Why did it not go sideways or upwards, he questioned, but constantly toward the earth's center?

During this fruitful period of his life, Newton laid the foundations for a new branch of mathematics called calculus. (Yes, he's to blame.) He also devised new theories regarding light and color and began his investigations into gravity and its effects on planetary movement. Two years after the university was reopened, Newton was appointed the Lucasian Professor of Math at Cambridge, a prestigious post that allowed him to continue his research.

In 1684, Edmund Halley (discoverer of the comet that bears his name) came to Newton with a question that had long vexed astronomers: What type of curve does a planet describe in its orbit around the sun? Isaac knew the answer to be an ellipse. Indeed, he had already performed the calculations but had characteristically misplaced them. He promised to send Halley a fresh calculation forthwith. Revisiting this question started Isaac down a path of research that in 1687 resulted in the publication of his greatest work: *Philosophie Naturalis Principia Mathematica* ("Mathematical Principles of Natural Philosophy"). Commonly called *Principia*, this extraordinary work is often considered the most important book in scientific history.

Newton moved to London in 1696, where he was appointed Master of the Mint and later elected president of the Royal Society, the leading scientific organization of its time.

Newton was also deeply religious and wrote extensively on matters of faith and about Judeo-Christian prophecy, which he believed was essential to the understanding of God. However, he privately rejected the doctrine of the Trinity and the worship of Christ as God. Nonetheless, Newton venerated the Bible and declared that evidence found in nature supports the biblical account of creation. "Gravity explains the motions of the planets," he wrote, "but it cannot explain who set the planets in motion. God governs all things and knows all that is or can be done."

FACTS IN THIS CHAPTER

Often you can recognize designers by their distinctive designs. One look at a distinctive building, car, or piece of clothing can help you learn something about the designer. Designers build their reputations on their ability to create things that are both beautiful and functional.

As you study this chapter, you will see that the universe exhibits highly complex design that points to a Designer who is powerful, intelligent, and has a purpose for the universe.

Let's start with what we know:

- There is a vast universe around us.
- The universe did not always exist; it had a beginning.
- The universe was finely tuned from the very beginning to support life on Earth.
- This fine-tuning is evidence of design, which implies a Designer.

This line of reasoning is called the Teleological Argument, from the Greek word *telos*, meaning "design" or "purpose."

THE TELEOLOGICAL ARGUMENT

As we've already seen, several scientific and philosophical arguments make the case that the universe had a beginning, that this beginning was from nothing, and that this beginning had a cause. But that's only part of the argument that points to a creator as the cause. Remember, that's our ultimate goal—to see if the evidence points to the God of the Bible.

Our second supporting argument, the Teleological Argument, says that the Big Bang was not a random event but one that was intentional and finely tuned. It points to numerous physical factors that suggest an intricate design to the universe. The Teleological Argument goes like this:

1. Every design had a designer.
2. The universe has highly complex design.
3. Therefore, the universe had a Designer.

The first premise is easily supported by observation of the way our world works—nothing we see that displays a design came into being without a designer. Therefore, we'll spend most of our time in this chapter proving the second premise, that the universe demonstrates highly complex design.

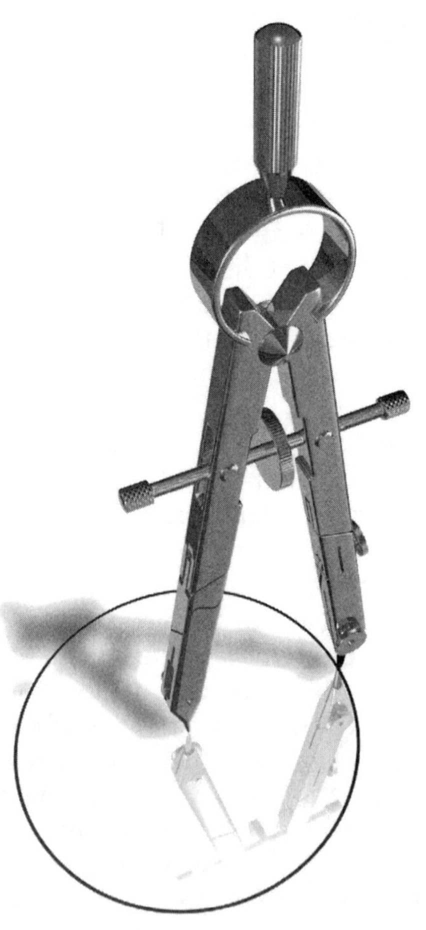

3. ***Explain William Paley's now-famous illustration and tell how it shows the validity of the first premise of the Teleological Argument.***

WHAT IS THE ANTHROPIC PRINCIPLE?

The term anthropic comes from the Greek word *anthropos*, meaning "mankind." The Anthropic Principle is a scientific observation that states that the universe is precisely tuned to support life on Earth. Any small variation in any of a number of factors could alter the delicate balance and cause the end of life on our planet.

It's as if there's a control room somewhere with hundreds of dials, all of which are adjusted to exactly the right settings for life within our universe to exist. In fact, many of these factors are interdependent. In other words, if just one of these universal constants was even slightly different, the change would affect the other constants and life and our universe would not exist.

Some of these physical factors are so precise (we've been calling them constants) that they defy any "chance" explanation. For example, if the gravitational force was altered by one part in 10^{40} (that's one part in 10 with 40 zeros following it), our sun would not exist and neither would we. How precise is one in 10^{40}? If you took a tape measure and stretched it across the known universe, then set the gravitational force at a particular mark on that tape measure, the "one part" would be represented by a single inch placed at precisely the right location on that tape measure. Move that imaginary section one inch to the right or left, and the universe could no longer exist! We don't have enough faith to believe that kind of precision happened without design.

4. ***How would you describe the Anthropic Principle to someone who is not a scientist?***

5. In what sense is Earth similar to a spacecraft such as Apollo 13?

ANTHROPIC CONSTANTS

Let's take a closer look now at some of these dials in the universe's control room. These anthropic constants make up the narrowly defined environmental conditions we need to survive. There are more than a hundred such constants, and more are being discovered every day. If you are interested in further study, read Hugh Ross's article "Why I Believe in Divine Creation" in the book *Why I Am a Christian: Leading Thinkers Explain Why They Believe*, edited by Dr. Geisler and Paul Hoffman.

Oxygen Level. One of the more obvious constants is Earth's oxygen level. All living things need to breathe. But if the amount of oxygen in our air were any less, then people and animals would suffocate, plants would die, and Earth would become a lifeless rock. On the other hand, if the level of oxygen in the air were any higher, then the atmosphere would be much too flammable and fires would rage across the planet uncontrollably. The chances are infinitesimal that our planet would have the perfect level of oxygen needed to sustain life unless someone had designed it that way.

Atmospheric Transparency. If the transparency of Earth's atmosphere were too dense, then it would deflect more of the sun's rays and the surface of the planet wouldn't receive the light and heat it needs to sustain life. If the atmosphere were any less dense, then we wouldn't be protected from the sun's radiation. All life would burn up, again leaving nothing more than a lifeless rock floating in space. Is it realistic to think that this perfect balance is the result of chance?

Moon-Earth Gravitational Interaction. Another anthropic constant is the interaction between Earth and its moon. In addition to helping us mark the passage of time, the moon's gravity affects the tides and even weather. If the moon's gravity were any stronger—that is, if it were closer to Earth or bigger than it is now—the atmospheric effects would cause massive damage. If the moon's gravity were any weaker—that is, if it were too far away or too small—the weather cycle would cease to function, making life on Earth impossible.

Carbon Dioxide Level. In addition to a breathable level of oxygen in the atmosphere, life as we know it also requires the right level of carbon dioxide. If there were any greater concentration of carbon dioxide in Earth's atmosphere, the air would be poisonous. If the concentration were any less, plants couldn't produce oxygen and people and animals would suffocate.

Gravity. Another major anthropic constant is the force of gravity. If it were even slightly stronger, all living things on our planet would be crushed. If gravity were even slightly weaker in the universe, planets and stars couldn't form, giving life no place to develop. So why is it that some people believe the universe came into being by mere chance?

6. ***The book cites five key Anthropic Constants that point to a distinctive design of the universe. List the five constants and explain how each one supports the precision and details of a divine design of the universe. Learn them and be prepared to cite them to an unbeliever as evidence of a divine Designer.***

7. ***In light of these constants, which takes more faith—believing that the universe came into being by chance or under the direction of an intelligent First Cause? Why?***

THE MULTIPLE UNIVERSE THEORY: IS IT VALID?

Some atheists try to counter the theistic implications of the Anthropic Principle with the Multiple Universe Theory, which states that there are an infinite number of universes out there and we just happen to be in the one that can sustain life. (Lucky us!) Although there's no evidence that other universes exist, that doesn't stop these people from insisting they're out there.

But this theory doesn't solve the problem. Just like positing that aliens were responsible for the beginning of life on Earth, adding multiple universes to the mix only increases the variables we have to account for. While the theory may sound plausible in the metaphysical realm, it doesn't coincide with what we see in the real world. For example, the Kalam Cosmological Argument showed that it is impossible to have an infinite number of finite things. A universe is a finite material thing; therefore it's impossible for there to be an infinite number of them.

Even proponents of the Multiple Universe Theory agree that it has problems. In 2006, Russian cosmologist Alexander Vilenkin admitted that even if multiple universes exist, the entire collection of universes would still require an absolute beginning. In his book *Many Worlds in One*, Vilenkin wrote, "It is said that an argument is what convinces reasonable men, and a proof is what it takes to convince even an unreasonable man. With the proof now in place, cosmologists can no longer hide behind the possibility of a past-eternal universe. There is no escape: They have to face the problem of a cosmic beginning."

8. ***Because the Multiple Universe Theory still needs to explain the cosmic beginning, what does that say about its ability to erase the need for God?***

WAS LIFE ON EARTH INEVITABLE?

Some atheists try to explain away the design of the universe by redefining the Anthropic Principle to mean that the conditions of the universe made mankind's arrival inevitable. In other words, the existence of mankind only proves that we are in the right universe, since different conditions could never have produced life and thus we would never have been here to know about them.

While it is certainly true that if the conditions were any different we wouldn't be here to know about them, that doesn't explain why the conditions of the universe are the way they are. Why is there a universe at all? And why did these extremely fine-tuned conditions for life arise? The most reasonable conclusion about the apparent design of the universe is that a Designer is responsible for it (especially in light of the fact that the Cosmological Argument has already given us evidence for a creator). So when we use the phrase "Anthropic Principle," we mean that the universe is precisely made enabling mankind to exist because a designer made it that way.

Some claim that another form of life entirely would have arisen had conditions been different. This is a faith-based assertion, and it says nothing about why the conditions of the universe are the way they are. It also doesn't account for the fact that the universe itself requires most of these constants regardless of whether life exists in it. In other words, if even a few of the constants in the universe were altered, not only would there be no life, but there would also be no universe! There would not even be chemistry! Nevertheless, some atheists still have faith that adding enough universes could enable all of this to happen by chance.

To see why this argument doesn't work, consider the game of poker. The chance of drawing a royal flush in a game of poker is one in 649,739. Now suppose two men are playing and one of them gets a royal flush. The other player might think, *Wow! That was a lucky hand.* But what if his opponent comes up with a royal flush in the next hand? And the hand after that? And the hand after that? The losing player is going to accuse his opponent of cheating!

Now imagine that his opponent responds, "Oh no, I'm not cheating. We just happen to live in a universe where I get four royal flushes in a row. And besides, you shouldn't be surprised you're seeing this, because if the conditions weren't right for me getting four royal flushes in a row, you wouldn't be here to observe it!"

What's the more reasonable explanation for the four royal flushes—that we live in the one universe (out of an infinite number of universes) where all the right conditions just happened to align or that the guy is cheating?

In a debate between atheist Richard Dawkins and Christian apologist John Lennox, Dr. Dawkins was asked, "Where did the laws of physics come from?" Dawkins said he had no idea, but he thought that suggesting God was the cause didn't help.

9. Explain how the claim that "If conditions had been different we would never have existed to observe them" fails to answer why conditions are the way they are.

10. Why not God? There are only two possible causes for the orderly and precise laws of nature: either intelligence or non-intelligence. Make a case that the laws of nature are better explained by a superior intelligence than by a random, non-intelligent cause.

WHAT DOES THE BIBLE SAY ABOUT THE TELEOLOGICAL ARGUMENT?

Our galaxy is enormous. There are about 100 billion stars in our galaxy, each separated by an average distance of around 30 trillion miles. Even though Isaac Newton and William Paley confirmed this through their scientific observations, the Bible directed us to look up to the heavens for proof of intelligent design long before any of these scientists existed.

11. Read Psalm 19. How does this chapter support the Teleological Argument?

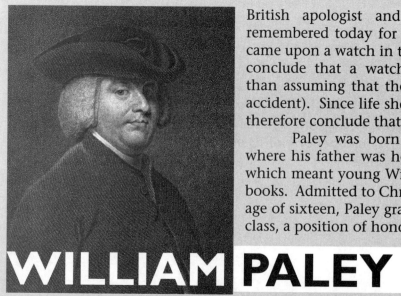

WILLIAM PALEY

British apologist and clergyman William Paley is remembered today for his watchmaker analogy: If you came upon a watch in the middle of a forest, you would conclude that a watchmaker had designed it (rather than assuming that the watch arrived fully formed by accident). Since life shows evidence of design, we must therefore conclude that life must have a Designer.

Paley was born in 1743 in northern England where his father was headmaster of a grammar school, which meant young William was always surrounded by books. Admitted to Christ's College in Cambridge at the age of sixteen, Paley graduated in 1763 at the top of his class, a position of honor called the senior wrangler. He returned in 1766 as a Fellow of Christ's College and lectured on metaphysics, philosophy, and the Greek New Testament.

After ten years as a professor, Paley left Cambridge to serve as a vicar, and then was appointed Archdeacon of Carlisle in 1782. While in Carlisle, Paley's friend and bishop,

12. Read Isaiah 40:25–26. How do these verses support the Teleological Argument?

The number of stars in the universe is about equal to the number of grains of sand on all the beaches on all the earth. And if you could fly at the speed of the space shuttle—about five miles per second—it would take you 201,450 years to complete a thirty-million-mile trip between just two of those stars. The Bible's use of the seemingly limitless expanse of the universe (heavens) helps us grasp what it means that God and His characteristics are infinite in scope.

Edmund Law, encouraged him to compile his philosophy lectures and publish them, offering his influence to arrange for a publisher. The result was *The Principles of Moral and Political Philosophy*, which was almost immediately made required reading at the universities in Cambridge.

In *Principles*, Paley spoke out strongly against slavery. The popularity of the book helped to bring public attention to the abolitionist movement. But some of his political views put him out of favor with church leaders, effectively bringing any hopes for career advancement to a halt. But Paley didn't seem to mind. He preferred a simpler life with time to study, write, and enjoy nature.

In 1790, Paley published *The Truth of the Scripture History of St. Paul*, which compared Paul's epistles with the book of Acts to show the historical accuracy of the New Testament. Paley also wrote *View of the Evidences of Christianity*, which was even more widely acclaimed. The Church of England appointed him to several positions around England, along with their incomes, yet Paley maintained a simple life.

Toward the end of his life, William Paley published his master work *Natural Theology: Evidences of the Existence and Attributes of Deity*. Here he put forth his ideas on the teleological argument for the existence of God, including his watchmaker analogy. This, too, was required reading at Cambridge for most of the nineteenth century—even Charles Darwin read it, commenting that it was one of the few works that was of benefit in his education.

13. Read Psalm 103:11. How much does God love those who fear Him? How does that make you feel, and how should it affect the way you live?

Long before the Anthropic Principle was discovered, C. S. Lewis, in his *Screwtape Letters*, had senior demon Screwtape advise his junior demon to keep people away from God by "pressing home on him the ordinariness of things. Above all, do not attempt to use science (I mean, the real sciences) as a defense against Christianity. They will positively encourage him to think about realities he can't touch and see. There have been sad cases among modern physicists." (The "sad cases" are those who have accepted the evidence they've seen and become Christians.)

In light of all the evidence for design in the universe, atheists have to have a lot of "faith" to reject belief in a Divine Designer. As the authors state, "This blind faith of the atheist reveals that the rejection of a Designer is not a head problem—it's not as if we lack evidence or intellectual justification for a Designer. On the contrary, the evidence is impressive. What we have here is a will problem—some people, despite the evidence, simply don't want to admit there's a Designer. In fact, one critic of the anthropic principle admitted recently that his real objection was 'totally emotional' because the principle 'smells of religion and intelligent design.'"

14. Has the scientific evidence you've seen so far convinced you that things aren't so ordinary—that there is a Divine Designer behind the universe? How?

YOU DO THE DIGGING

If we found a diamond-studded Rolex in the woods, we wouldn't assume it was the result of some combination of natural forces. We would recognize that it had been constructed with a clear design. And if there is a design, there must be a designer.

Throughout the ages, scientific evidence has pointed to God as the Intelligent Designer of our universe; so has the Bible, telling us to look to the heavens as proof of a Creator whose creation of the universe demonstrates His wisdom and power.

Now it's time to for you to do some digging on your own. Pick at least one of the following assignments and complete it before moving on in the workbook.

Assignment 1: Atheists cannot explain the extreme fine-tuning of the universe, which includes the laws of nature. Read the paper and watch the video about the Transcendental argument for God presented on the Christian Apologetics and Research Ministry website (http://carm.org/transcendental-argument). Then write a one-page paper explaining why theism explains immaterial and absolute laws, such as the laws of logic and laws of mathematics, better than atheism.

Assignment 2: Research and describe five other fine-tuned physical factors about our universe. For more, see Hugh Ross's video "Why I Believe in Divine Creation." Or you can visit his website at www.reasons.org.

Assignment 3: Watch the movie *Apollo 13,* taking note of how many environmental conditions affected the astronauts. Write a one-page summary of these conditions.

Assignment 4: Watch one of the debates between atheist Richard Dawkins and Christian John Lennox (visit www.CrossExamined.org and search for "Lennox Dawkins debate.") Summarize the main points each man makes. Who do you think had the better points and why? What did you think of Lennox's argument that the rational intelligibility of the universe and our ability to reason is better explained by theism than atheism?

TOOK

WHAT DO I DO NOW?

On a clear night, away from the lights of the city, you can see more than a thousand stars at a time with the naked eye. These heavenly bodies maintain their relative position or orbit around other bodies in the same patterns year after year. These stars and planets obey the laws of physics, so where did the laws of physics come from? Why are they so precise and orderly? The very laws of nature seem to be the product of the mind of a Designer.

The Anthropic Principle shows that without a Designer there would be no universe. It's not just the fact that there would be no life if some of the constants were not as they are—there would be no universe or laws of nature! So the Teleological Argument points out the precision with which the universe began and continues to operate. That's strong evidence that there is a Designer.

THINKING ABOUT WHAT YOU LEARNED

Answer the following questions to sum up what you have learned in this chapter.

A. List five major points you would like to remember from this chapter.

B. Summarize the five constants discussed in this chapter, using no more than a sentence each.

C. Why does God tell us to compare Him to the heavens?

D. There are only two possible causes for our precise universe—intelligence or non-intelligence. Discuss why an intelligent cause is the better explanation.

THAT'S ASTRONOMICAL!

Astrophysicist Hugh Ross has calculated the probability that these and other constants—122 in all—would exist for any planet in the universe by chance (i.e., without divine design). Assuming there are 10^{22} planets in the universe, his calculations show there would only be one chance in 10^{138}—that's one chance in ten with 138 zeros after it! There are approximately only 10^{70} atoms in the entire universe. In effect, this means there is zero chance that any planet in the universe would have the life-supporting conditions found on Earth—unless there is an intelligent Designer behind it all.

In light of these numbers, it takes much more faith to be an atheist than a Christian. Yet atheists persist, even inventing theories like the Multiple Universe theory—which is purely theoretical and not backed by any evidence—in what seems a desperate attempt to avoid the obvious. It seems then that the atheists' problem is not one of reason, but of the heart. They remain unwilling to follow the evidence to the obvious conclusion that there is a Designer—the God of the Bible.

Photo: NASA/JPL-Caltech

CHAPTER 5

THE FIRST LIFE: NATURAL LAW OR DIVINE AWE?

BEFORE STARTING THIS CHAPTER

- Read chapter 3 of *I Don't Have Enough Faith to Be an Atheist* (IDHEF), pages 113–135.

ROAD MAP OF THE "TWELVE POINTS THAT PROVE CHRISTIANITY IS TRUE"

This chapter covers the following points:

3 The theistic God exists, as evidenced by
a) the beginning of the universe,
b) the design of the universe
c) ***the design of life,*** and
d) moral law.

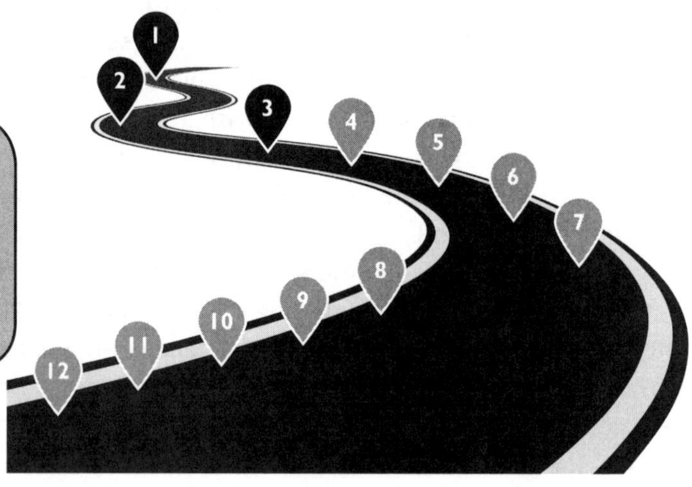

KEY TOPICS

After completing this chapter, you should be able to:

- Describe two possibilities for the origin of life.
- Explain how DNA reveals the specified complexity of life.
- Show how the Principle of Uniformity can be used to discover what caused the first life.
- Show why rejecting spontaneous generation and positing an intelligent cause to life is not "God of the Gaps" reasoning.
- Explain why giving more time to allow life to spontaneously generate contradicts the Second Law of Thermodynamics.
- Describe whether "chance" is a valid explanation for how life began.
- Give at least two reasons why materialism is not reasonable.

KEY TERMS

Write the definitions for these words found in your reading:

Spontaneous generation

DNA

Specified Complexity

Principle of Uniformity

Naturalism

Panspermia

Reductionism

Materialism

QUESTIONS THAT GRAB YOUR MIND

How did the first human come to exist? How did the first life form emerge? Is the origin of life just an accident, or did someone create it on purpose? This is one of the five most consequential questions in life, and answering it correctly is key to understanding the Box Top to life.

1. Why is it important to understand the origin of life?

SO WHAT?

Your belief about the origin of life affects how you view your own life. If everything that exists is the result of a cosmic accident and humans evolved from primordial goo, then life has no ultimate meaning. If humanity is nothing but a cosmic accident, then you are nothing but a highly evolved collection of cells whose ultimate fate is to return to dust. But if we were created, then you and everyone you know are endowed with rights, meaning, and purpose. What you believe matters.

TWO POSSIBILITIES FOR THE ORIGIN OF LIFE

When it comes to the origin of life, there are really only two possibilities: Either life is the product of intelligence or it is not. Either some kind of intelligence created life or it came together through the confluence of natural forces. While many atheists admit there is no good naturalistic explanation for the origin of life, they still insist that spontaneous generation must have occurred at some point, possibly in a warm pond millions of years ago. They insist on this view despite its lack of evidence because they have ruled out intelligent design in advance and therefore refuse to consider it as a real possibility. This is a philosophical presupposition that guarantees a naturalistic conclusion, and one that requires unreasonable faith to follow.

The fact is that the creation-versus-evolution debate is not so much a debate over evidence as it is over philosophy. Everyone is looking at the same evidence. So the debate really comes down to two major philosophical issues: 1) What causes will we consider possible before we look at the evidence? And 2) how should we interpret the evidence once we've gathered it? As we will see, philosophy and personal bias have more to do with "scientific" conclusions than most people think.

This chart summarizes the positions each view holds on the origin of life:

NATURALISM	INTELLIGENT DESIGN
Only natural causes are possible.	Natural and intelligent causes are possible.
The first life arose spontaneously by chance from non-living chemicals.	Even the simplest life has characteristics that are the products of intelligence and cannot be explained by natural causes.
Adding long periods of time increases the chances for spontaneous generation.	No amount of time is enough to allow spontaneous generation to occur.
The creation-versus-evolution debate is about religion versus science.	The creation-versus-evolution debate is about good science versus bad science.
Although spontaneous generation isn't supported by empirical observation, it is still the best explanation for life's origin.	Based on the principle of uniformity (the present is the key to the past), intelligent design is the best explanation for life's origin.

Many Darwinists start with false philosophical assumptions based on naturalism, or materialism, and insist that science is the only source of objective truth (which is a self-defeating proposition because the claim itself is philosophical and not scientific). Intelligent Design (ID) proponents recognize that science depends on philosophy and so is only one means of finding truth. Intelligent design proponents also recognize that philosophical assumptions can dramatically impact scientific conclusions.

2. ***What two things must exist before new life forms can come into existence? (Note: Both of these things display design and thus require a designer.)***

FACTS IN THIS CHAPTER

As we have seen, when we look through telescopes at our massive universe, we see highly fine-tuned design. In this chapter, we will see that when we look into a microscope at even the tiniest life form, we see amazing evidence of design there too.

DNA AND SPECIFIED COMPLEXITY

In 1953, James Watson and Francis Crick isolated the structure of DNA (deoxyribonucleic acid), which contains the chemicals that encode instructions for building and replicating all living things. Bill Gates, founder of Microsoft, has said, "DNA is like a software program, only much more complex than anything we've ever devised." Indeed, the "code" present in the rungs of DNA's double-helix ladder is similar to those used by computer programmers. Computers do not have any built-in intelligence, so they must rely on instructions from a program that has been carefully designed by an intelligent being. Every living being has DNA encoded in its cells, and that code contains the set of instructions comprising the unique genetic makeup of that being.

Genetics is the study of how living organisms inherit traits from their ancestors. This helps explain why you look like your parents or grandparents, for example. Genetic information has been carried by their DNA and copied across one or more generations, with some traits being more dominant than others. (If your parents have brown eyes, you probably do too.) DNA is made up of a sequence of simple units (A, T, C, and G), and the specific order of these units spell out instructions in the genetic code. Just like reading this book requires you to know what the particular sequence of letters mean in any word, so your body is able to "read" the sequence of units in its DNA and decode the genetic instructions. The instructions about your particular traits are contained in segments of DNA called genes.

The sequence of the four-letter alphabet of DNA contained within a living cell determines the unique genetic makeup of that cell and thus the organism as a whole. This is known as *specified complexity*, which means 1) that the makeup of DNA is complex and 2) that it contains a specific message. The DNA of just the cell nucleus of one tiny amoeba contains more information than all thirty volumes of the *Encyclopedia Britannica* combined. And if you were to spell out all the A, T, C, and G units in the entire amoeba, the letters would fill a thousand sets of encyclopedias.

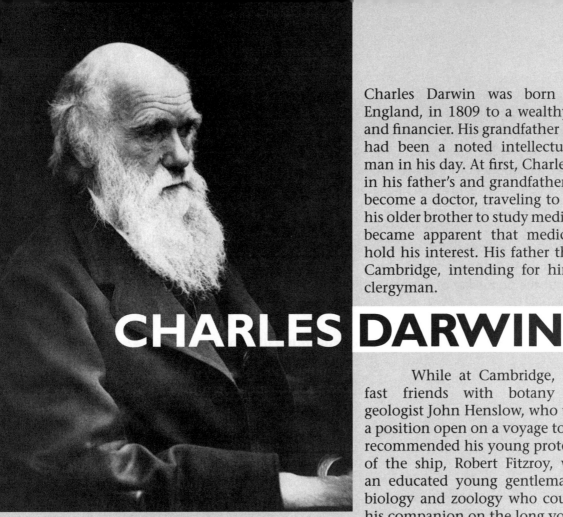

Charles Darwin was born in Shropshire, England, in 1809 to a wealthy society doctor and financier. His grandfather Erasmus Darwin had been a noted intellectual and medical man in his day. At first, Charles tried to follow in his father's and grandfather's footsteps and become a doctor, traveling to Edinburgh with his older brother to study medicine. But it soon became apparent that medicine just didn't hold his interest. His father then sent him to Cambridge, intending for him to become a clergyman.

CHARLES DARWIN

While at Cambridge, Darwin became fast friends with botany professor and geologist John Henslow, who upon hearing of a position open on a voyage to South America, recommended his young protégé. The captain of the ship, Robert Fitzroy, was looking for an educated young gentleman interested in biology and zoology who could also serve as his companion on the long voyage. Darwin fit the bill splendidly, and after being accepted, he set out on the HMS Beagle in 1831 for what would become a nearly five-year-long expedition.

The voyage gave Darwin an opportunity to indulge his first love: observing the world around him. He took exacting notes of everything he came across on the journey and collected specimens as often as he could. Periodically, his notes and specimens were shipped back to Cambridge for further study. Given the variety of plants and animals he encountered, Darwin became convinced that the different species must have developed gradually, through a series of small changes over time. He found his study of the Galapagos Islands to be particularly fascinating and helpful in cementing his theories.

When the Beagle finally returned home to England, Darwin found he had already become something of a celebrity. His mentor Henslow had compiled the notes Darwin had sent back and circulated them among the scientific community. Almost immediately after his return, Darwin began editing his notes for publication and lecturing on his findings.

His expedition on the Beagle had planted the seeds for his theories of evolution and natural selection, and he spent the next two decades refining his ideas, incorporating input from other scientists as well as working-class people such as farmers and horse breeders. In 1859, Darwin published his most famous work, *On the Origin of Species by Means of Natural Selection, or the Preservation of Favored Races in the Struggle for Life*. Although the work was well received in intellectual and scientific circles, it caused a great deal of controversy elsewhere. Many felt his theories directly contradicted the story of creation in Genesis and implied that human beings were no better than animals themselves.

Darwin's theory of evolution inspired many other intellectuals who were eager to explain life without God. Despite the many problems and counter evidence discovered since 1859, Darwin's theory still dominates secular science education today.

The origin of the DNA code is a supreme problem for atheists. To say that materials can create a code is like saying that an iPod can create its own music. (If it could, you wouldn't have to pay all that money to iTunes!) The DNA code, like a song from iTunes, is immaterial. It is a digital code that is the product of a mind. (A great book on this topic is *Signature in the Cell* by Dr. Stephen Meyer, a proponent of Intelligent Design.)

The DNA code, while expressed in chemicals, is not determined by random physical forces any more than the order of the words in this sentence is determined by random physical forces. In other words, just as the laws governing ink and paper cannot explain the order of the letters in this sentence, the laws of physics, chemistry, and biology cannot explain the order of the letters in your DNA. A code is always the product of an intelligent mind. So for atheists, who have ruled out the possibility of design in advance, the complexity and order of DNA is very hard to explain.

3. In light of the genetic code, why is so-called simple life not really simple?

WHAT CAUSED THE FIRST LIFE?

Since no human observed the origin of the first life, how can we know how the first life came into being? Well, the origin of life is a forensic question, so we can employ the same scientific principles that are used every day by our criminal justice system.

The central principle of forensic science is the Principle of Uniformity, which states that causes in the past were like the causes we observe today. So if the cause of something in the past was due to natural laws, it should be the same today. Likewise, if something today requires an intelligent cause, then it must also have required an intelligent cause in the past.

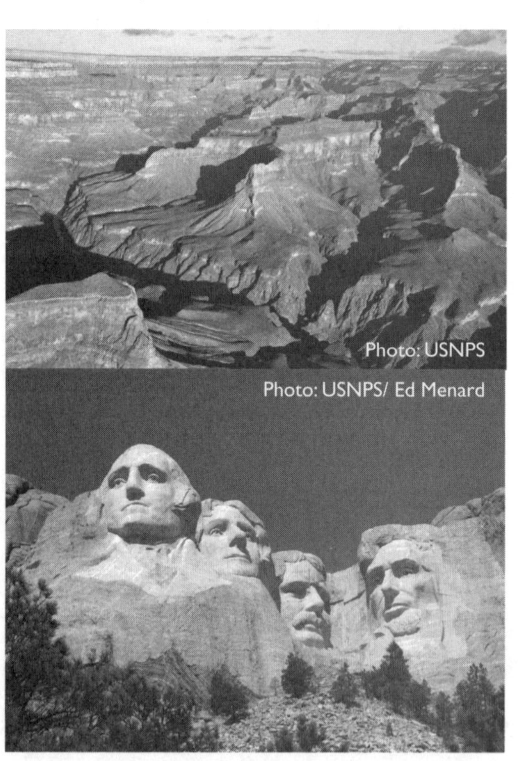
Photo: USNPS

Photo: USNPS/ Ed Menard

The book references two examples—the Grand Canyon and Mount Rushmore. Human beings didn't observe the origin of the Grand Canyon, but based on studies in geology, we can safely assume that the Grand Canyon was caused by natural forces (in this case, a lot of water). On the other hand, the Principle of Uniformity leads us to conclude that the presidential faces on Mount Rushmore could not have been formed by natural forces. Intelligence is the only viable explanation for something that contains such specified complexity.

So when we find so-called simple life forms containing such specified complexity, the Principle of Uniformity should lead us to conclude that intelligence is its cause (that is, if our own naturalistic philosophy doesn't get in the way).

Science is a search for causes. There are two types of causes: intelligent and non-intelligent (or natural). There are also two types of science: empirical and forensic. Empirical science is used to study present, repeatable events (those things we can witness through our senses), whereas forensic science is used to study past, unrepeatable events (those we must use logic to determine).

4. ***List two additional examples of effects with natural causes besides the Grand Canyon.***

5. ***List two additional examples of effects with intelligent causes besides Mount Rushmore.***

SPONTANEOUS GENERATION

The spontaneous generation of life has never been observed, though not for lack of trying. Scientists have attempted to combine chemicals to simulate the environment that they theorize would have been necessary for spontaneous generation to happen. Their attempts have failed. The inability of the brightest scientists to create even the simplest life form is evidence that "simple life" is not simple at all. Moreover, if human intelligence hasn't been able to create life, why should we expect non-intelligent natural processes to do so?

There is also a "chicken and egg" problem for those who advocate spontaneous generation. The question is which came first, proteins (which are critical to the formation of DNA) or DNA (which is critical to the formation of proteins)? One must already be in existence for the other to be made.

Some may argue that just because we haven't found a natural explanation for the existence of life doesn't mean we won't find it in the future. While it is possible that one day we could find a natural explanation, it does not seem likely. There are only four known natural forces—gravity, electromagnetism, and strong and weak nuclear forces—and they appear to be repetitive forces that do not create the unique messages (specified complexity) found in life. The Second Law of Thermodynamics also weighs against order arising from disorder. If anything, life is highly ordered. How could non-living chemicals organize themselves into life?

As we have discussed, people sometimes accuse Christians of committing the "God of the Gaps" fallacy by plugging God in wherever there is a gap in knowledge. However, and *this is essential*, the conclusion that life was created by an intelligent being is not a "God of the Gaps" argument. When you see "John loves Mary" written in the sand on the beach and conclude that the message was caused by an intelligent being, you did not do so because you lacked a natural explanation for its existence but, rather, because such a message was *positive*

FRANCIS CRICK & JAMES WATSON

Photo: Public Library of Science (CC BY 2.5)

Molecular biologists Francis Crick and James Watson are credited with discovering the double-helix structure of DNA, arguably the most important scientific discovery of the twentieth century. For this discovery, Crick and Watson were awarded the 1962 Nobel Prize in physiology.

Francis Crick was born in England in 1916. Always attracted to science, Crick entered University College of London in 1933 and graduated four years later. Though first drawn to physics, he instead chose a field that he felt had more potential for great discoveries—biology. In 1951, Crick began working at the Cavendish Laboratory in Cambridge, spending two years using X-ray diffraction to take pictures of the structure of proteins.

Twelve years younger than Crick, Watson's scientific career began in America. He was a bright young boy who loved bird watching with his father. At the age of fifteen, he enrolled in the University

evidence for an intelligent being. Likewise, it is not because we lack a natural explanation for the massive amounts of information contained in life forms that leads us to believe in a supernatural cause. Rather, we do so because such information is positive evidence for an intelligent cause. To believe that a thousand sets of encyclopedias could be the result of natural forces is like believing that the Library of Congress is the result of an explosion in a printing shop! That's a "science of the gaps" position, and we don't have enough faith to believe that.

6. Why is positing intelligent design of the first life not "God of the Gaps" reasoning?

of Chicago. Watson went on to study at Indiana University where he earned his PhD at the age of twenty-two.

Watson's post-doctorate work took him to Cambridge, where he became friends with Francis Crick. Discovering they were both fascinated by the structure of molecules, Crick and Watson joined forces to discover the specific structure of DNA. They were on the clock—American biologist Linus Pauling was close to his own solution. But Crick and Watson were determined to get there first. They succeeded in March 1953, deducing DNA's double-helix shape from X-ray diffraction photos of proteins taken by Dr. Rosalind Franklin at King's College in London, a rival laboratory. Although the immediate response to their discovery was subdued, its significance eventually earned them and colleague Maurice Wilkins a Nobel Prize nine years later.

With their careers soaring, both men moved to the United States. Crick took a prestigious position at the Salk Institute for Biological Studies in California, where he turned his attention to neurobiology and the study of human consciousness. His 1994 book *The Astonishing Hypothesis* revealed his materialist view of reality: that we have no real consciousness or free will because only materials exist and, therefore, everything is determined by physics. For all his scientific brilliance, Crick didn't seem to realize his astonishing hypothesis is logically self-defeating. If we have no free will—if all thoughts are completely determined by chemical reactions—then we have no grounds to believe his thoughts and hypotheses are true because they were completely determined by chemical reactions.

Watson became director of the Cold Springs Harbor Laboratory in New York, a position he held for nearly forty years, pointing the lab's research toward finding a cure for cancer. Watson was also influential in starting the Human Genome Project with the goal of mapping the genetic heritage of people groups around the world.

Crick and Watson's first DNA model is now on display at the National Science Museum in London.

INTELLIGENT CAUSES VS. SUPERNATURAL CAUSES

The Rosetta Stone. Photo: Albeins (cc-by-3.0)

ID (Intelligent Design) theorists have made the case that the proper distinction in the debate is between natural and intelligent causes, not natural and supernatural causes. That certainly makes sense in scientific endeavors such as archaeology, forensic criminal investigations, cryptology, and even SETI (the real-life Search for Extraterrestrial Intelligence, as depicted in the movie *Contact*). This distinction is not being "intellectually lazy," as atheist Richard Dawkins has declared, nor is it some kind of God-of-the-gaps argument. We don't assume, for example, that the Rosetta Stone is a result of an intelligent being because we lack a natural explanation for it but, rather, because the inscriptions are positive, empirically detectable evidence for an intelligent cause.

There does come a point, however, when we need to make a distinction between natural and supernatural causes. Certainly that seems to be the case with the creation and fine-tuning of the universe. There can be no natural cause for the universe because nature didn't exist prior to the Big Bang. Nature itself was created at the beginning of the universe—it was the effect. Since space, time, and matter were created with extreme precision, the cause behind them must be spaceless, timeless, immaterial, and intelligent. This requires not just an intelligent cause but also a supernatural one.

Cosmology is one thing, you may say, but what about biology? Again, the evidence points toward the supernatural as the ultimate cause of all living things, especially the genetic code. The genetic data doesn't necessarily tell us whether the cause of the genetic code exists inside or outside the natural world—for example, some claim that this code could have been planted by an intelligent alien species that exists in the natural universe. However, if no known natural forces can create the genetic code, then no known natural forces could have created the intelligent aliens who are suspected of having created the genetic code. Therefore, we must ultimately arrive at a supernatural cause for the genetic code, not just an intelligent one.

When you consider the background information brought to us by cosmology, it seems that the best candidate for authorship of the genetic code is the same spaceless, immaterial, timeless, and intelligent being who created the universe. So while natural-versus-intelligent causes is the proper distinction for some ID questions, when it comes to ultimate ID questions, the proper distinction is natural-versus-supernatural.

Ultimately the evidence also points to a personal supernatural force—someone who exists beyond nature, beyond space, time, and matter, but also possesses the volition to choose to create. As we progress through this curriculum, we'll see that this being actually is the God of the Bible.

7. ***When scientists reason, they often work backward from the effect to its cause. What effects tell us that there must be an ultimate Designer who is not just intelligent but also supernatural?***

PANSPERMIA

Many think that the creation/evolution debate is a debate between religion and science, but it isn't. It's about good science versus bad science. It's not about faith versus reason; it's about reasonable faith versus unreasonable faith. Spontaneous generation cannot be supported by empirical observation or forensic science principles—it's just all atheists have left after willfully ruling out any kind of intelligent cause for life.

The evidence is so strong for an intelligence cause (as opposed to naturalism) that evolutionists have gone so far as to suggest that alien beings deposited the first life on Earth. Fred Hoyle invented this theory, called panspermia (or "seeds everywhere"), after calculating that the probability of life arising by spontaneous generation was effectively zero. But this simply takes the question back a step to who made the intelligent aliens? (This is different from asking who made God, because an eternal God does not require a beginning. Intelligent aliens, however, do require a beginning.) If natural forces cannot create life on earth, then why should we expect natural forces to create alien life elsewhere? Faith is the foundation of this atheist position.

8. ***Why is the creation-versus-evolution debate not over religion versus science, but over good science versus bad science?***

9. What makes panspermia a weak explanation for the origin of life?

REDUCTIONISM

Reductionism is the false belief that you can reduce life, and everything else, to its nonliving chemical components. The problem with this belief is that DNA proves that life is more than a conglomeration of nonliving chemicals. Life contains a message that is in the DNA, but those chemicals do not cause the message. A reductionist would say that everything about a book can be reduced to ink and paper. But such an assertion is nonsense. The message in a book, like the message in DNA, points to an intelligence beyond its mere chemical elements. In fact, while information can be expressed through chemicals (like ink and paper or DNA), the source of that information must exist outside of the components.

10. Why isn't reductionism a valid explanation for the origin of life?

TIME, CHANCE, AND THE SECOND LAW OF THERMODYNAMICS

When pressed with evidence showing that life could only have begun through an intelligent source, Darwinists try to defend their position with two dubious explanations. Neither adequately answers the question of how life came to begin in the universe.

First, they say that given enough time, life will eventually evolve from nonliving chemicals. The problem with this theory is that everything we observe in the world around us tells us that natural laws tend to bring things toward disorder rather than order. This is an aspect of the Second Law of Thermodynamics. How did life arise from nonliving chemicals without intelligence when nonliving chemicals are susceptible to the Second Law? The truth is, the longer we wait for nonliving chemicals to generate life, the more disorderly the chemicals will become. Thus there must be some intelligent cause beyond natural laws to provide the order and information needed to create life.

Second, Darwinist suggest that life came into being by chance. The problem with leaving the creation of life to chance is that you need about two hundred protein molecules, each consisting of one hundred amino acids, to come together just to have the elements necessary to produce the most basic life form. But there's not enough time or resources in our entire galaxy to produce even one protein by chance, much less life itself. In effect, the probability of life originating by chance in the universe is zero.

11. ***Briefly define the Second Law of Thermodynamics and explain why giving more time to allow life to spontaneously generate contradicts this law.***

12. ***Why isn't leaving the origin of life up to chance plausible? What does the book say about "chance"? Does it have any causal power?***

CAN SCIENCE ALONE REALLY ACCOUNT FOR EVERYTHING?

Darwinists want to explain everything using science. Using science to search for causes by observation and repetition is just one of the ways we can discover truth, but it is not the only way. As we have seen, we can also employ the laws of logic and historical evidence to discover truth.

While science is a great tool we can use to learn truth, we need to understand that science cannot be done without philosophy—philosophical assumptions underlie the search for causes. You must assume some things to be true in order to conduct an experiment. If your philosophical assumptions are wrong, your scientific conclusions may be wrong as well. If a person begins with the assumption that only natural causes are possible, then no amount of evidence to the contrary will convince that person of the existence of a Creator.

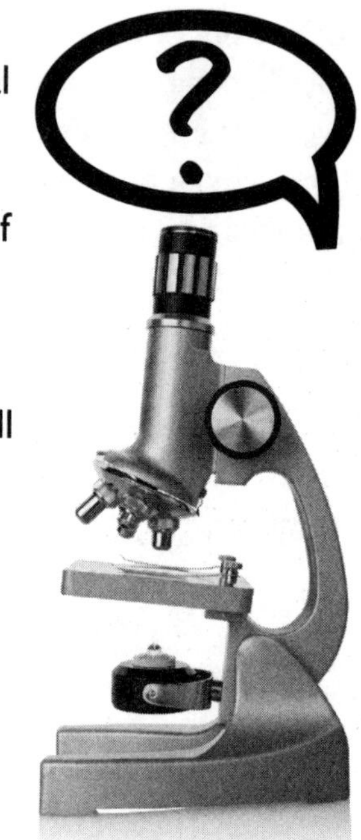

The fact is that science doesn't really say anything—scientists do. All data must be interpreted, and that is done by people who call themselves scientists. When scientists undertake to study a biological life form, the creature doesn't come with a label that says "Made by God" or "Evolved." The scientist must look at the data and make an interpretation, and that involves philosophical reasoning skills. When those scientists let their personal preferences dictate their assumptions or interpretation of the evidence, then their ideology is dictating their conclusions, not the other way around. Ironically, that's exactly what many secular scientists accuse religious people of doing!

13. *What philosophical assumption do Darwinists make regarding causes before they even look at the evidence?*

14. *How do those philosophical assumptions affect their conclusions?*

YOU DO THE DIGGING

The case for Intelligent Design is fully supported by good science. But naturalists appear to be too influenced by their preconceived materialistic philosophy to apply good science to the question of the origin of life. Not only can they not explain the origin of life using natural law, but the complexity of DNA and the messages written into the smallest elements of human cells is evidence for Intelligent Design. However, the Darwinists ignore the evidence and take it on faith that one day they will find a natural explanation. Thus, the Darwinian theory of the origin of life is based on a kind of faith and is little more than a secular religion disguised as science.

Now it's time to for you to do some digging on your own. Pick at least one of the following assignments and complete it before moving on in the workbook.

Assignment 1: Visit the Crossexamined.org website and read Frank Turek's article "Science Doesn't Say Anything, Scientists Do." From what you learn in the article, describe how a scientist's ethics, philosophy, worldview, and even his desire for fame and fortune may influence and color his conclusions or interpretations.

Assignment 2: National Geographic is an institution that produces a large amount of information on the study of Earth and the life on it. It's also an institution steeped in naturalism. Find a National Geographic article on the origin of life on the Internet or at your library. Write a one-page paper documenting and refuting the article's main points.

Assignment 3: Go to www.discovery.org and search for a recent article on the origin of life. After reading it, summarize the major points made in the article in one page or less. What kind of evidence did the author present? How did the author's worldview come through in the article?

TOOK

WHAT DO I DO NOW?

Previous chapters have focused on the evidence for the beginning and intelligent design of the universe. This chapter has examined the simplest components of life (which are not "simple" at all). As we have seen, it's important to consider the context in which the evidence you are reviewing exists, whether you're looking at the whole of the universe or a single cell. We have learned there is overwhelming scientific evidence of intelligent design. We have also learned that naturalistic biologists often come to their "scientific" conclusions due to their prior philosophies of naturalism and materialism.

Discovering the most reasonable view of the origin of life is foundational to building the rest of your view of life—which "box top" you are using. Now it is time to apply what you have learned to the world you live in.

THINKING ABOUT WHAT YOU LEARNED

Answer the following questions to sum up what you have learned in this chapter.

A. *Why is it reasonable to conclude that there must be a supernatural intelligent cause for the first life?*

B. *How might a scientist's worldview affect the way he or she does science?*

C. Now that you know that "Science doesn't say anything—scientists do," how can you use this understanding to respond to people who say, "Science disproves God" or "Science proves evolution"?

D. How is the suggestion that life was brought here by aliens a tacit admission that intelligence is detectable in nature?

DON'T FORGET!

The debate about how life originated has raged for centuries. Both sides have accused the other of narrow-mindedness. Too frequently people who believe in intelligent design have been accused of being brainwashed by religion. You have already seen in this study that this charge is far from accurate. The evidence we've seen for intelligent design did not begin with the Bible but started with observations from the world around us and used science and logic to unlock the truths you have learned.

The evidence points to a design that is too complex and too well planned to have happened by accident. The characteristics of the "first cause" are exactly the characteristics theists ascribe to God. As Geisler and Turek stated, "These characteristics are not based on someone's religion or subjective experience: They are drawn from the scientific evidence we have just reviewed about ordinary things we can observe. As scientist Ariel Roth put it, 'God never performed a miracle to convince an atheist, because his ordinary works provide sufficient evidence.'"

CHAPTER 6

NEW LIFE FORMS:

FROM THE GOO TO YOU VIA THE ZOO?

BEFORE STARTING THIS CHAPTER

- Read chapter 3 of *I Don't Have Enough Faith to Be an Atheist* (IDHEF), pages 137–167.

ROAD MAP OF THE "TWELVE POINTS THAT PROVE CHRISTIANITY IS TRUE"

This chapter covers the following points:

3 The theistic God exists, as evidenced by
a) the beginning of the universe,
b) the design of the universe
c) ***the design of life,*** and
d) moral law.

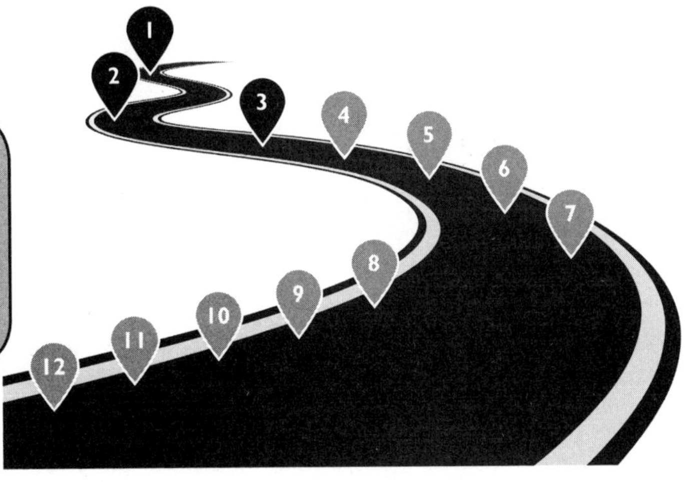

KEY TOPICS

After completing this chapter, you should be able to:

- Explain the difference between *microevolution* and *macroevolution*.
- Define natural selection and explain its relationship to evolution.
- Give five reasons for why natural selection cannot produce new species.
- Describe the significant support for Intelligent Design theory provided by the fossil record.
- Discuss why Darwinism cannot explain the dissimilarity between living things.
- Explain three objections Darwinists typically have to Intelligent Design.
- Discuss why, in spite of all the evidence, Darwinists still believe in evolution.

KEY TERMS

Write the definitions for these words found in your reading:

Macroevolution

Natural Selection

Microevolution

Genetic limits

Cyclical change

Irreducible complexity

Nonviability of transitional forms

Molecular isolation

Intelligent Design

QUESTIONS THAT GRAB YOUR MIND

Where did the universe come from? Why is the universe so finely tuned? How did the first life come into being? We have seen that the best answer to these questions is a theistic God. But some Darwinists act as if they can sidestep these questions by simply stating that God doesn't exist because new life forms can be explained without God through the process of macroevolution.

There are two big problems with this line of reasoning—problems so big you could drive a universe through them! First, the fact is that biology can't even get started without space, time, and matter (which, as we've seen, require a cause outside of all three). And second, new life forms can't "evolve" unless there is a first life from which to evolve!

We'll see in this chapter that macroevolution does not appear to be true. But even if it proved to be true, that wouldn't mean atheism is true. A creator/designer is necessary to explain the universe and first life regardless of how new life forms develop.

What is the truth about new life forms? Did we all descend from the first life through some kind of natural evolutionary process? Or was there a creator who brought new life forms into existence? What you will hear on almost every college campus, in nearly all museums, and over and over again on television is that there was no creator or designer. Instead, all life forms—from amoebas to snakes to humans—evolved naturally from a single common ancestor.

Someone once said, "It's not what we don't know that is the problem, but what we think we know that isn't so." Could macroevolution be one of those "facts" that many people think is true but really isn't? We think it takes a lot more faith to believe in macroevolution than to believe there was an intelligent designer. What do you think?

1. Do you think a Christian can believe in macroevolution? Why or why not?

SO WHAT?

How often have you been in a conversation with someone and they told you to prove your statement or belief? Just what do they mean when they say that? When someone asks where you came from, you might answer, "From my mom and dad." If they wanted you to go further back than a generation, you might be able to tell them who your grandparents or even great-grandparents were. You might even have some yellowed photographs documenting your recent heritage. The people in these photographs might wear very different clothes and hairstyles, but they still look like people—like you.

MICROEVOLUTION VERSUS MACROEVOLUTION

Take a look at this chart, which compares the two major views about the origin of new life forms.

DARWINISM	INTELLIGENT DESIGN
New life forms evolved by natural selection (survival of the fittest).	New life forms have never been observed to arise from other life forms. Life has only been observed to come from the same type of existing life.
New life forms evolved by natural selection (survival of the fittest).	Irreducible complexity seems to preclude new life forms from arising by slight, successive changes.
The origin of new life forms via evolution is proven by the evolutionary fossil record.	Fossil remains are inadequate to establish ancestral relationships. The Cambrian explosion is more consistent with immediate creation rather than gradual evolution.
Only natural causes are considered possible.	Natural and intelligent causes are considered possible.
The debate over the origin of life is between religion and science.	The debate over life's origins is about good science versus bad science. Darwinists are practicing bad science by ruling out intelligent causes.
Observable micro changes can be extrapolated to prove that unobservable macroevolution occurred.	While microevolution has been observed, it cannot be used as evidence for macroevolution, which has never been observed.
Intelligent Design advocates don't have any evidence to support their views—they simply repeat what the Bible says.	While ID may arrive at conclusions consistent with the Bible, ID theory is supported by empirically detectable evidence and does not rely on the Bible.

2. Briefly explain the difference between microevolution and macroevolution.

3. What two events must Darwinists explain before getting into the debate over whether macroevolution is plausible?

BOOK

FACTS IN THIS CHAPTER

You've just defined the difference between microevolution and macroevolution. This is a good beginning in our quest to understand the fundamental differences between Darwinism and Intelligent Design. But Darwinists also face some significant problems in defending their assertion that all life forms share a common ancestor and have descended without the aid of an outside intelligence. Your study here will shine a light on the glaring problems Darwinists often try to hide when defending their views.

STEPHEN JAY GOULD

Photo: Kathy Chapman Online (CC by 3.0)

American paleontologist and evolutionary biologist Stephen Jay Gould was one of the most influential and widely read writers of popular science of his generation. As a scientist, he is perhaps best known for developing the theory of *punctuated equilibrium*, which states that evolution happened in short spurts rather than one continuous upward progression.

Born in New York in 1941, Gould grew up in a secular Jewish home. At five years old, he saw his first dinosaur skeleton and decided he would grow up to be a paleontologist. Gould earned his PhD from Columbia University in 1967 and soon after became a professor at Harvard, where he remained for the rest of his career.

Concerned that the fossil record didn't show the transitional forms Darwinism had predicted, Gould and colleague Niles Eldredge modified the theory of evolution. Instead of viewing evolution as a gradual upward climb from simple life forms to complex ones, they theorized that rapid spurts of evolution must have occurred, separated by long periods of stasis where nothing happened. Calling their theory "punctuated equilibria," in 1972 Gould and Eldredge published a paper outlining their ideas. Their theory made a splash in scientific circles, providing the foundation for the field of paleobiology where scientists apply modern biology methods to the study of fossils. However, some evolutionists believed their approach was wishful thinking and didn't solve the dilemma of "missing links" between species. Nevertheless, the theory pushed Gould and Eldredge into the public eye.

In addition to teaching at Harvard, Gould wrote science books for non-scientists. He wanted to make the sciences—and the theory of evolution, in particular—accessible to anyone, regardless of their formal education. He published his first book in 1977 and over the next twenty-five years wrote or contributed to hundreds of peer-reviewed papers and more than twenty books, including the award-winning *The Mismeasure of Man* and the best-seller *The Panda's Thumb*. He wrote regular essays for *Natural History* magazine and made numerous television appearances, becoming one of the most frequently cited evolutionary scientists.

He also developed what he believed was the solution to the debate between science and religion. He called it *non-overlapping magisteria* (NOMA), meaning that science and religion formed entirely separate areas of thought (magisteria), neither of which overlapped with the other. Therefore, science couldn't discuss topics that belonged to religion and religion had no voice in matters that pertained to science. Gould, however, neglected to state just where the boundary line should be drawn.

To honor Gould for his contributions to science and for popularizing Darwinism, he was elected to the National Academy of Sciences in 1989 and named Humanist of the Year in 2001 by the American Humanist Association. Suffering from cancer, after having beaten it twenty years earlier, Gould died in 2002, having just published a restatement of his evolutionary theories.

4. ***Geisler and Turek say that while natural selection may be able to explain the survival of a species, it cannot explain the arrival of the species. What does that mean?***

5. ***The textbook presents five reasons why natural selection is an inadequate explanation for the arrival of new life forms. Give a brief description of each below:***

   Genetic Limits

   Cyclical Change

   Irreducible Complexity

   Nonviability of Transitional Forms

   Molecular Isolation

WHY CAN'T DARWINISM EXPLAIN DISSIMILARITY?

Darwinists say that the similarities of living things—usually with respect to homology (body type) and the genetic code (DNA)—is evidence of common ancestry and macroevolution. Although it *could* be evidence of common ancestry and macroevolution, that's not the only possibility. Instead of pointing to a common ancestor by unguided macroevolution, this evidence could also point to a common designer by special creation.

Remember, science doesn't say anything; scientists do. And many scientists carry philosophical presuppositions that allow them to rule out intelligent causes before properly considering all the evidence. Is it any wonder, then, that many scientists interpret the evidence to conclude that similar body type and DNA *must* be evidence of common ancestry and unguided macroevolution? That's their only option because they've ruled out the one remaining alternative!

Taken alone, evidence from homology and DNA could point equally to a common ancestor or a common designer. But in light of the five reasons that cast doubt on natural selection, the evidence seems to tilt decidedly toward a common designer. Moreover, it's not the similarities between living things that need to be explained but, rather, the vast *dissimilarities* between living things that Darwinists must explain from an evolutionary perspective.

Yes, it's true that humans bear a resemblance to apes, but so what? We certainly don't look like snakes and trees, yet Darwinists say we share a common ancestor with them too. So how do Darwinists explain the vast dissimilarity between supposedly ancestrally related creatures such as seahorses, whales, Venus flytraps, peacocks, mildew, rock fish, Bermuda grass, and humans? Pointing to DNA and homology isn't convincing, but that's their basic argument.

On top of that, the reasoning behind Darwinism is inherently circular. Darwinists say that we know all of Earth's creatures share a common ancestor by way of unguided macroevolutionary processes because of DNA and homology. And how do we know that DNA and homology all point to a common ancestor? Because macroevolution is true. That's circular reasoning!

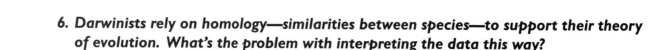

6. ***Darwinists rely on homology—similarities between species—to support their theory of evolution. What's the problem with interpreting the data this way?***

DARWINIAN OBJECTIONS TO INTELLIGENT DESIGN

If there is a lack of evidence for macroevolution, then what *is* the truth? Atheist Richard Dawkins admits that if gradualism (Darwinism) is not true, we are forced to accept a miraculous explanation. That would imply the existence of God, which, as we'll see in the next section, is one of the main reasons atheists continue to insist that Darwinism is true.

As Dawkins knows, if natural forces did not cause new life forms, then intelligence caused them. That's the only other alternative. And as we have seen, not only do we lack evidence that natural laws could do the job, but the characteristics of life provide empirically detectable evidence for intelligent design.

Yet Darwinists still object to Intelligent Design theorists, claiming that ID isn't science (based on their own narrow definition of science); that ID commits the God-of-the-gaps fallacy (although the evidence points *toward* design); that ID is religiously motivated (yet ID relies purely on empirically detectible evidence); or that ID can't be true because the design of some life forms isn't perfect (yet "perfect" design cannot be known without knowing the intentions of the designer, and less-than-perfect design is still design).

Although these objections may seem formidable at first glance, a quick peek "behind the curtain" proves that they are based on faulty logic.

7. ***How would you respond to the following statements?***

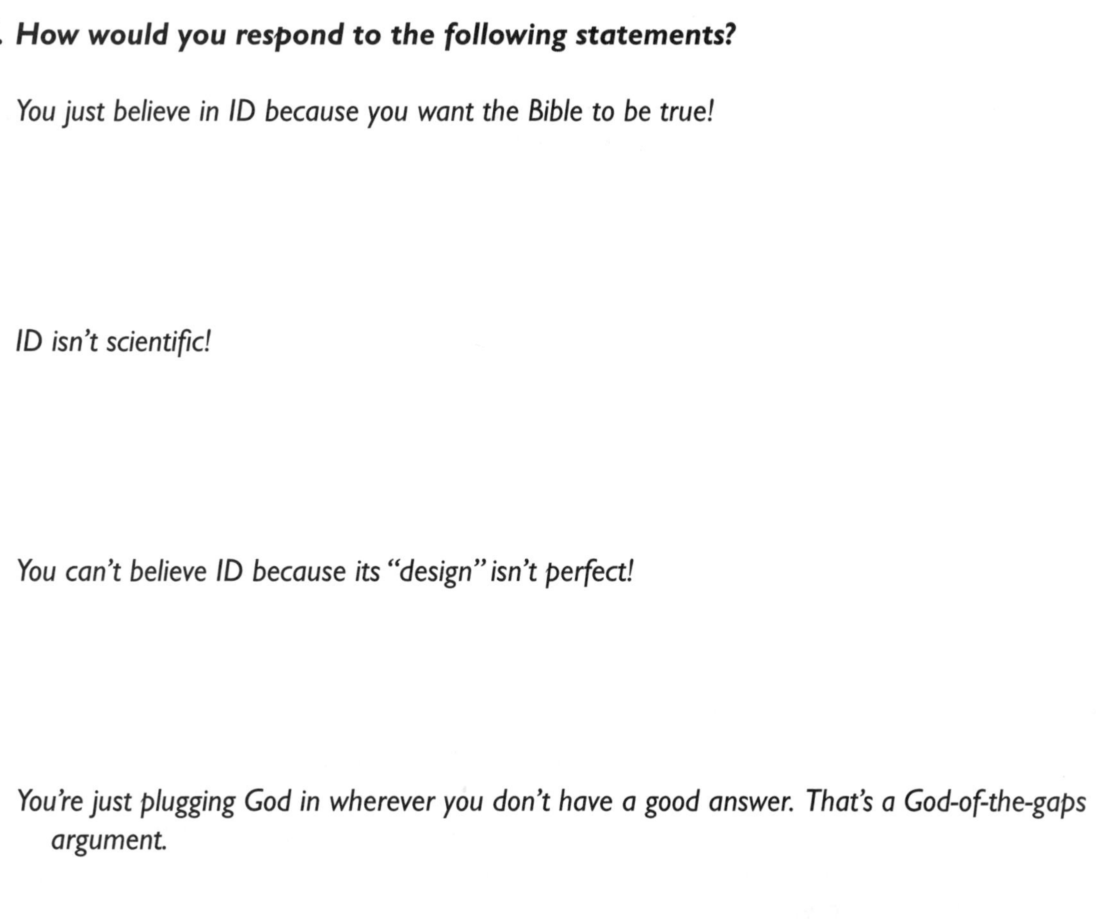

You just believe in ID because you want the Bible to be true!

ID isn't scientific!

You can't believe ID because its "design" isn't perfect!

You're just plugging God in wherever you don't have a good answer. That's a God-of-the-gaps argument.

SO WHY DO DARWINISTS STILL BELIEVE IN EVOLUTION?

Despite overwhelming evidence in favor of Intelligent Design being the cause of new life forms, Darwinists continue to stand firm in their belief that no intelligence was involved. In fact, some Darwinists are downright hostile toward anyone who suggests that intelligent design is even possible. (See the movie *Expelled* for a popular treatment of this.)

8. ***Look back at pages 161–165 in the book. List four possible reasons for why Darwinists maintain their worldview in spite of the evidence.***

9. ***What is the common theme among all four of these reasons? Why is resisting that "one thing" so important to Darwinists?***

YOU DO THE DIGGING

As we saw in this chapter, there are at least five reasons to believe natural selection cannot produce new life forms. Additionally, the fossil record does not support Darwinism, but is more consistent with creation. The vast dissimilarity of living things also seems beyond the reach of natural causes. Again, the evidence unquestionably points toward an intelligence creating life on earth.

In spite of all the evidence, Darwinists continue to cling to their theory. Darwinism is treated as fact rather than theory on television, at museums, in magazines, and at colleges and universities around the world.

Photo: Shane Pope (CC BY 2.0)

RICHARD DAWKINS

Outspoken British atheist and biologist Richard Dawkins has become a leader of the fight against Creationism and Intelligent Design, especially since the publication of his 2006 book *The God Delusion*, which posited that religious faith is a mass delusion.

Born in 1941, Dawkins was raised in a nominally Anglican home. In his teens, though, he decided that evolution and natural selection provided better explanations for the universe than creation and turned away from faith in the existence of God. He studied zoology at Balliol College, Oxford where he was tutored by Nikolaas Tinbergen, winner of the 1973 Nobel Prize for physiology. Dawkins focused on ethology, the scientific study of animal behavior, using his experiments to hone his view of evolution. He continued as a research student under Tinbergen's supervision, earning his doctorate in 1966.

After spending two years as an assistant professor of zoology at the University of California at Berkeley, where he participated in several anti-Vietnam War protests, Dawkins returned to Oxford as a lecturer in 1970. In 1995, Dawkins was honored as the first Simonyi Professor for the Public Understanding of Science, a position dedicated to one who has made "important contributions to the public understanding of some scientific field."

Dawkins's most well-known contributions were two theories that modified traditional Darwinism in an attempt to explain the process of natural selection more fully. The first was the theory of gene-centered evolution, presented in his book *The Selfish Gene*. This theory suggested that individual genes should be considered the units of natural selection rather than whole organisms. The second theory he is known for (which he helped popularize but did not invent) is the idea of memes. Dawkins defined a meme as the behavioral equivalent of a gene—just as genes transmit information from generation to generation, so a meme could transmit an idea or character trait from person to person. He believed that concepts such as altruism and even religion were memes, or idea genes, that could be passed around, growing and changing as they went. He saw this theory as providing a natural explanation for non-material things.

Although he retired from teaching in 2008, Dawkins continues to write and speak. He has declared that atheism is the sign of a healthy, independent mind and that faith—which he defines as belief not based on evidence—is one of the greatest evils in the world. He once wrote, "It is absolutely safe to say that if you meet somebody who claims not to believe in evolution, that person is ignorant, stupid, or insane (or wicked, but I'd rather not consider that)." He also admitted that atheism provides no grounding for objective morality, while at the same time calling religious upbringing "child abuse" and publishing his own ten commandments in *The God Delusion*.

A gifted writer, Dawkins serves as editor for numerous secular and atheistic journals and magazines, including *Free Inquiry* and *Skeptic*, and to date has published a dozen books (such as *The Blind Watchmaker*, an attempted refutation of Paley's argument for design in the universe) and nearly as many documentaries. He also supported an atheistic ad campaign launched in 2008 in London, where the phrase "There's probably no God, so stop worrying and enjoy your life" was placed on buses throughout the city.

Now it's time to for you to do some digging on your own. Pick at least one of the following assignments and complete it before moving on in the workbook.

Assignment 1: Darwinist Jerry Coyne has written a book titled *Why Evolution is True*. Biologist Jonathan Wells of the Discovery Institute wrote a rebuttal titled "Why Darwinism is False" (available at www.discovery.org). Read Wells' rebuttal and summarize his arguments in a one- to two-page paper.

Assignment 2: Find an article, story, or TV show that provides supposed evidence for Darwinism. Examine the main points it uses as evidence for Darwinism and write your own one- to two-page rebuttal.

Assignment 3: Do an online search for "Phillip Johnson and Methodological Naturalism" (the same Phillip Johnson who wrote *Darwin on Trial* and several other books refuting Darwinism). Read one of the articles you find on the topic, and then write a one-page paper stating how naturalistic philosophy has influenced scientific conclusions regarding evolution.

Assignment 4: Watch the DVD "Darwin's Dilemma" and summarize its main points in outline form. Why is the Cambrian Explosion problematic for Darwinism, and how does it point to Intelligent Design?

TOOK

WHAT DO I DO NOW?

The creation/evolution controversy can appear daunting and complicated. Biology is complicated, but the arguments for macroevolution are quite simple. Most of macroevolutionary theory rests on two basic arguments:

1. Anatomical and molecular similarities (similar body plans and DNA)
2. Extrapolating microevolutionary changes to macroevolutionary changes

Do these arguments prove macroevolution? No, because the data needs to be interpreted correctly. This is where philosophical reasoning comes in. No one can do science without philosophy because the data does not interpret itself. Darwinists present lots of supposed evidence, but most of it is unsubstantiated, circular, or the product of naturalistic philosophical presuppositions. In addition, Darwinists tend to dismiss the evidence against their theory, such as the five reasons we've already discussed.

It's also important to understand that even if macroevolution were true, it would not preclude the need for a creator and designer. As we have emphasized repeatedly, biology is only one aspect of reality that all worldviews need to explain. Where did the highly fine-tuned universe come from? How about the first life itself? Where did the genetic code originate? What's the source for the laws of logic, the laws of nature, and the laws of morality? They are all much better explained by theism than by atheism—not because we just haven't found a natural cause yet, but because the evidence points to an intelligent cause.

The culture treats macroevolution as a given and anyone who disbelieves it as ignorant. This may be the first place you and your faith are attacked. With that in mind, it's essential that you be ready to point out the problems with Darwinism while providing a defense of Intelligent Design.

THINKING ABOUT WHAT YOU LEARNED

Answer the following questions to sum up what you have learned in this chapter.

A. *Darwinists often use the fossil record as proof for evolution. Why are fossil remains inadequate to establish ancestral biological relationships? (See IDHEF, pages 153–154.)*

B. *Briefly explain the difference between empirical science and forensic science (IDHEF page 156). Why are the two used in different situations?*

C. What reason do the authors give for why theistic macroevolution isn't a viable option? (See IDHEF, page 166.)

D. Compare the two lists in the summary on pages 165–167 in the book. Which viewpoint requires more faith to believe? Which side do you come down on and why?

ASK THE RIGHT QUESTIONS!

When someone makes a truth claim, it's not your job to refute it—it is his job to support it. With that in mind, if someone says "I believe in evolution," ask these three questions (which, by the way, are useful for any topic, not just evolution).

1. ***What do you mean by that** (in this case, "evolution")? Get clarification about what the person means and how he is defining his terms. If he means microevolution or simply change over time, fine. But if he is using evolution to mean macroevolution, then he is going to have to provide some evidence to back up his claims.*

2. ***How did you come to that conclusion?** Use this question to encourage the person to support his claims with evidence. Much of the time you will find that he is relying not on evidence, but on the popular opinion that macroevolution is true and Christianity is false. Making him think through the evidence for his beliefs could help him see the holes in his theory.*

3. ***Have you ever considered . . . ?*** *Complete the sentence by offering evidence for design or creation. You could say, "Have you ever considered that a common genetic code could be evidence of a common creator?" or "Have you ever read the book* Icons of Evolution?*" This is a polite way to provide evidence for ID.*

For more on how to use questions effectively, check out *Tactics: A Game Plan for Discussing Your Christian Convictions* by Gregory Koukl. His website, www.str.org, also offers other good apologetics materials. You can also visit www.Crossexamined.org and click on "Resources and Links" to find other materials to help you share your faith with others.

CHAPTER 7

MOTHER TERESA VERSUS HITLER

BEFORE STARTING THIS CHAPTER

- Read chapter 7 of *I Don't Have Enough Faith to Be an Atheist* (IDHEF), pages 169–193.
- Read Appendix 1, pages 389–401.

ROAD MAP OF THE "TWELVE POINTS THAT PROVE CHRISTIANITY IS TRUE"

This chapter covers the following points:

The theistic God exists, as evidenced by
a) the beginning of the universe,
b) the design of the universe
c) the design of life, and
d) ***moral law***.

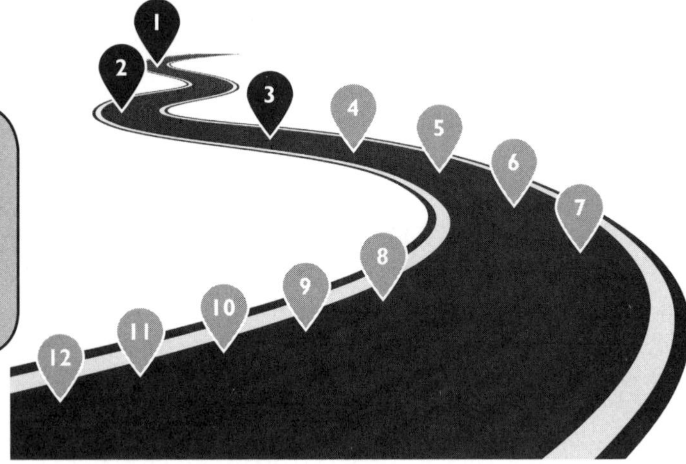

KEY TOPICS

After completing this chapter, you should be able to:

- Define a third argument for the existence of a theistic God—the Moral Law—and give evidence to support it.
- List eight reasons that support the existence of the Moral Law.
- Explain several distinctions between absolute and relative morality.
- Refute several theories Darwinists use to deal with the question of morality.
- Describe several consequences that result from Darwinian ideas about morality.

KEY TERMS

Write the definitions for these words found in your reading:

Moral Law

Situational Ethics

QUESTIONS THAT GRAB YOUR MIND

Are laws against murder and other crimes just based on someone's opinion? Is it simply a society's opinion if they decide it's okay to kill innocent people who are considered unworthy or a nuisance? What about laws condemning rape, slavery, or child abuse? If societal opinion changes, is it okay to change the laws to permit such behavior? Who decides what is right and wrong? Is it Mother Teresa or Billy Graham? Is it Hitler? Is it you? Me? Who gets to decide?

You might have heard someone say, "I should be able to do whatever I want as long as it doesn't hurt anyone." Although on the surface this appears to be a harmless philosophy, there are some major flaws with this type of thinking. How does this person define "whatever I want"? What happens when what he or she wants affects or violates what *you* want—who takes precedence? And what about a definition of "not hurting anyone"? What is this person's standard for deciding what "hurt" encompasses? What if the person he is hurting is himself? Does an outsider have the right to step in and prevent him from harming himself? And how can you be sure that what you do doesn't "hurt" others? Might a seemingly harmless action actually inadvertently "hurt" someone later? After all, we can't see the future. And come to think of it, who said it is wrong to "hurt" others? Why do they get to tell me what I ought to do?

Without an objective, absolute Moral Law, we leave ourselves open to whatever others may think is "right" for them at the time. Hitler believed exterminating the Jews and other undesirables was the right thing to do so that he could build his "master race." But after the war, the Allies judged many Nazi leaders guilty of war crimes. This could only have taken place if they recognized the existence of a real, unchanging standard of right that was higher than the opinions of the German government.

1. Do you agree with the statement there is nothing objectively wrong with murder, rape, torture, or child abuse unless God exists? Why or why not?

SO WHAT?

In contrast to the previous chapters, where we discussed several scientific arguments for the existence of a theistic God, this chapter focuses on a philosophical argument for a theistic God. This is the argument from morality. Evidence for this argument is something we've all recognized since we were very small children. As soon as a child is old enough to know what murder is, he or she knows that murder is wrong. Early on you understood when you and others were being treated unfairly. In fact, one of the first things every kid says is "That's not fair!" Where does that come from? And why do most people believe that certain behaviors are objectively right while others are objectively wrong?

Why do we seem to know the good and right things to do but then so often don't do them? And why do most people understand that "good" usually means helping people and "bad" usually means hurting them? Christians believe it's because of the Moral Law that is written on our hearts. It is a prescription to do good that has been given to all humanity by God. The Moral Law means there are basic principles of right and wrong that are binding on everyone, whether people will admit to it or not.

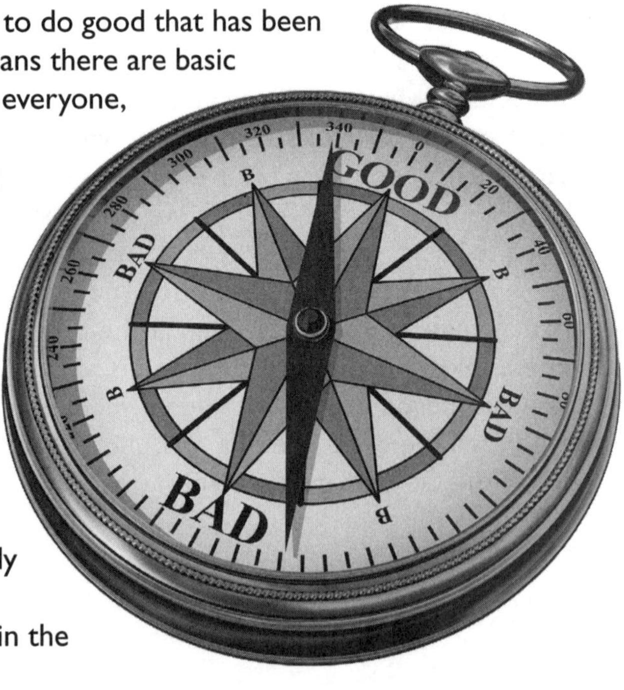

Some atheists deny this Moral Law, saying that there are no absolute moral laws or obligations. They say we are all the result of an evolutionary process, and therefore the only guiding principle is survival of the fittest. The natural conclusion of this argument is that people are no better than the slime from which they evolved. Following this logic, murder and rape are not objectively wrong. They may be socially inconvenient or unfashionable, but they are not objectively morally wrong.

If you truly believe that people are made in the

image of God—that they have infinite worth endowed by their Creator—then that will affect how you treat them. On the other hand, if you truly believe that people are nothing more than intelligent apes, that philosophy will lead you to treat them very differently.

While social outcomes of beliefs are important and will be discussed, they are not the focus of this chapter. Nor will this chapter make the claim that atheists don't know morality or can't act morally. Atheists, like everyone else, do know right from wrong and can act morally. But the focus of this chapter is to show that the existence of God best explains the existence of objective morality.

THE MORAL LAW

Let's take a moment to review our two previous arguments for the existence of a theistic God. The first was the Cosmological Argument, which said that if the universe had a beginning then it must also have had a cause. This argument established that the cause of the universe must transcend space, time, and matter. The second argument was the Teleological Argument, which said that the fine-tuning of the universe and the specified complexity of life require an intelligent designer.

The third argument is the Moral Law. It goes like this:

1. Every law has a law-giver.
2. There is an objective Moral Law.
3. Therefore, there is a Moral Law-giver.

Just like the other initial premises, the fact that every law must have a law-giver is self-evident. So in order for the conclusion to be true, we must prove the existence of an objective Moral Law.

2. Why is the existence of a Moral Law an argument for a theistic God?

MOTHER TERESA

The name Mother Teresa has become synonymous with charity and morality around the world. But who was the woman who inspired this reputation?

Mother Teresa was born Agnes Gonxha Bojaxhiu in 1910 in what is now Skopje, Macedonia. After losing her father when she was nine, she was raised as a devout Roman Catholic by her mother. As a girl she was fascinated by stories of missionaries in far-off lands, and when she turned eighteen she left home to become a nun. After learning English at Loreto Abbey in Ireland, she traveled to Calcutta, India, where she would teach children at a convent school.

There she took her religious vows, choosing the name Teresa in honor of the patron saint of missionaries. For the next twenty years, Teresa ministered at the Loreto convent school in Calcutta and was eventually nominated as headmistress, a position she held for two years.

In 1946, Teresa received a second calling from God, pointing her toward missionary work among the poorest of the poor, those considered outcasts by Indian society or those too poor to have anywhere else to go. After two years of training, Teresa, then thirty-eight years old, exchanged her nun's habit for a plain white sari with a blue border and set out for the slums of Calcutta. For months she lived as the poor lived, having to beg for food and supplies. But by 1949, a small group of women had joined her in her work, and a year later Teresa was able to start her own order, which she called the Missionaries of Charity. This group would care for "the hungry, the naked, the homeless, the crippled, the blind, the lepers, all those people who feel unwanted, unloved, uncared for."

What began with thirteen women blossomed over the next few decades. In 1952, Teresa opened her first hospice to give the poor a place to die in peace and dignity. Leprosy clinics soon followed, spreading across India. She opened her first orphanage in 1955. The Missionaries of Charity eventually spread to other countries, and today operates more than 600 missions, schools, and shelters in more than 120 countries.

Teresa saw it as her job to help anyone in need, including war refugees and disaster victims. She even brokered a temporary cease fire during the Siege of Beirut in 1982 so that she could rescue a group of children trapped in a hospital behind enemy lines. Mother Teresa received numerous awards in recognition of her service, including the Nobel Peace Prize in 1979. Yet despite her fame, she continued to work among the poor, saying, "Love has no meaning if it isn't shared. Love has to be put into action."

Following her death in 1997, Pope John Paul II gave her the title "Blessed Teresa of Calcutta."

FACTS IN THIS CHAPTER

Now it is time to dig deeper to get more answers and understand some of the facts behind the Moral Law. We will ask questions like *How do we know the Moral Law exists?* and *What is the confusion between absolute and relative?* You will also discover what Darwinists believe about the Moral Law. Finally, we will tie it all together with the fact that ideas have consequences.

If you adopt the Darwinist philosophy that morals are relative, then that will dictate how you see and respond to everything around you. Your opinions and desires will be your subjective guideline because you believe that your chemical makeup alone determines how you see right and wrong. On the other hand, if you recognize that there is an objective Moral Law given to us by our Creator, you will have an objective standard against which to judge your behavior.

HOW DO WE KNOW THE MORAL LAW EXISTS?

Can we prove to you that an objective Moral Law exists? No. Just as we can't prove to you that the Law of Non-contradiction exists, neither can we empirically prove that the Moral Law exists. It is something that is self-evident. Certain moral principles are known by all and binding on all. There only needs to be one such principle to show that God exists. For if there is a Moral Law prescription, there must be a Moral Law prescriber.

Many such principles exist. For example, we all know that torturing babies for fun is morally wrong. It's not just a matter of opinion—it is wrong for all people, at all times, in all places. This is what philosophers call "a properly basic moral belief." We would need vast external evidence to the contrary to cause us to discard what seems to be universally morally true.

3. ***How do we know that the Moral Law is undeniable? How could you demonstrate to someone that they really do believe in moral absolutes?***

4. ***The book uses an illustration of comparing two maps of Scotland to a real place called Scotland. How is this used to illustrate that an objective morality exists beyond mere human opinion?***

ABSOLUTE VERSUS RELATIVE MORALITY

If there really is an absolute Moral Law, then why do so many people claim that morality is relative? Sometimes it is due to a failure to make proper distinctions; other times it is based on wanting to assert their own will rather than being in submission to God.

I Don't Have Enough Faith to Be an Atheist discusses six distinctions between absolute and relative morality that people blur or ignore in their determination to follow their own desires:

- Absolute morals versus changing behavior
- Absolute morals versus changing perceptions of the facts
- Absolute morals versus applying them to particular situations
- An absolute command (what) versus a relative culture (how)
- Absolute morals versus moral disagreements
- Absolute ends (values) versus relative means

5. ***Pick two of the six distinctions between absolute and relative morality and explain them using examples.***

6. Match one of the distinctions listed above to each of the following claims.

This is the twenty-first century. Premarital sex is fine, even healthy.

Not supporting government-funded health care means you don't care about the poor.

Morality is all relative—just look at how people disagree about homosexuality.

What if you have to lie to save someone's life? Shouldn't you do it?

I can prove morality is relative—we used to believe slavery was fine and now we don't.

THE EUTHYPHRO DILEMMA

If you say that God is the source of objective morality, you may hear atheists bring up what is known as "the Euthyphro dilemma" from one of Plato's writings. The dilemma goes like this: Does God do something because it is good (which would imply there is a standard of good beyond God), or is it good because God does it (which would imply that God arbitrarily makes up morality)?

But this is not an actual dilemma at all. There is a third alternative. When it comes to morality, God doesn't look to another standard beyond Himself, nor is He arbitrary. The third alternative is that God's character is the standard. The buck has to stop somewhere, and it stops at God's unchanging moral nature. In other words, the standard of rightness we know as the Moral Law is derived from the very nature of God Himself—infinite justice and infinite love.

HOW DO DARWINISTS DEAL WITH THE QUESTION OF MORALITY?

Darwinists have a difficult time dealing with the moral argument. Some say that because only material things exist, and morals are not material in nature, there can be no morality. However, materialism is a philosophical assertion that cannot be proven and is ultimately self-defeating. We couldn't know anything—including Darwinist theory—if all our thoughts were solely the product of material forces. Moreover, logic and math are clear counter examples to materialism—the laws of logic and math aren't material, but Darwinists have no problem relying on those. It is self-defeating to reason that only materials exist when the very process of reasoning uses the immaterial laws of logic!

Other Darwinists admit morality but claim evolution gave it to us to help us to survive—that we need to "cooperate" with one another or we wouldn't survive. There are several problems with this approach.

First, moral laws are not chemical or biological; they are immaterial and come from personal agents. Chemicals cannot tell you what to do. In fact, chemistry and biology are both *descriptive*, not *prescriptive*. They describe what *does* survive, not what *ought* to survive. Why should humans survive and thrive as opposed to any other life form?

Second, who said survival is our goal? There is no real "good" without an objective moral law. And if survival is our goal, then should we commit rape to survive? Should we murder the weak to enable the rest of us to survive? That was Hitler's idea.

Third, we all know that sacrificing yourself to save someone else is the highest expression of love—far higher than mere survival. (In fact, Jesus did this for us!)

Fourth, because evolution is a process of change, then morals must change, too, in which case rape may one day be considered "good."

Finally, why should anyone cooperate with others if cheating or killing others helps him survive? The Russian dictator Joseph Stalin didn't cooperate with anyone—he killed all his enemies and died comfortably of old age in his bed.

A CRITICAL DISTINCTION

Atheists often think Christians are saying that they can't know morality or be moral unless they believe in God. That is not what we are saying. We are saying that while atheists can *know* morality without God, they can't *justify* morality without God. This is a critical distinction.

It is the difference between epistemology (how we can know the Moral Law) and ontology (its existence). Even if we come to our own moral conclusions due to genetic or environmental factors, that doesn't mean there is no objective Moral Law outside ourselves. You may have learned your multiplication facts from your fourth-grade teacher (epistemology), but the laws of multiplication existed independently of you or your teacher knowing them (ontology). Likewise, you may learn morality from many different sources (God, parents, society, etc.), but morality exists only because God exists whether you know it or not.

7. ***You witness a plane crash into a lake, and ignoring your own instinct for survival, you dive in to rescue the drowning passengers because it is the right thing to do. How does this reaction show that morality is not based on our instinct toward self-preservation?***

8. ***A Darwinist claims that morality is just a social construct that has arisen naturally so we can all get along together. After you ask him, "What do you mean by that? And how did you come to that conclusion?" what would you say to refute his position if he continued to assert it?***

THE CONSEQUENCES OF DARWINIAN IDEAS ABOUT MORALITY

Darwinists state that morality is naturally derived. If that is the case, then morality is neither objective nor absolute. The natural conclusion is that there is no God and humans are no better than dogs or pigs. As the book points out, others have even advocated rape and murder because it is the natural outworking of the evolutionary process. In fact, rape and murder are to be expected because they are the result of chemical reactions in the criminal's brain brought about by natural selection.

It is important to understand the difference between *assertions* and *arguments*. An assertion states a conclusion (e.g., "morality is objective") without offering evidence. An argument states a conclusion and then supports it with evidence. Many times Darwinists make assertions about subjects where their worldview cannot offer proof. The fact is that there is no empirical or forensic evidence supporting the claim that natural selection can account for new life forms, much less morality. Darwinists assert that morals have evolved naturally because they believe man has evolved naturally.

9. ***In your own words, give three reasons why evolution cannot account for objective morality.***

ADOLF HITLER

In today's culture, the name Adolf Hitler calls to mind the worst of humanity. Born in Austria in 1889, Hitler was the fourth of six children, only two of whom lived to adulthood. His family moved to Germany when he was three years old. Young Adolf had an artistic streak and wanted to pursue painting, but his father disagreed and made him attend a technical school. In retaliation, he performed poorly, determined to show his father that he had made the wrong decision. After his father's death in 1903, Hitler was asked to leave first one school, then another, because of disruptive behavior.

Moving to Vienna in 1905, Hitler twice applied to the Academy of Fine Arts, but was rejected both times because of his lack of skill and general knowledge—the years spent acting out against his father's wishes prevented him from being able to follow his artistic dreams. Hitler then spent several years living on the streets of Vienna and Munich, working odd jobs and selling watercolors.

In 1914, when war broke out, he joined the German army and spent several years serving in France and Belgium. He was decorated for bravery, receiving the Iron Cross. After Germany's defeat, Hitler became involved in the German Worker's

10. Why can't non-theists justify that anything—including murder, rape, or the Holocaust—is absolutely wrong?

Party, later to become the Nazi Party. He went to work full-time for the party, making rousing speeches and gathering support. He even designed the party's banner—a black swastika in a white circle on a red background. By the summer of 1921, Adolf had risen to a position of leadership.

Two years later, Hitler and the party stormed a beer hall during a meeting of an opposing political party and declared themselves the new government. Referred to as the Beer Hall Putsch, the coup failed. Hitler was arrested, tried for treason, and sentenced to five years in prison. While there, he wrote his manifesto, *Mein Kampf*, in which he detailed his plans for making Germany the dominant nation in the world, including plans for ensuring the racial purity of the German people. The book was published in 1925, shortly after Adolf had received a pardon and early release.

Taking advantage of the worldwide Great Depression, during which millions were thrown out of work and several major banks collapsed, Hitler used the socialist German Worker's Party to advance politically, eventually gaining enough support to be appointed Chancellor of Germany in 1933. He then manipulated events to gain complete control of the leadership of Germany. By August 1933, Hitler had set himself up as dictator and declared the Nazi Party to be the only legal political party in Germany.

His plans for Germany centered on war. He expanded the armed forces and then began taking control of the smaller nations around Germany—Austria, Czechoslovakia, then Poland—sparking World War II. In the meantime, Hitler introduced laws depriving German Jews of their citizenship. He planned to deport all European Jews to Siberia, but when his invasion of the Soviet Union failed, a "final solution of the Jewish question" was proposed. Although no specific order from Hitler authorizing the mass killings has been found, he approved the killing squads and concentration camps that targeted Jews, and he was kept well informed about their activities. Between 1939 and 1945, the Nazis were responsible for the deaths of about 6 million Jews, two-thirds of the Jewish population in Europe.

The German war machine began suffering crippling losses in 1943. By April 1945, Hitler knew the end was near. In a bunker beneath Berlin, he committed suicide. Germany surrendered a few days later. Hitler's legacy was a war that left more than 50 million dead and a philosophy that would set the standard of evil for generations to come.

YOU DO THE DIGGING

The Darwinian assertion that morality is relative has serious consequences. Darwinists rely on natural selection to explain behavior, saying that since only material things exist, all behavior must be genetically determined. Logically then, a murderer or thief is just obeying his genes and therefore isn't responsible for his behavior or choices.

Without an objective Moral Law, we would have 7 billion different standards of what constitutes acceptable behavior. The results of that would be catastrophic for any nation and its people. If there isn't an objective standard of right and wrong, then anything goes.

Without an objective source of morality, all so-called moral issues are nothing more than personal preferences. If there is no moral standard outside of ourselves, then the Holocaust and the life work of Mother Teresa are the same—neither right or wrong, and can only be judged according to each person's opinion.

This assertion that morality is relative is lived out all around us, taught in our colleges and universities, and promoted in our television shows and movies. You will need to study and prepare yourself to refute this assertion with a strong argument for the Moral Law.

Now it's time to for you to do some digging on your own. Pick at least one of the following assignments and complete it before moving on in the workbook.

Assignment 1: Read the full text of the Declaration of Independence and then write a two-page paper about the moral statements it makes. List at least five ways it supports an objective Moral Law and compare those to the eight ways we know that Moral Law exists from pages 172–181 of the book.

Assignment 2: Give three examples of core moral values that are shared among several cultures. Write a one-page paper explaining how these moral standards are consistently found within each of those cultures (even though they may be applied differently in each).

Assignment 3: Write an informal essay explaining how you would respond to someone who claimed that all morality is subjective. What arguments would you make and what examples would you use to combat this assertion?

Assignment 4: Check out the apologetics resources at CrossExamined.org and find an article on the moral argument for God. Read the article and then write a one-page review, summarizing the article's main points.

WHAT DO I DO NOW?

An objective Moral Law is written on the hearts of all people everywhere. Everyone knows basic moral principles, even though many people suppress them in order to do what they want. In fact, we often make excuses for violating the Moral Law, something we wouldn't do if morality was merely a matter of personal opinion.

Even though some people may believe that morality is relative, core moral values transcend time and cultures. Moral values are absolute, even if our understanding of them, or of the circumstances in which they should be applied, is not absolute. People do not *determine* what is right or wrong; they simply *discover* right and wrong. Atheists know right and wrong because the Moral Law is written on their hearts just like everyone else's. But in the end, although they may believe in an objective right and wrong, they have no way to justify it unless they admit there is a moral law-giver.

Finally, every time an atheist complains about something being evil or unfair, they are presupposing the existence of God. Why? Because evil is a lack of good. There can be no objective evil unless there is objective good. And there can be no objective good unless there is a standard of good outside of ourselves—beyond mere human opinion. That standard is God's very nature. You could put it this way: The shadows (evil) prove the sunshine (good). Just like there can be sunshine without shadows but no shadows without sunshine, so there can be good without evil but no evil without good. And there can't be objective good without God. So when an atheist claims that evil disproves God, he is borrowing from God in order make the argument! He's borrowing a standard of good, which only exists if God exists.

THINKING ABOUT WHAT YOU LEARNED

Answer the following questions to sum up what you have learned in this chapter.

A. *How do a person's reactions prove that he unconsciously follows an objective Moral Law, even if he denies its existence consciously (IDHEF, pages 173–175)?*

B. The Declaration of Independence begins with these words: "We hold these truths to be self-evident, that all men are created equal, that they are endowed by their Creator with certain unalienable rights, that among these are life, liberty and the pursuit of happiness." What does this statement say about the Moral Law? How does it compare to what we read in Romans 2:14–15?

C. What is the difference between an assertion and an argument?

D. Atheists often say there is no God because of all the evil in the world. How does this argument backfire on the atheist? Explain how the existence of evil points to the existence of God.

ASK, "WHAT IS YOUR STANDARD?"

When discussing how morality points to God, it's sometimes better to ask questions rather than make statements. At a recent presentation on a college campus, an atheist was trying to tell Frank that he had an objective standard for morality without God. When asked what that standard was, the young man said, "Whatever society decides is morally correct."

So Frank asked him, "Are you saying that if a Nazi society decides to murder Jews then the murder of Jews is objectively morally right?"

The young man hesitated, blushed, and quivered a bit before he said, "Yes."

At that point, his friend sitting right next to him looked at him and yelled, "No!"

The young atheist knew the correct answer was no, but he chose to suppress that truth in order to be consistent with his atheism.

Once an atheist admits that his view supports Nazism, every sane person in the room knows he's lost the argument. But sometimes you need to ask the question in order to reveal it.

Of course, even if the Nazis had won the war and brainwashed everyone to believe that murdering Jews was right, that would not make it right. If God exists, then the obligations of the Moral Law are binding on all people, at all times, in all places—even if everyone disagrees with them or denies they exist. God has had a long history of patient dealings with disobedient humans. In fact, that's why He sent His perfect Son, to rescue us from our disobedience.

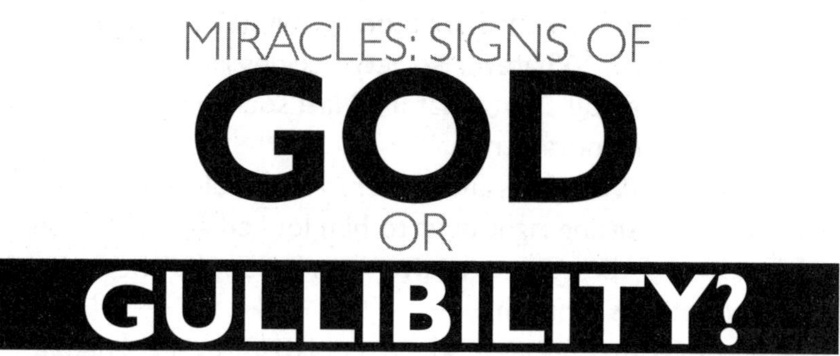

BEFORE STARTING THIS CHAPTER

- Read chapter 8 of *I Don't Have Enough Faith to Be an Atheist* (IDHEF), pages 197–217.

ROAD MAP OF THE "TWELVE POINTS THAT PROVE CHRISTIANITY IS TRUE"

This chapter covers the following points:

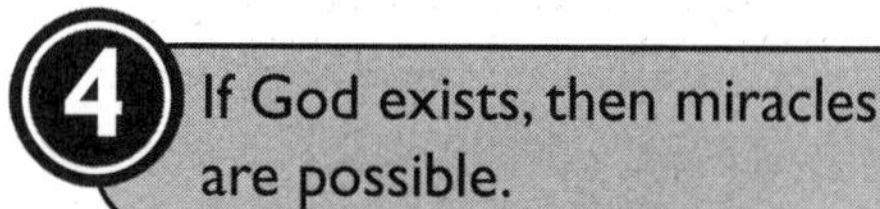

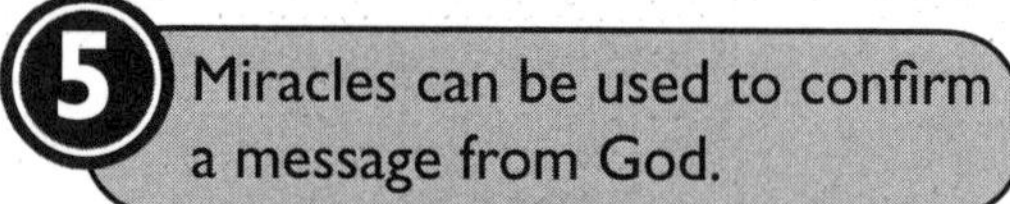

5
Miracles can be used to confirm a message from God.

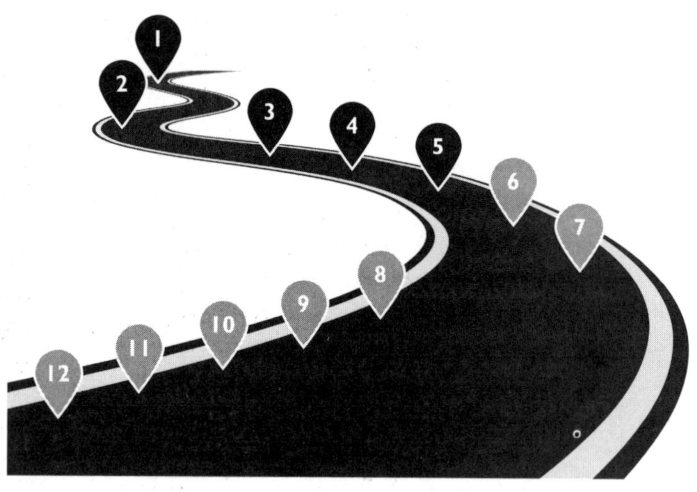

KEY TOPICS

After completing this chapter, you should be able to:

- List the characteristics of the theistic God shown by the Cosmological, Teleological, and Moral Arguments.
- Explain the difference between general revelation and special revelation.
- Explain why only a theistic religion could be true.
- Identify the greatest miracle in the Bible.
- Explain and refute two objections to miracles.
- Describe what constitutes a miracle of God and contrast that with other "unusual" types of events.
- Explain the main purpose of miracles in biblical times.

KEY TERMS

Write the definitions for these words found in your reading:

General revelation

Special revelation

Miracle

Providence

Psychosomatic

Magic

Anomaly

HOOK

QUESTIONS THAT GRAB YOUR MIND

Nowadays people find it hard to believe that anyone can believe in miracles. After all, everything's been explained by science, right? Didn't we give up superstition during the Enlightenment? And if the Bible is true, why don't we see public displays of miracles all the time? Were people in biblical times just uninformed and gullible?

With so much prevailing opinion weighing against supernatural occurrences—especially the resurrection of Jesus—it's sometimes hard to even get a discussion about God started.

1. Why do you think many people today have a hard time believing in miracles?

SO WHAT?

If miracles are not possible, then much of the Bible is false. The book is filled with miracles. Yet many in the academic community think it's foolish to believe in miracles. According to their worldview, miracles don't happen. In other words, they philosophically rule out the possibility of miracles in advance.

This anti-supernatural bias is admitted explicitly by James Tabor, chairman of the Department of Religious Studies at the University of North Carolina at Charlotte, in his book *The Jesus Dynasty*. Speaking of the claim that Jesus was born of a virgin, Tabor writes, "The assumption of the historian is that all human beings have both a biological mother and father, and that Jesus is no exception. That leaves two possibilities—either Joseph or some other unnamed man was the father of Jesus."

If Jesus really was born of a virgin, how could Tabor ever discover it? He couldn't because he's already ruled out the possibility. We'll see in this chapter that ruling out miracles in advance is a foolish thing to do. Why? Because if God exists, then miracles are possible. In fact, the greatest miracle in the Bible has already occurred, and we have scientific evidence for it.

THE CHARACTERISTICS OF GOD

Thus far our study has focused on three arguments for God that are crucial to our understanding of the meaning of life: the Cosmological, Teleological, and Moral Arguments. Each shows us something vital about the characteristics of the First Cause, whom we know as God.

2. What attributes of the First Cause do we discover from each of the following arguments? (See IDHEF, pages 197–198.)

Cosmological

Teleological

Moral

3. How do these attributes match the attributes of God found in the Bible?

FACTS IN THIS CHAPTER

Why is it significant that the Cosmological, Teleological, and Moral Arguments show us beyond a reasonable doubt that there is a theistic God? It's important that reason and evidence show the existence of a theistic God because it changes our view of the world and begins to provide answers to the "box top" of life. It also provides a way to answer the five most consequential questions in life based on natural revelation.

Logically, if theism is true, then any nontheistic worldview (anything based on the belief in no God or many gods) cannot be true. And as we will see in this chapter, since God exists, miracles are possible. Since the greatest miracle of all—the creation of the universe out of nothing—has already occurred, every other miracle in the Bible is at least possible. (As we progress through this study, we'll see evidence that other biblical miracles actually occurred.)

We have discovered the characteristics of the theistic God through what He has made and how He has made it. The previous arguments have shown us the character of the theistic God apart from the Bible. In other words, we have not assumed God exists because the Bible says so. We have shown that a being with characteristics closely aligned to those of the God of the Bible actually exists through *general revelation*. (The revelation from Scripture about God is called *special revelation*.)

4. Summarize the evidence we've collected so far that shows why theism is true.

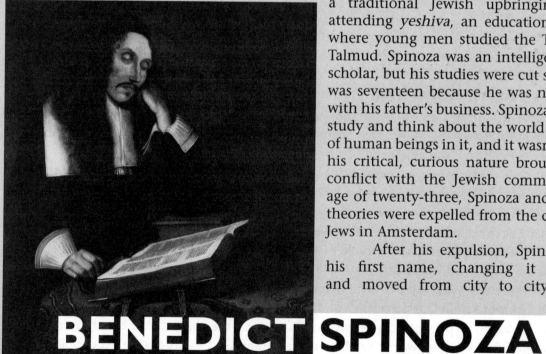

Benedict Spinoza (1632–1677) was a Dutch Jewish philosopher whose ideas were condemned by many of his day because his notions ran counter to biblical teachings. His rationalist philosophies laid the groundwork for the eighteenth-century cultural movement called the Enlightenment, or the Age of Reason.

As the son of a wealthy merchant, young Baruch (Spinoza's given name) received a traditional Jewish upbringing, including attending *yeshiva*, an educational institution where young men studied the Torah and the Talmud. Spinoza was an intelligent and gifted scholar, but his studies were cut short when he was seventeen because he was needed to help with his father's business. Spinoza continued to study and think about the world and the place of human beings in it, and it wasn't long before his critical, curious nature brought him into conflict with the Jewish community. At the age of twenty-three, Spinoza and his heretical theories were expelled from the community of Jews in Amsterdam.

After his expulsion, Spinoza Latinized his first name, changing it to Benedict, and moved from city to city throughout

BENEDICT SPINOZA

WHY CAN'T A NONTHEISTIC RELIGION BE TRUE?

All our evidence so far points to the irrefutable fact that a theistic God exists. If that is the case, then any nontheistic religion is built on a false foundation. (See page 198 of the book for a list of major nontheistic religions.) That means that while nontheistic religions have the potential to teach some things that are true, they are grounded on false beliefs concerning the existence and nature of God. Therefore, they aren't reliable ways to look at the world around us.

Only theism fits all the facts so far. The three major theistic world religions are Islam, Judaism, or Christianity. But which one is the right one? While it is possible that none of the three are completely true—maybe they have theism right but not much else—if one of them really is true, we'll see how we can discover that in an upcoming section.

WHY CAN'T A POLYTHEISTIC RELIGION BE TRUE?

So why can't polytheism be true? Why can't there be many gods instead of just one? There are a couple of reasons why polytheism can be ruled out. First, there can only be one infinite being. Why? Because, logically, in order to distinguish one being from another they must differ in some way. If they differ in some way, then one lacks something the other one has. If one being lacks something the other one has, then the lacking being is not infinite because an infinite being, by definition, lacks nothing. So there can be only one infinite being. (This rules out Q from the Star Trek universe as being truly infinite—though he'd never admit it!)

the Netherlands. While making his living as a lens grinder, he continued to develop his theories. Spinoza believed that the universe and everything in it were all different forms, or modes, of one unified substance. He believed this substance, which he called God or Nature, was responsible for creating all life, but was abstract and impersonal. He also believed in *determinism*—that whatever happened was predetermined by how the universe was set up. According to Spinoza, this meant there was no divine providence guiding events but, rather, everything happened the way it must.

Spinoza published his first book of philosophy in 1670. But the response was so unfavorable that he decided to hold off on publishing his next big project, *Ethics*, which would come to be considered his magnum opus. *Ethics* was published after his death in 1677 by his friends, who prepared the manuscript in secret for fear that the authorities would confiscate and destroy Spinoza's work.

Philosophers today credit Benedict Spinoza with being the catalyst for the Enlightenment as well as modern biblical criticism (the forensic study of the biblical texts and manuscripts, most often in an attempt to discredit the Bible). As the world slowly moved from belief in the truth of the Bible to belief in science, Spinoza's influence spread beyond the field of philosophy, influencing such people as novelist George Eliot, scientist Albert Einstein, and even Arne Naess, the founder of the modern Deep Ecology movement that exalts nature above human beings.

Spinoza's ideas can also be found in New Age philosophy and pantheism, the belief that the universe and God are one and the same. People throughout modern history have been drawn to Spinoza's ideas because they allowed for a First Cause that didn't make any demands on the way people live. If God is merely the impersonal everything, then He requires neither obedience to a set of rules nor a personal relationship. Under these conditions, there is also no need for a savior, since everything that happens is determined by the universe, doing away with sin and guilt as well as good and evil.

Second, the Teleological Argument reveals that the universe and life are the product of a single mind. There are too many precise, interdependent constants and interacting biological machines for either the universe or life to be the product of diverse intelligences. Therefore, the theistic God is the only infinite being, ruling out polytheism.

5. Explain why the following are not theistic religions:

Hinduism

Secular Humanism

Mormonism

6. How would you share with a friend why two infinitely perfect beings cannot logically co-exist?

7. Why can't Satan be equally as powerful as God, as dualism says?

THE PURPOSE OF MIRACLES

Because the theistic being predicted by our three arguments has all the characteristics of the God of the Bible, we would expect that He would reveal more of Himself and His purpose for the universe and our lives. Understanding how this theistic God would communicate with us can help us understand which theistic religion—Islam, Judaism, or Christianity—is true. Special revelation is the key to answering the question of which of the many world religions is true.

Jesus Walking on the Water by Aivazovsky.

You have already seen that God communicates to us through creation and conscience (general revelation). And since God has not chosen to speak face to face with every person—for the very real reason that standing in the presence of God might overwhelm us and negate our free will—He would choose another means to communicate the specific plans He has for us. The most likely way He would communicate with us would be through the written word because it can be very precisely passed on from one generation to another, keeping His message pure. But since each of the three theistic religions has its own religious book—Islam has the Quran, Judaism has the Torah and the Talmud, and Christianity has the Bible—which book, if any, is the one true message from God?

Think about it this way: How could you prove to someone that you are who you said you are? You would offer something unique that would authenticate who you are—some reliable form of identification, or the testimony of a credible person, or knowledge that only you would know. It would have to be something unique to you. The same is true when it comes to communication from God.

For God to show which book or message is truly from Him, He would need to do something unique—something only He could do in order to authenticate His message. Miracles are the unique evidence God uses, since only God—who is the only being not bound by the laws of the universe—can do them. Miracles are acts of God to confirm a word from God to the people of God. They are signs that confirm the sermon. So through miracles, God has demonstrated to the world which book or person actually speaks for Him.

But how can we believe in miracles in today's secular culture? Think about this question first: What is the greatest miracle in the Bible? Christians normally say it's the Resurrection. But when you think about it, the Resurrection is relatively minor compared to what God accomplished in the very first verse of the Bible: "In the beginning, God created the heavens and the earth" (Genesis 1:1). If that verse is true, then every other verse that follows is possible, including Jesus' resurrection from death to life.

So how can we support miracles in today's show-me culture? We use good reason, philosophy, and scientific evidence from the Cosmological argument to prove that the first verse of the Bible is true! So when people tell us they don't believe in miracles, we can respond, "Look around you. You're living in one. This entire universe is a miracle! It came into being out of nothing."

Since the greatest miracle of all has already occurred—and we can prove it without even appealing to the Bible—we can move on to examining if more miracles have occurred since the first one. If they have, which theistic religion do they authenticate? We'll get to that later in this study.

8. Why are miracles the best way for God to confirm His message to us?

OBJECTIONS TO MIRACLES

Despite the evidence found in general and special revelation, many thinkers throughout history have objected to miracles. The book covers two of the major ones. Let's look at Spinoza's objection first.

Benedict Spinoza argued that since natural laws are immutable, there is no way natural laws can be overpowered in the kinds of ways miracles require. Although this sounds convincing at first glance (and has influenced the thinking of many intellectuals since the late 1600s), a logical examination of the argument shows that Spinoza used circular reasoning. The proof is set up in such a way that miracles can only be discredited.

Another reason why Spinoza's objection doesn't work is that it gives natural laws too much credit. The law of gravity is considered a universal natural law, yet we overpower it in small ways every day, every time we catch a ball, pick up something we dropped, or jump in the air. Natural laws can only describe what usually happens. They are not unbendable rules that dictate what must happen without exception.

9. How would you explain to a friend why Spinoza's objection to miracles fails?

David Hume offered the argument that miracles are not credible. According to his thinking, because the evidence for the regular is always greater than the evidence for the rare, a wise man shouldn't believe in miracles. The problem with this argument is that the evidence for the common is not always greater than that for the uncommon. Events such as the formation of the universe, the rise of the first life, and even Hume's own birth were one-time-only events, yet we have no trouble believing they happened because we can see the forensic evidence left behind by these singular events.

So although Hume's argument may seem like sound reasoning on the surface, it ultimately fails to disprove the existence of miracles. The truth is that we need only one counterexample to disprove his entire theory. Geisler and Turek give us four counterexamples:

1. The origin of the universe happened only once.
2. The origin of life happened only once.
3. The origin of new life forms also happened only once.
4. The history of the world is made up of rare, unrepeatable events.

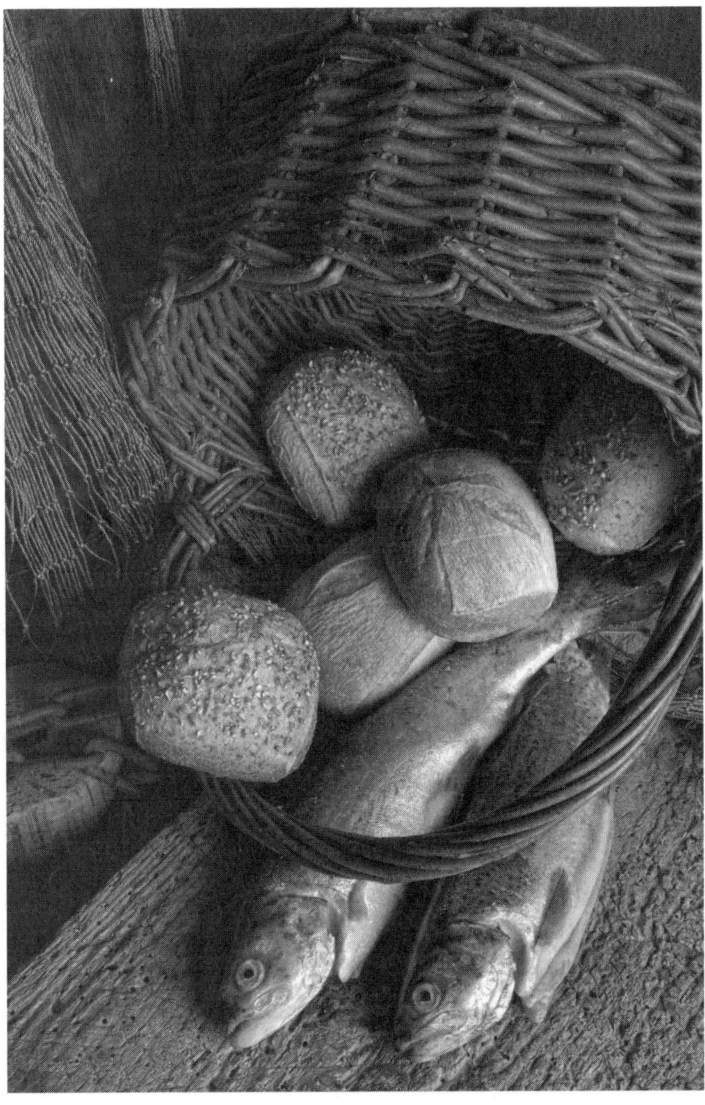

In addition, Hume's argument makes two mistakes. First, it confuses believability with possibility. Hume is saying that since miracles are rare, and therefore not believable, they aren't possible. But many things happen every day that are difficult to believe. This is where we get the saying "Truth is stranger than fiction." Just claiming that something probably couldn't happen doesn't make it impossible.

Second, Hume confuses probability with evidence. Instead of examining each miraculous occurrence on a case-by-case basis, Hume generalizes, lumping all the uncommon events together and weighing them against all the common events. Since by definition more common events occur each day, Hume implies that their quantity somehow makes them more believable.

10. Give two counterexamples from your personal life to show that Hume's third premise in his argument against miracles is false.

11. According to C. S. Lewis, how is Hume arguing in a circle? (See IDHEF, pages 207–208.)

GENUINE MIRACLES FROM GOD VERSUS FAKES

For a "miracle" to be an unmistakable sign from God, it needs to meet certain criteria. A miracle must be unique, easily recognizable, and something only God can do (that is, unexplainable by natural laws, forces, etc.).

A miracle should also display or contain the following elements:

1. Instantaneous beginning—a powerful act that could not be started naturally
2. Intelligent design and purpose—it must have an obvious purpose such as confirming a truth, verifying a messenger of truth, or bringing glory to God
3. Promotion of good or right behavior—in other words, it cannot be connected with error or immorality

All these criteria are drawn from what we learn about God by looking at the natural world, but they line up perfectly with the characteristics of God as described in the Bible.

There are at least six different categories of unusual events:

	DEFINITION	POWER	TRAITS	EXAMPLE
ANOMALY	Freaks of nature	Physical	Natural event with a pattern	Bumble bee
MAGIC	Sleight of hand	Human	Unnatural and man-controlled	Rabbit in a hat
PSYCHOSOMATIC	Mind over matter	Mental	Requires faith; fails for some sickness	Psychosomatic cures
SATANIC	Evil power	Psychic	Evil, falsehood, occult, & limited	Demonic influence
PROVIDENTIAL	Prearranged events	Divine	Naturally explained; spiritual context	Fog at Normandy
MIRACLE	Divine act	Supernatural	Never fails, immediate, lasts, & glorifies God	Raising the dead

12. Explain how a miracle is different from each of these other unusual events.

A miracle is different than anomalies because:

A miracle is different than magic because:

A miracle is different than a psychosomatic event because:

A miracle is different than satanic signs because:

A miracle is different than providence because:

THE PURPOSE OF MIRACLES IN BIBLICAL TIMES

Some people wonder why we no longer seem to witness big public miracles such the parting of the Red Sea or the feeding of the 5,000 that were described in the Bible. If we don't experience them ourselves, why should we believe these miraculous events occurred in the past? This kind of question is based on two common mistakes. First, many people think that because they have never seen a miracle, that means miracles are not real or have never happened. But there are plenty of events that we don't doubt happened, even though we didn't see them with our own eyes.

Second, they are under the mistaken impression that miracles happened continuously in the Bible. If you search for miracles in the Bible from the time of Moses to the life of Jesus, there are about 250 miraculous events. That's about one miracle every six years on average. Not that they occurred evenly like that; rather, they were clustered together during certain periods.

Of the recorded miracles God did through people, most occurred within very small windows of history during three distinct time periods: the lifetime of Moses, the lifetime of Elijah and Elisha, and the lifetime of Jesus and the apostles. Why? Because during those times God was confirming new truth and new messengers to proclaim that truth. A new revelation needs new confirmation so the people of God can be sure they are receiving a new word from God.

Biblical history indicates that often long periods of time passed without miracles occurring because God was not confirming any new revelation then.

So why don't we see extraordinary biblical-type miracles today? It's not because God cannot do any, because He certainly has the power. (And perhaps He sometimes does—modern Christians debate that.) But if He does not display His power through big public miracles like the parting of the Red Sea, it might be because all the truths He wanted to reveal have already been revealed and confirmed. If there's no new revelation, there's no need for new confirmation.

13. According to Exodus 4:1–8, Numbers 16:5–33, 1 Kings 18:21-39, Matthew 12:40, and Luke 7:20–22, what was the purpose of miracles in these instances?

14. Many people claim they would believe if God performed a great miracle for them. But there's a difference between believing that God exists and putting your trust in Jesus. You can believe that God exists and still not be saved (James 2:19). Do miracles always motivate a belief in the son of God? Give a couple of examples from the life of Jesus to explain your answer.

WHO CONTROLS MIRACLES?

Some Christians today claim that if you are not healthy and wealthy it is because you just don't have enough faith. If you have enough faith, they say, "miracles" are guaranteed. Not only does this false theology overlook the fact that many Christians are called to suffer (1 Peter 2:19–21), but it also overlooks the fact that neither Jesus nor His disciples were healthy and wealthy. In fact, many of the disciples were beaten, tortured and killed for following Christ. Don't tell us they didn't have enough faith!

People don't control the dispensing of miracles. God has always had the final say in the miraculous. When He provided miracles through His apostles and prophets, God was still in control. Notice that miracles in the Bible were never done for entertainment or simply for the personal benefit of the one through whom the miracle was done. For example, Paul couldn't heal his own "thorn" in the flesh (2 Corinthians 12:7–10). Miracles were done as signs from God to point back to God, and they were always under God's control.

You will also notice that the miracles of Christ validate His claim to be the Messiah. Christ's miracles showed His power over nature (e.g., walking on water, calming the storm), His power over sickness (healings), and His power over death (Resurrection). These are signs of the Messiah and an indication of the restoration the Messiah will accomplish. One day the Messiah will return to completely restore this fallen natural world and forevermore put an end to sickness and death. If He has the power to create the universe out of nothing, He has the power to restore it to perfection.

LOOK

YOU DO THE DIGGING

Examining the evidence to know that a theistic God exists is important, especially with respect to the possibility of miracles. It means, for example, that if God wanted to interact with us, He could use any means He desired. He already has shown Himself through the creation of the universe (Romans 1:20) and by the Moral Law written on our hearts, thus

There are many nontheistic religions in the world, each claiming to offer the way to divine enlightenment and inner peace. Some emphasize finding the god within you. Others hope to lead you to the realization that god is in everything around you. But as the Cosmological, Teleological, and Moral Arguments show, religions that don't worship a theistic God do not adequately explain the world around us.

NONTHEISTIC RELIGIONS

Photo: dknisely (CC BY 2.0)..

Let's look first at Buddhism and Hinduism. Popular in India and Southeast Asia, these religions both replace worship of a deity with a personal journey toward virtue (salvation by works), one that continues endlessly through reincarnation. Until you get it right, you will be reborn again and again, with your new status being determined by how many good deeds you did in your previous life. While Buddhists and Hindus deny the existence of an intelligent, personal God, different sects believe in higher beings, either enlightened humans (like Buddha) or a unifying force or supreme reality (like Brahman).

Another pair of religions with similar teachings is Confucianism and Taoism, which are popular in Asia. Both teach that each person must earn his or her displaying His key characteristics. And if He wanted to communicate further with us, He could do that as well. But we would need a way to confirm or authenticate that it was His message, not an imposter's, that we received. One way God could do that would be through miracles. As mentioned before, He already created the universe, so lesser miracles are well within His power.

A true miracle would be an act only God could perform. That means that it would point back to His characteristics, such as supernatural power, intelligent design, and the promotion of moral behavior. It is by these characteristics that miracles can be distinguished from other types of unusual events.

Many people deny the existence of miracles, claiming that they are the result of illusion, magic, superstition, or imagination. It is important for you to do your own research about miracles since, after all, you are living in a universe that came into existence by a miracle from God.

Now it's time for you to do some digging on your own. Pick at least one of the following assignments and complete it before moving on in the study.

Assignment 1: Research and write a three-page paper on a contemporary Christian "faith healer." What evidence did you find that substantiates his or her claims? If all contemporary Christian faith healers are false/true, does that mean the miracles in the Bible are false/true?

salvation by obeying the guidelines for living created by each founder. Confucius taught his followers to live in peace with all people and to honor family and the ancestors. He believed that widespread peace could be achieved if people behaved according to their potential. In contrast, Lao Tzu, founder of Taoism, taught that the key to achieving enlightenment was to avoid conflict and violence. Only by passive acceptance could people become virtuous.

A nontheistic religion currently popular in the United States is New Age. This belief system, though individual in application, centers around the idea of pantheism. This means that truth resides in every person, so whatever someone decides to do or believe is right for him or her. The New Age believer's ultimate goal in life is to gain perfect awareness of his or her divine consciousness. They believe that when enough people achieve this awareness, a new utopian age will be ushered in. New Agers are often drawn to ecological concerns (since god is in the trees and animals) and to ideas like astrology and reincarnation. New Agers see God not as a personal being, but an impersonal force (think *Star Wars*).

Another nontheistic American religion is Mormonism. Although Mormonism tries to set itself up as a form of Christianity, it actually is polytheistic. Mormonism asserts that the god of our planet was once a man and that some Mormons will become gods themselves. It also denies the deity of Jesus, the inerrancy of the Bible, and teaches that salvation must be earned through continuous effort and virtuous living. Only perfect obedience can assure a Mormon that his or her sins will be forgiven. The Book of Mormon also doesn't have a reliable historical foundation, containing many nineteenth-century references that contradict its supposed ancient origin.

In today's politically correct culture, it's easy to fall for the viewpoint that all religions contain some merit and should thus be tolerated. However, while all people are of equal value, all ideas are not. Truth doesn't change, and what people believe will affect the way they live. Only by living according to the truth can a person hope to find true meaning and purpose in life as well as eternal hope.

Assignment 2: Select three miracles from the Bible and answer the following questions about each one:

1. What characteristic(s) of God does this miracle demonstrate?
2. How was it unique, easily recognizable, and something only God can do?
3. Which of the following criteria for a true miracle does it include and how?
   a. Instantaneous beginning of a powerful act
   b. Intelligent design and purpose
   c. Promotion of good or right behavior

Assignment 3: Select three of the unusual events from among anomalies, magic, psychosomatic, satanic signs, and providence. Write a one-paragraph summary of each, defining what makes that event unique and what power source it draws from, giving real-world examples of that event. Finish up by describing how each compares to a true miracle.

Assignment 4: Research David Hume and write a two-page paper on his life, beliefs, and legacy. Include the following components:

1. His birthplace and childhood
2. A list of his major works
3. People who influenced him
4. A brief outline of his career
5. His religious and philosophical beliefs related to the existence of God

WHAT DO I DO NOW?

You now know that the characteristics of the biblical God can be discovered through natural revelation as shown in the Cosmological, Teleological, and Moral arguments. These combine to show us that we live in a theistic universe. We will learn in the next chapters which of the three theistic world religions—Islam, Judaism, and Christianity—is the one true theistic religion. For now, we know that since God exists, miracles are possible. And a true miracle would include some or all of God's characteristics, such as supernatural power, intelligent design, and the promotion of moral behavior.

But think for a minute. Why does it matter that miracles are from God? Who cares if this earth came into being via a miracle or just some accident? How do the miracles that happened more than 2,000 years ago impact your life today? And why did God choose to communicate to us through miracles? You will run into people every day who have never thought through these questions and the significance of the answers. Yet they are living and breathing because God designed their bodies that way and enabled them to enjoy Him and His creation.

So as you consider what you will do with what you have learned about miracles, think about the people around you. They are looking for answers to the big questions in life—where they came from, who they are, and why they are here. If you think about the importance that miracles play in answering each of those questions, you will begin to understand the significance of knowing that the theistic God can and has performed miracles that impact us all.

THINKING ABOUT WHAT YOU LEARNED

Answer the following questions to sum up what you have learned in this chapter.

A. *How would you answer a friend who told you that only fools believe in miracles? What questions would you ask of this friend? What evidence would you present in support of miracles? How would you explain the purpose of miracles?*

B. *Briefly summarize why the authors say only a theistic religion can be true.*

C. *How can we tell real miracles from fake ones? What criteria must a real miracle meet that other "miracles" wouldn't?*

D. The authors use the illustration of two boxes—one closed, one open—to explain the difference between a naturalistic worldview and a theistic worldview. Why have naturalistic intellectuals closed their minds to the possibility of the existence of God and miracles? How does this impact the way they live?

LET'S REVIEW!

So far in this study we have seen that a theistic God exists and that miracles are possible. Use the following diagram to see the logical flow of the points we've made in the last few chapters. Start at the bottom—the foundation for everything else—and move upward to trace how we will arrive at our final conclusion. Notice that the evidence and points are on the left and the IDHEF chapter numbers are on the right. These set the framework for the facts and the overall layout of the book.

The argument for the reliability of the Bible—our conclusion—builds from the arguments for the existence of a theistic God to the historical evidence about Jesus we'll examine in the coming chapters. In fact, you can collapse the twelve points into two major points: 1) A theistic God exists and 2) Jesus proved He was God. That's why we spend so much time on the question of God's existence and question of who Jesus was and is.

Before we move on, let's look at a summary of the points we've covered so far:

1. For the Bible to be true, truth must exist. The Bible can't be true if there is no truth. It is a self-defeating argument to claim that there is no truth, so truth must exist and we must be able to know it.
2. For the Bible to be true, God must exist. There can't be a Word from God if there is no God. Using the Cosmological, Teleological, and Moral arguments, we've established that a theistic God exists.
3. For the Bible to be true, miracles must be possible. Since the evidence shows that the greatest miracle in the Bible (the creation of the universe from nothing) has already occurred, the other miracles are also possible.

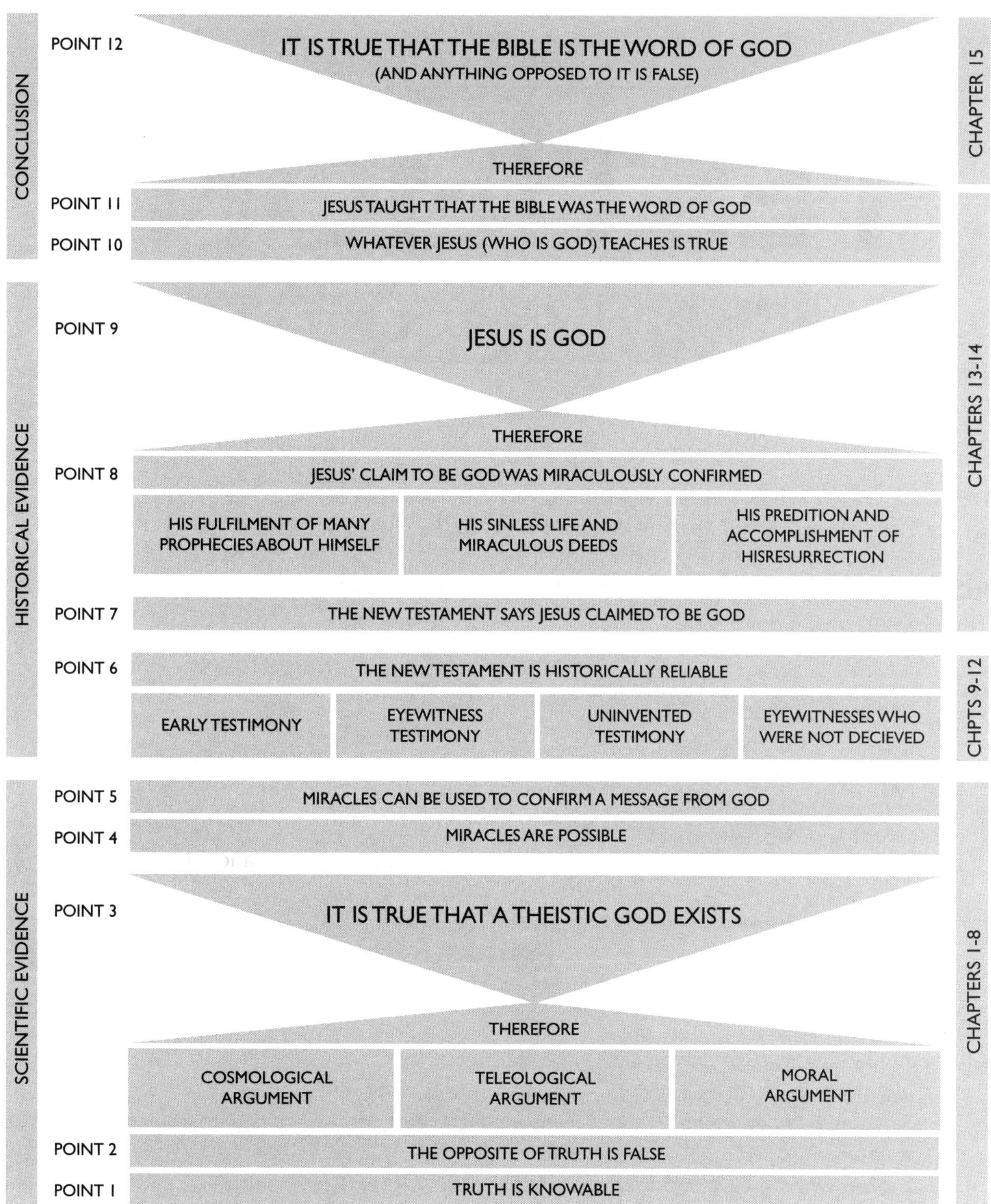
CONCLUSION
POINT 12
IT IS TRUE THAT THE BIBLE IS THE WORD OF GOD
(AND ANYTHING OPPOSED TO IT IS FALSE)
THEREFORE
CHAPTER 15
POINT 11
JESUS TAUGHT THAT THE BIBLE WAS THE WORD OF GOD
POINT 10
WHATEVER JESUS (WHO IS GOD) TEACHES IS TRUE
HISTORICAL EVIDENCE
POINT 9
JESUS IS GOD
THEREFORE
CHAPTERS 13-14
POINT 8
JESUS' CLAIM TO BE GOD WAS MIRACULOUSLY CONFIRMED
HIS FULFILMENT OF MANY PROPHECIES ABOUT HIMSELF
HIS SINLESS LIFE AND MIRACULOUS DEEDS
HIS PREDITION AND ACCOMPLISHMENT OF HISRESURRECTION
POINT 7
THE NEW TESTAMENT SAYS JESUS CLAIMED TO BE GOD
POINT 6
THE NEW TESTAMENT IS HISTORICALLY RELIABLE
EARLY TESTIMONY
EYEWITNESS TESTIMONY
UNINVENTED TESTIMONY
EYEWITNESSES WHO WERE NOT DECIEVED
CHPTS 9-12
SCIENTIFIC EVIDENCE
POINT 5
MIRACLES CAN BE USED TO CONFIRM A MESSAGE FROM GOD
POINT 4
MIRACLES ARE POSSIBLE
POINT 3
IT IS TRUE THAT A THEISTIC GOD EXISTS
THEREFORE
COSMOLOGICAL ARGUMENT
TELEOLOGICAL ARGUMENT
MORAL ARGUMENT
CHAPTERS 1-8
POINT 2
THE OPPOSITE OF TRUTH IS FALSE
POINT 1
TRUTH IS KNOWABLE

Our task now is to discover if any other miracles since the first one have occurred. That will tell us which theistic religion is true. We will begin with a look at the New Testament documents.

CHAPTER 9

DO WE HAVE EARLY TESTIMONY ABOUT JESUS?

BEFORE STARTING THIS CHAPTER

- Read chapter 9 of *I Don't Have Enough Faith to Be an Atheist* (IDHEF), pages 221–249.

ROAD MAP OF THE "TWELVE POINTS THAT PROVE CHRISTIANITY IS TRUE"

This chapter covers point 6:

The New Testament is historically reliable, as evidenced by
a) early testimony,
b) eyewitness testimony,
c) authentic testimony, and
d) eyewitnesses who were not deceived.

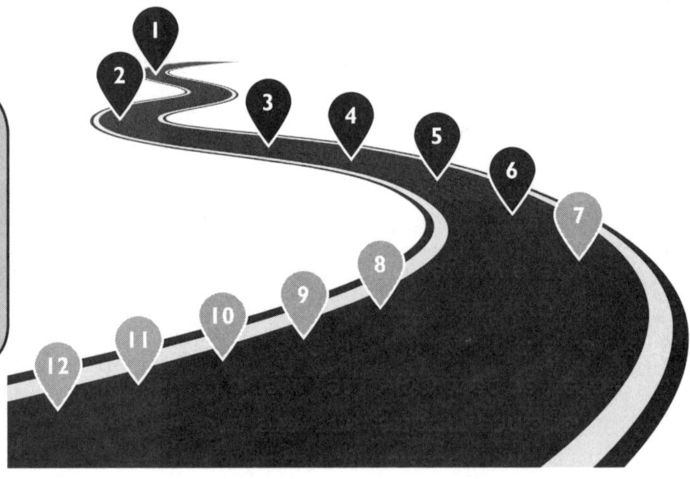

KEY TOPICS

After completing this chapter, you should be able to:

- Identify at least three early non-Christian sources who mention Jesus.
- Summarize what we learn about Jesus from the early non-Christian sources of historical writings.
- Explain why we have accurate copies of the New Testament.
- Know the truth about "misquoting Jesus" and the accuracy of New Testament reconstruction.
- Defend the historical reliability of the New Testament.
- List two objections against the reliability of the New Testament documents.
- Explain why the dates of the New Testament documents are important to establishing reliable historical knowledge about Jesus and the early church.

KEY TERMS

Write the definitions for these words found in your reading:

Manuscripts

Historical reliability

AD

BC

HOOK

QUESTIONS THAT GRAB YOUR MIND

Out of all the history you've studied—the history of your family, your state, your nation, and your world—how much of it have you verified as true? Did you ever check any of the eyewitness testimonies to the historical facts? Do you know for certain that those witnesses can be trusted? Most people have learned historical facts without ever questioning them, being more concerned with passing a pop quiz than with verifying sources. But what evidence do you have that the so-called eyewitnesses did in fact experience the events they related? And even if they were eyewitnesses, can they be trusted to tell the truth?

Although few people would put their high school history text under such scrutiny, many are highly skeptical about the truth and reliability of the Bible. People may not question an apocryphal story about Abraham Lincoln or Alexander the Great, but they'll try to punch every hole they can in what the Bible says. After all, what Alexander the Great did or didn't do won't really affect you or your future. But whether the Bible is true can change the course of your life dramatically. The more there is at stake, the more skeptical people get. Most people understand that if the Bible is true, the implications for them are great (even if they don't *want* to submit to those implications).

As we will see, the more we question the documentation of the Bible, the more we'll see that it does tell us the historical truth. That's critical because without credible historical evidence we could not know if there was a person named Jesus who made the claims He did.

The primary evidence we will look at is the written testimony about Jesus. If the testimony of people who personally witnessed and wrote about the life and works of Jesus is credible, then we are one step closer to knowing the truth about who Jesus is—and one step closer to discovering the "box top" we've been seeking.

1. Christianity is based on verifiable historical claims. How does that differ from most other world religions?

The writings of first-century Roman-Jewish historian Josephus have been heralded and criticized throughout history, and his *Antiquities of the Jews* is one of the few non-biblical sources to confirm Jesus' historical existence.

Josephus was born in Jerusalem to a prominent family in AD 37. His father, Matthias, was a descendant of the priestly line, and his mother was a Jewish noblewoman. Josephus received a good education as befitted his social stature, and by all accounts he was a good student. Born at a time when the land of Palestine was uneasily ruled by Rome, Josephus became caught up in the First Jewish-Roman War (AD 66–73), sometimes called the Great Revolt. He served in the region of Galilee as a commander but was captured a year into the war when, faced with defeat, his men chose to draw lots and kill one another,

TITUS FLAVIUS JOSEPHUS

SO WHAT?

If Christianity is true, the eternal implications make this the most important fact in the universe. If Christianity is false, it is irrelevant. So how do we discover if it is true? Unless God reveals Himself to us directly, the only way we can know if Christianity is true is to do good historical research. Unlike most other religions, Christianity can be verified or falsified by discovering whether or not certain historical events took place, such as the Resurrection.

EARLY NON-CHRISTIAN SOURCES

Skeptics often accuse Christians of using circular reasoning to prove that Jesus lived. They claim that Christians use the Bible to prove that Jesus lived, and use Jesus to prove the truth of the Bible. This, of course, misunderstands what scholars do and the nature of the New Testament documents.

Rather than being a single book, the Bible is actually a collection of documents, many of them historical in nature. As we will see, the evidence shows that the New Testament documents are not merely moral writings on the level of *Aesop's Fables*, tales that teach life lessons but aren't true. Instead, most of them are historical documents containing verifiable eyewitness testimony, and they tell us the truth about what really happened in the first century.

It's still a good idea to ask if there are non-Christian sources that mention Jesus and if they align with what is taught about Him in the Bible. There actually are ten ancient non-

leaving Josephus as the sole survivor.

Josephus offered to advise his captor, General Vespasian. Josephus had seen the high cost of opposing the might of Rome and decided that the only intelligent course of action was to submit to Roman rule and assimilate into Roman culture. Josephus served Vespasian and his son Titus for many years, even acting as negotiator between Titus and the Jewish leaders during the Siege of Jerusalem in AD 70. In recognition of his service, Josephus became a Roman citizen, taking the Latin name Titus Flavius Josephus in honor of his sponsor. He was granted a pension and a house in Palestine.

Thanks to his powerful patrons, both of whom would become Roman emperors, Josephus was allowed to live in Palestine unmolested, despite the fact that many Jews considered him a traitor to his homeland. Thus protected, Josephus undertook to write a history of the war. *The Jewish War* was published in AD 75 as a seven-volume overview of the causes and sequence of the Jewish revolts. Then, in an attempt to explain Jewish culture and law to the Romans, Josephus spent the next twenty years compiling *The Antiquities of the Jews*, a twenty-one-volume work that covered the history of the Jewish people from creation to his present day. It was in volume eighteen that Josephus mentioned a young miracle worker from Galilee by name, providing modern historians and scholars with definitive extra-biblical proof that Jesus existed.

Although Josephus claimed to be creating a balanced account of history, many in Palestine accused him of having a pro-Roman bias. Yet as an eyewitness to many of the events that he detailed, Josephus's writings provide an invaluable glimpse into the turbulent times at the beginning of Christianity. And his descriptions of places were so accurate that modern Israeli archeologist Ehud Netzer was able to discover Herod's Tomb using his writings as a guide.

Christian sources, all written within 150 years of Jesus' life, that give us glimpses into the lives of Jesus, the disciples, and the early church. So just as we compiled external evidence for truth, God, and miracles, we will now look at the surviving evidence for Jesus that exists outside the Bible.

FACTS IN THIS CHAPTER

Establishing a foundation of credible non-Christian historians who corroborate the historical evidence that Jesus lived is only part of the eyewitness testimony. The most significant testimony comes from the New Testament documents. Therefore we need to know if they are historically reliable. To do this we must ask two questions:

1. *Do we have accurate copies of the original documents that were written in the first century?*
2. *Do these original documents speak the truth?*

If we are going to believe the New Testament, then both of these questions have to be answered affirmatively. We don't have the original scrolls on which each New Testament document was written. We have only copies. So first we need to see if we can reconstruct the originals, and then we need to discover if the originals told the truth.

DO WE HAVE ACCURATE COPIES OF THE NEW TESTAMENT?

The New Testament is made up of twenty-seven different documents written by eight or nine different writers over a period of twenty to fifty years. Although we have only copies of the original writings, this isn't unusual for ancient writings. We are able to reconstruct what the original documents said from manuscripts from near the time of the originals. In fact, the New Testament is by far the most well-supported ancient document due to the quality and quantity of existing manuscripts.

The number of manuscripts containing all or part of the New Testament far exceeds what any other ancient document can boast. There are nearly 5,700 partial or complete New Testament manuscripts in Greek alone, and another 9,000 manuscripts written in other languages. The closest ancient equivalent is Homer's Iliad, with a total of 643 manuscripts.

The New Testament also has the support of very early manuscripts—copies made within a generation or so of the originals. This adds to the manuscripts' authenticity because errors were less likely to have been introduced

Fifth-century copy of the book of Mark.

between the originals and these copies. The earliest existing New Testament manuscripts date to about twenty-five years after the originals they were based on. In contrast, the existing manuscripts for the Iliad were written 500 years after its original.

According to New Testament manuscript scholar Daniel Wallace, a newly discovered first-century manuscript of the Gospel of Mark—the earliest New Testament manuscript yet uncovered—will be revealed in a new book early in 2013. Wallace points out that if one were to stack all the currently existing manuscripts of a typical ancient writer such as Josephus, the stack would be about four feet high, whereas the stack of New Testament manuscripts would be over one mile high! Wallace is currently leading the effort at the Center for the Study of New Testament Manuscripts (visit csntm.org) to take digital photographs of all of the 2.6 million pages of existing Greek New Testament manuscripts.

CORRECTION: On page 228, the book cites Charles Leach, author of *Our Bible: How We Got It*, saying that the early church fathers quoted all but eleven verses of the entire New Testament in their writings. We have since learned that the early church fathers actually cited about 46 percent of the New Testament—still an impressive amount. Due to the wealth of manuscript evidence, this new insight does not change the overall conclusion that the New Testament can be reconstructed accurately.

2. ***Why is it important that Josephus and other non-Christian writers mentioned Jesus?***

3. ***List at least six facts about Jesus Christ we can learn from the ten ancient non-Christian sources that mention Him.***

4. ***Some messages get distorted when passed orally from person to person. Why does this problem not affect the New Testament documents?***

5. ***Why might the loss of the original documents actually help preserve their actual message? (See IDHEF, page 229.)***

NEW TESTAMENT RECONSTRUCTION: IS IT ACCURATE?

Using the facts you've learned about the New Testament manuscripts, we can now discuss how scholars go about reconstructing the original New Testament. The abundance of copies makes it easier to reconcile those copies and reconstruct the original documents. The minor differences found between the copies are compared to one another, so it is easy in most places to see what the original likely said. The fact is that there are relatively few places of uncertainty in the New Testament text, and none of them affect any essential Christian doctrine.

Despite this overwhelming evidence, people still try to cast doubt on the authenticity and reliability of the New Testament. In 2005, agnostic professor Bart Ehrman made a name for himself as a critic of the New Testament documents when he published *Misquoting Jesus*, a best-selling book that questioned whether we can accurately reconstruct the original New Testament documents. In saying this, Ehrman appeared to be at odds with most New Testament scholars—both liberal and conservative—who have long agreed that the great number of manuscripts (many of which you can view at csntm.org) make reconstruction of the original quite certain.

But Ehrman only appeared to be at odds with most everyone else. His mentor, Dr. Bruce Metzger of Princeton University, was the greatest manuscript scholar of the last century. In fact, Ehrman dedicated *Misquoting Jesus* to Metzger. The same year Ehrman published *Misquoting Jesus*, he helped his mentor update and revise Metzger's *The Text of the New Testament*, which is the classic work on the subject of New Testament reliability. In that revised edition, Metzger concluded that the New Testament documents can be reconstructed accurately, a fact Ehrman admitted in the appendix for *Misquoting Jesus*:

> Bruce Metzger is one of the great scholars of modern times, and I dedicated the book to him because he was both my inspiration for going into textual criticism and the person who trained me in the field. I have nothing but respect and admiration for him. And even though we may disagree on important religious questions—he is a firmly committed Christian and I am not—we are in complete agreement on a number of very important historical and textual questions. If he and I were put in a room and asked to hammer out a consensus statement on what we think the original text of the New Testament probably looked like, there would be very few points of disagreement—maybe one or two dozen places out of many thousands. The position I argue for in *Misquoting Jesus* does not actually stand at odds with Prof. Metzger's position that the essential Christian beliefs are not affected by textual variants in the manuscript tradition of the New Testament.

So why did Dr. Ehrman deliberately give casual readers of *Misquoting Jesus* the impression that the New Testament cannot be reconstructed accurately, while admitting in the appendix that it could? Was he simply interested in gaining notoriety or in selling books? We don't know. But we find the contradiction here quite telling—the man who gained international attention for casting doubt on the authenticity of the New Testament text, upon further review, doesn't really doubt it himself. Therefore, neither should you.

6. ***When reconstructing the New Testament documents, what kind of differences do scholars find? Do any of these differences affect essential Christian beliefs?***

THE HISTORICAL RELIABILITY OF THE NEW TESTAMENT

So if we can show that we have accurate historical manuscripts of the New Testament, the next question we need to ask is whether the events described in the New Testament really happened. In other words, is the basic story fact or fiction? Can we corroborate any of the historical events described in the books with outside sources? We are not arguing here for inerrancy—that's a discussion for later in the book—just historical reliability.

There are seven primary tests historians use to determine whether or not a historical document can be believed:

1. Is there early testimony? Did the testimony closely follow the events themselves?
2. Is there eyewitness testimony? Did the people testifying actually witness the events?
3. Is there testimony from several unconnected sources? Are there multiple people independently testifying to the same thing?
4. Are the eyewitnesses trustworthy? Does the character of the witnesses make them reliable and believable?
5. Can we corroborate the testimony with outside sources? Are there historical and archeological sources that back up the witnesses' stories?
6. Is there testimony from hostile sources? Can the opposition corroborate any part of the witnesses' testimony?
7. Are there embarrassing details in the testimony? Does the eyewitness testimony contain claims that would make the people involved look foolish or untrustworthy (parts that a person making up or retelling a story would probably leave out)?

These tests, when applied to the New Testament manuscripts, prove that the New Testament is historically reliable. We'll apply these seven tests to the New Testament in a few pages, so stay tuned.

OBJECTIONS TO NEW TESTAMENT RELIABILITY

In today's secular colleges and universities, professors often imply or state that the Bible cannot be trusted. *I Don't Have Enough Faith to Be an Atheist* identifies some of the common objections these professors and skeptics bring to bear on the New Testament. It is important that you understand these objections and how to refute them because you may have to defend your belief in the reliability of the Scriptures somewhere down the road.

One of the most common objections is that we cannot trust the New Testament documents because they were written by biased and converted people who were not objective. While it's certainly true that the New Testament writers were converted people, that doesn't mean they lied or exaggerated. This objection ignores some obvious questions: Why were they converted? Why would they lie? To get themselves beaten, tortured and killed? Not likely.

It's more likely that the New Testament writers strived to be accurate in their reporting to ensure that their extremely important message could not be not easily dismissed or disbelieved. They certainly had no reason to say Jesus had risen from the dead if He really did not. Because they faced persecution and death for declaring Christ's resurrection, they would more likely leave that part out for their own safety.

7. How would you respond to a friend who said the following?

There's no way the Bible can be trusted, with its stories about people coming back to life and worldwide floods. It's more like legend than history.

You can't trust what the New Testament writers said. They were just making up stories so people would follow them.

Everyone knows there's no way to know what really happened in history, so there's no way to prove if the Bible is true or not.

ARE THE NEW TESTAMENT DOCUMENTS EARLY?

Let's take a closer look now at the first of the seven tests for whether an historical document can be considered reliable: Were the original documents written relatively close to the time of the events they describe?

8. *Briefly summarize the evidence we have documenting why:*

All the New Testament books had to have been written by AD 100 (IDHEF, pages 235–237).

Most, if not all, had to have been written by AD 70 (IDHEF, pages 237–239).

Several critical books had to have been written before AD 62 or even earlier (IDHEF, pages 239–241).

9. ***Scholars agree that a creed appearing in I Corinthians 15 dates to before AD 40, not long after the Resurrection itself. What is the significance of this and the forty other creeds found elsewhere in the New Testament?***

YOU DO THE DIGGING

We have seen that there is ample evidence supporting the New Testament documents. Even though we no longer have the originals, we can reconstruct their message by comparing and cross-checking the thousands of manuscripts that do survive. We have also learned that the New Testament documents were written a short time after Jesus' death and contain even earlier source material, some of which goes back to Jesus' lifetime.

Now it's time to for you to do some digging on your own. Pick at least one of the following assignments and complete it before moving on in the study.

Assignment 1: Write a two-page paper on the reliability of the New Testament as compared to other ancient documents. Include important information such as the dates of these writings, the authors, the number of copies, and the time gap between copies.

Assignment 2: Write a two-page paper on why the New Testament documents are a very reliable source of information about Jesus and far better than any known non-Christian sources. Specifically target your paper to refute the charge that the New Testament writers were biased (so we can't trust what they wrote).

Assignment 3: Dr. Gary Habermas has identified more than forty creeds in the New Testament documents. Find ten of them (check out his book *Historical Jesus* or visit www.GaryHabermas.com). Then write a paragraph for each creed, discussing its significance and how it helps establish the historical reliability of the New Testament.

Assignment 4: Find Dan Wallace's review of Ehrman's *Misquoting Jesus* online. (Dan Wallace is a scholar of New Testament manuscripts and professor at Dallas Theological Seminary). Outline Wallace's critique of *Misquoting Jesus*, and then write a summary of his arguments and conclusions.

WHAT DO I DO NOW?

What if you were in an automobile accident and were wrongly accused of causing the wreck? You would need reliable testimony of what actually happened to cause the accident. The facts provided by your witnesses could be used in court to prove who was at fault and who was not. In court, the more eyewitnesses you have, and the more credible they are, the better your chances of proving your point.

The same is true of the New Testament. Even though we don't have the original documents, we have many copies of those originals and much eyewitness testimony of the events recorded in the New Testament concerning Jesus. And those writings are all very early—within forty years of his life and death.

If you profess to be a Christian, you may be challenged on these points, especially at a secular college. Can you defend your faith by showing that we have an accurate copy of the original New Testament documents? Your articulate and informed defense may one day be used to convince an opponent or bystander of the truth of the Bible. What you do can and will have eternal consequences.

CLEMENT OF ROME

Clement of Rome was an early church father who held a high position in the first-century church in Rome. His writings substantiate the existence, historicity, and truth of the New Testament.

From the historical and religious documents and letters of the time, we are able to piece together a few facts about Clement's life. He was said to have been a companion and student of either the apostle Paul or the apostle Peter or both and was appointed to lead the church at Rome by Peter himself. (Today, the Catholic Church counts Clement as the second or third Bishop of Rome after Peter.)

The best evidence regarding Clement's life and ministry is found in a letter he wrote in the name of the Roman church to the Christian church at

A. List the fourteen people named by the apostle Paul who were eyewitnesses to the resurrection of Jesus (IDHEF, pages 242–243).

Corinth, the same church that received the epistles of 1 and 2 Corinthians from Paul. Though the letter doesn't contain his name anywhere, several of Clement's contemporaries, such as Irenaeus and Origen, clearly identify Clement as the author. Other works attributed to him are more difficult to verify.

In this letter, Clement writes to calm a dispute that had arisen between two factions in the Corinthian church. Some innocent leaders had been deposed, disrupting the order and structure of the local church. Clement speaks of proper discipline in the church, stressing humility and meekness in the Christians' behavior toward one another. To illustrate his points, Clement quotes from the Old Testament as well as several New Testament books, including as Paul's first letter to the Corinthians and the books of Romans, Hebrews, James, and 1 Peter. These quotes are what make this early letter so interesting to historical critics, because it proves that Clement wrote after these books were already established parts of the New Testament.

Although the exact date of the letter is unknown, Clement does apologize for his delay in dealing with the Corinthian dispute, as the church at Rome was dealing with troubles of its own. Based on the time of Clement's death, it is most likely that he was referring to the persecution of the Christians in Rome under the emperor Domitian, which ended between AD 95 and 96. The most likely date, then, for Clement's letter is between AD 96 and 98. After the New Testament documents, this time frame makes Clement's letter one of the earliest surviving Christian writings.

This letter was highly thought of by other early church fathers. Indeed, evidence exists that the letter was regularly read in churches nearly one hundred years after Clement's death. Although not much detail about his life has remained, Clement, as a personal associate of the apostles, played a vital role in corroborating the truth of the New Testament documents and the Christian faith. He died around AD 100, possibly as a martyr.

B. When people say things denying Christianity, it is not your job to refute what they say, but rather, it's their job to support their statements. So if someone were to say, "The New Testament can't be reliable because it's been changed throughout the centuries," how would you answer that person? (Remember the three questions we talked about earlier: The first two ask for clarification and evidence from the person, and the third is your opportunity to offer the truth.)

C. What is the importance of the creed found in 1 Corinthians 15:3–8? (See IDHEF, pages 241–243.)

D. What three explanations do the authors give for why the New Testament documents weren't written earlier? (See IDHEF, pages 245–246.)

FIVE POINTS TO REMEMBER!

It's easy to see how people can be so skeptical today. With all the lies circulated about the Bible on television and the Internet, it's no wonder people have trouble believing anything! We are surrounded by people making promises they don't keep, stories about events that turn out to be lies, and people trying to cover up crimes they have committed.

In addition, most young people attend secular high schools, colleges, and universities full of skeptics trying to convince them that what they believe isn't scientifically or historically sound. But the truth is that the Christian faith is not based on biases, but on evidence.

To help you in your discussions, memorize the following:

1. We have about 5,700 copies of the New Testament documents—many more than exist for any other ancient book, including those by Homer, Plato, or Tacitus. As a result, we can reconstruct the original text with great accuracy.
2. Most of the supposed "errors" in the biblical manuscripts turn out to be spelling and word order differences, none of which affect a single doctrine of the Christian faith. Even the skeptic Bart Ehrman, author of *Misquoting Jesus*, agrees with this.
3. We have the written testimony of ten non-Christian sources from within 150 years of Jesus, some of those from sources hostile to Christianity.
4. Most, if not all, of the New Testament books were written before AD 70, which puts them within forty years of the life of Jesus. And the numerous creeds contained in the writings are of very early origin.
5. All of this was written during the lives of the eyewitnesses, making historical revisionism very difficult if not impossible.

You now have ample evidence to support the early testimony of the New Testament writers regarding Jesus Christ. Your challenge will be to take these facts to those who want to know the truth but may not be easily convinced.

CHAPTER 10

DO WE HAVE EYEWITNESS TESTIMONY ABOUT JESUS?

BEFORE STARTING THIS CHAPTER

- Read chapter 10 of *I Don't Have Enough Faith to Be an Atheist* (IDHEF), pages 251–274.

ROAD MAP OF THE "TWELVE POINTS THAT PROVE CHRISTIANITY IS TRUE"

This chapter covers point 6:

The New Testament is historically reliable, as evidenced by
a) early testimony,
b) eyewitness testimony,
c) authentic testimony, and
d) eyewitnesses who were not deceived.

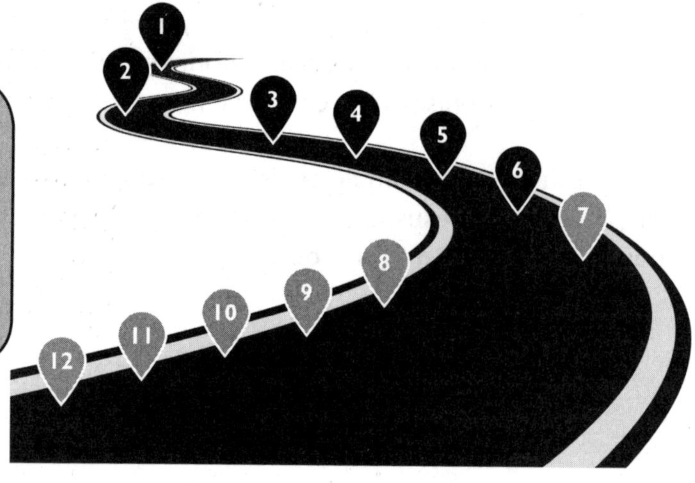

KEY TOPICS

After completing this chapter, you should be able to:

- List five New Testament verses that support the eyewitness accounts about Jesus.
- Provide two proofs that the New Testament writers really were eyewitnesses or had access to eyewitness testimony.
- Describe the implications of the eighty-four facts found in the last sixteen chapters of Acts.
- Explain two ways we can know that Luke's Gospel is as reliable and accurate as the book of Acts.
- List three details from the Gospel of John with supporting verses that prove John was also an eyewitness of Jesus.
- Explain the significance of the references to real historical figures in the New Testament.

QUESTIONS THAT GRAB YOUR MIND

Think back to exactly two weeks ago today. Who did you talk to and what did you discuss? It's probably difficult to remember, unless something dramatic happened that impacted you personally. You might remember visiting someone, having an intense disagreement, or seeing something spectacular. But what about a year ago today? Ten years ago? Unless it was a milestone event in your life, you've probably forgotten the details of those dates.

Can you remember where you were on September 11, 2001? If you are old enough, you probably can recall the details of that day. Why? Because the terrorist attacks were a dramatic "impact event"—an event that had a great emotional impact on many Americans. The details of that experience, or any impact event, may be forever seared into your mind.

Think of the events recorded in the New Testament the same way. If those events really happened—people healed or brought back to life, Jesus walking on water and feeding the masses, the crucifixion and resurrection, the intense persecution that followed the birth of Christianity—do you think the eyewitnesses would have had any trouble remembering them? We don't think so. Those experiences would have been seared into their minds because they were impact events.

As we'll see in this chapter, the New Testament writers who recorded these events not only claimed to be (or at least know) eyewitnesses, they also recorded details that *proved* they were eyewitnesses. These details are corroborated by archaeology and other historical documents.

1. Why is eyewitness testimony to the life of Jesus important?

SO WHAT?

You may have lived most of your life not questioning whether the facts about Jesus are true. But when you get into college or enter the workforce, you will run into views quite the opposite of yours. Some of the people who hold those opposing views, including professors, may actively try to talk you out of Christianity. They may mock and challenge your views. They may insist that Jesus was just a nice person or a "good religious leader." Or they may claim that He didn't really exist at all.

If you are not prepared with an intelligent defense of Christianity (as the Bible itself commands), then you will not be able act as God's ambassador who can help change lives forever. You can't give what you haven't got. So now is the time to prepare yourself to show that the New Testament documents actually do tell us the truth about events in the first century.

FACTS IN THIS CHAPTER

This chapter continues to investigate the historical facts that support the credibility of the New Testament documents. Here we will look at the second historical test: Do the New Testament documents contain eyewitness testimony?

EYEWITNESS ACCOUNTS OF JESUS

As mentioned earlier, the more eyewitnesses of an event, the better the reliability of their testimony. The fact that there are multiple eyewitnesses makes it easier to determine what really happened and harder to fake a story. If the witnesses' testimony aligns on the major events (though not necessarily every detail), then you have greater assurance that their testimony is credible.

Herod's Family Tomb in Jerusalem.

Rising from relative obscurity to become one of the most powerful rulers of his day, Herod the Great was known as a ruthless and cunning king. He and his sons dominated the Middle East during Jesus' lifetime, leaving their mark on history forever.

HEROD THE GREAT

Herod was born in 72 BC, the second son of ambitious Antipater. As Edomites descended from Jacob's brother Esau, Antipater and his sons were considered foreigners by the Jews. But Antipater had curried favor with Julius Caesar, so when Caesar defeated Pompey and took control of Rome, Antipater was made chief minister of Judea with the right to collect taxes. Using his political savvy, Antipater also managed to have his sons appointed to high political positions in Judea.

After an uprising resulted in his older brother's death, Herod petitioned

So the New Testament contains numerous eyewitness claims. The next question we have to ask is what evidence do we have that the New Testament writers really were eyewitnesses or had access to eyewitness testimony? After all, it's one thing to claim to be an eyewitness; it's another thing to prove it.

2. Name four New Testament writers who personally saw the resurrected Christ.

Rome for the title King of Judea. His petition was granted, and Herod returned to Judea to take control of his new kingdom. Though only twenty-five at the time, Herod proved an able military leader and cunning diplomat.

Herod was now responsible for keeping peace between the Jews and the Roman occupation. The Jews resented their Roman masters, and the Romans thought the native people rebellious and stubborn. Thus it took Herod the next twelve years to consolidate his kingdom. He made a brilliant match with Mariamne, a Jewish heiress from the dynasty of the high priests. Their marriage put him in position to choose the next high priest while giving him respectability in the eyes of the Jewish people.

Herod also went to extravagant lengths to honor Rome, building cities and monuments to Caesar's heir and successor, Augustus, and holding games in his honor. Under Herod's rule, Judea began to prosper, with both the Roman and Jewish factions of the population living side by side in a precarious peace. In 20 BC, he began construction of his grandest achievement. Finished in AD 63, Herod's Temple was the most beautiful building in all Judea, made of white marble overlaid with pure gold. Although an impressive gift to his people, the building of the temple didn't endear Herod to the Jews the way he had hoped. They still saw him as a foreign conqueror and the puppet of Rome.

Though politically successful, Herod was surrounded by rumors of conspiracy and was suspicious of the members of his own family. After the high priest's death, he was forced to appoint his wife's younger brother to the position. Herod then killed him when he became too popular.

Herod slowly became more and more paranoid, executing anyone who appeared to threaten his rule, including his wife Mariamne and his two favorite sons. The slaughter of the innocents, as told in Matthew 2:1–16, happened near the very end of his life and prompted Joseph to flee to Egypt with Mary and Jesus.

3. ***This chapter provides a list of verses that contain eyewitness claims. Pick two of them, record the references below, and summarize how they enhance our confidence in the truth of the New Testament message.***

DID THE NEW TESTAMENT WRITERS USE EYEWITNESS TESTIMONY?

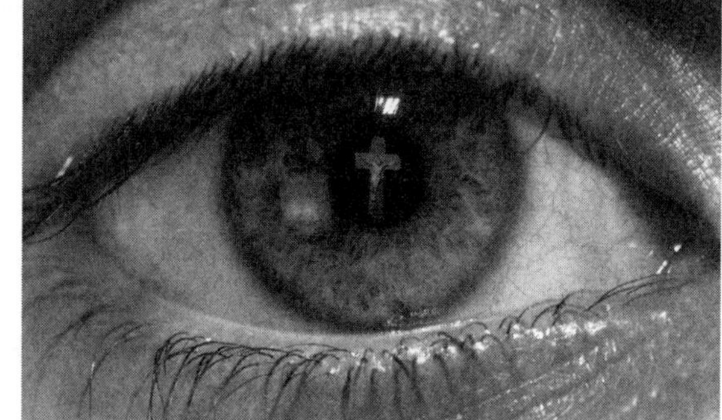

In a courtroom, an eyewitness is expected to provide the judge and jury with detail about what he or she saw, enabling them to make a decision about the guilt or innocence of the defendant. Because a trial relies on forensic evidence, the more detail the eyewitness can add that can be substantiated, the more his or her testimony will be valued as accurate.

It is this kind of detail that makes the New Testament writers believable. Not only did they provide details of a kind that could only be known to someone who had lived the events they described, but they also referenced historical people, places, and events that can be corroborated. In fact, the New Testament includes challenges to the readers of their era to verify the facts for themselves. The writers pointed their readers to other witnesses who were still alive, saying that the events of the life of Christ and the early church weren't done in secret, but out in the open. This is a pretty bold (almost foolhardy) strategy if the disciples were perpetuating an elaborate hoax.

EYEWITNESS DETAILS IN THE BOOK OF ACTS

In the midst of eighty-four confirmed eyewitness details, Luke records thirty-five miracles in the last sixteen chapters of the book of Acts. All of these miracles are recorded in the same historical narrative that has been confirmed as authentic eyewitness testimony. Although New Testament critics (who are already set against the possibility of miracles) feel that this discounts the rest of the book, the question we need to ask is why Luke would be so careful to document trivial details such as the depth of the water or the direction of the wind and not be equally careful with his description of these thirty-five miracles? Based on Luke's track record, we can only assume that the miraculous events he described took place, just as the everyday ones did.

4. ***Summarize four of the eighty-four facts that stood out the most to you (see IDHEF, pages 256–259). How could you use them in a discussion with a friend?***

Fact 1:

Fact 2:

Fact 3:

Fact 4:

5. ***How does knowing that Luke wrote with such precision impact your confidence in the truth of the Bible? Does the fact that he also described miracles change your confidence in any way? Why or why not?***

IS THE GOSPEL OF LUKE AS RELIABLE AS THE BOOK OF ACTS?

The book of Acts is a continuation of the Gospel of Luke. The author begins Acts by saying, "In *my former book*, Theophilus, I wrote about all that Jesus began to do and to teach until the day he was taken up to heaven." Since Luke's Gospel is also addressed to Theophilus, it is clear that this is the former book to which he is referring. In essence, Luke wrote a two-volume account of the events surrounding the birth of the church. The Gospel of Luke gives details of Jesus' life, death, resurrection, and ascension, while the book of Acts records what happened after Jesus returned to heaven, including the growth of the church until about AD 62.

Luke writes in Luke 1:3, "Since I myself have carefully investigated everything from the beginning, it seemed good also to me to write an orderly account for you, most excellent Theophilus." Because Luke writes with such precision in the book of Acts, shouldn't we expect that same accuracy from the Gospel of Luke?

6. ***Name three facts from Luke's Gospel that have been verified.***

7. ***If Luke is telling the truth, what does that say for the storyline in the Gospels written by Matthew and Mark?***

EYEWITNESS DETAILS IN THE GOSPEL OF JOHN

John's overall approach to telling about the life of Jesus is different than the other three Gospels. In fact, some critics believe that the Gospel of John was written much later and that much of it was invented rather than recorded by an eyewitness and therefore cannot be trusted. But is this true? How accurate was John as a historian, and what evidence do we have to show he was an eyewitness?

Although John's Gospel does not include quite as many geographical, topographical, and political details as the book of Acts, there is still sufficient evidence to verify that John's Gospel contains numerous eyewitness details.

8. ***Summarize three of the fifty-nine facts and unlikely inventions that stood out the most to you from pages 263–268 of the book. How could you use them in a discussion with a friend?***

Fact 1:

Fact 2:

Fact 3:

9. ***How do these facts impact your confidence in the fourteen miracles (including the Resurrection) recorded in John's Gospel?***

WHAT IS THE SIGNIFICANCE OF REFERENCES TO HISTORICAL FIGURES?

Not only are many of the sociological and geographical details in the New Testament confirmable, but so are the lives of many of the historical figures the New Testament writers mention. There are more than thirty important people named in the New Testament who were also mentioned by other historians of the day. These include people like Herod the Great and his family, Pontius Pilate, and the Jewish high priest Caiaphas. In many cases, these were powerful Roman officials who would not have taken kindly to the spreading of untruths about their lives and decisions, especially to promote what they saw as a threatening political movement.

10. Why is it unlikely that the New Testament writers would include actual historical figures in an invented story?

11. Briefly describe the discovery of the Caiaphas Ossuary and its significance.

12. The book talks about how the New Testament testimony contains "historical crosshairs." What does this mean? Identify two of these "historical crosshairs" and their significance.

THE "ONE SOURCE" THEORY

It's often assumed by critics of the New Testament that it comes from a single religious source rather than a collection of historical documents from multiple, independent sources. But to believe this, skeptics must let their presuppositions determine their interpretation of the facts, rather than relying on the facts to determine their interpretation. From the facts we have studied already in this chapter, it is clear there is too much historical accuracy and unique eyewitness testimony in the New Testament for it to have been pulled from a single source. Eight or nine independent authors (depending on who wrote Hebrews) penned this collection of historical documents. It was not written or edited by a single person, or even by a committee. Although the New Testament writers describe many of the same events, their descriptions contain several lines of independent eyewitness testimony and enough similarity to corroborate multiple events, yet enough dissimilarity to make a single source for these accounts unlikely.

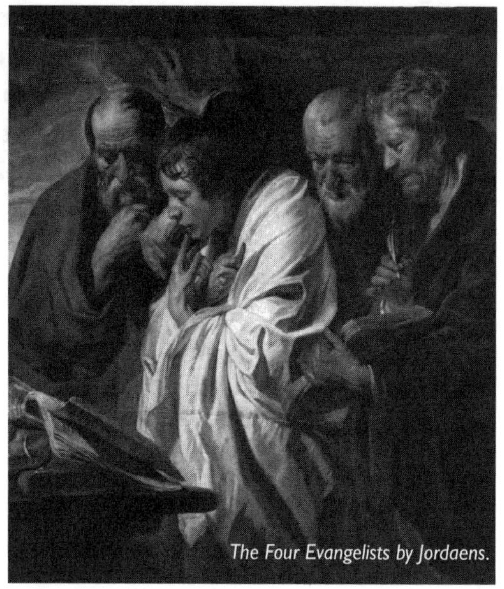
The Four Evangelists by Jordaens.

13. How do we know that the New Testament documents contain independent eyewitness testimony?

14. Novels such as* The Da Vinci Code *suggest that the New Testament documents reveal a false story that's part of a grand church-manufactured conspiracy. Give several reasons why this is not plausible.

15. The New Testament writers claim to be eyewitnesses several times. Paul even does so before King Agrippa, claiming that "the King is familiar with these things, and I can speak freely to him. I am convinced that none of this has escaped his notice, because it was not done in a corner." If this exchange is historically accurate as recorded in Acts 26, why is this strong evidence that the Resurrection actually happened?

16. How would you respond if someone said to you, "The Bible is just a religious book—you can't trust its view of historical events"? (Don't forget to start with the three questions!)

YOU DO THE DIGGING

As we have seen, the twenty-seven New Testament books were written soon after the events they describe, and we find the same basic storyline when combining references from several non-Christian sources. This is foundational to proving that the New Testament contains credible documentation about the life of Jesus. Chapter 10 strengthens this foundation by examining the wealth of eyewitness details included in the New Testament. The second half of Acts alone contains at least eighty-four historically confirmed eyewitness details. In addition, Luke's Gospel corroborates the same basic storyline found in the Gospels of Matthew and Mark. John's Gospel also includes at least fifty-nine historically confirmed or probable eyewitness details. Finally, epistles written by Paul and Peter provide the fifth and sixth testimonies of the Resurrection.

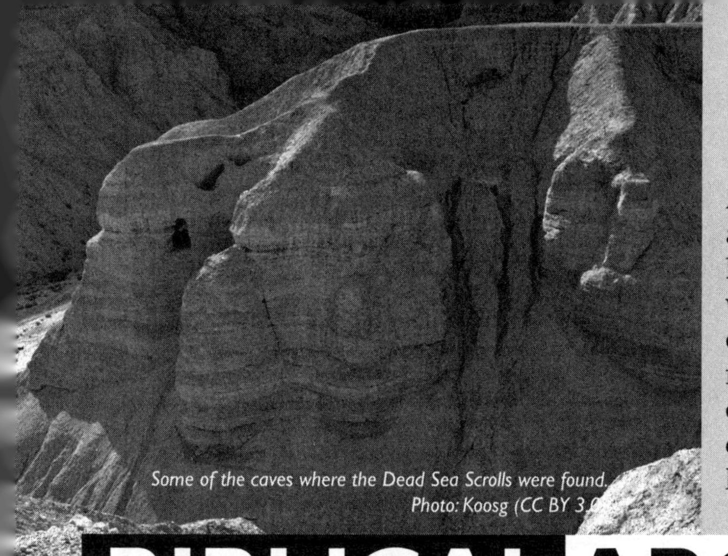
Some of the caves where the Dead Sea Scrolls were found.
Photo: Koosg (CC BY 3.0)

Archeology is the study of the buildings, artifacts, and inscriptions ancient peoples left behind. Biblical archeology focuses on what we can learn about biblical events and characters from external historical sources, not only to gain a better understanding of the cultural and historical context of the events described in the Bible, but also to assess its historical validity.

BIBLICAL ARCHAEOLOGY

An archeologist studies the clues left behind in the dirt and stone to decipher how ancient peoples lived and worked, what they ate, how their societies functioned, and what contributions they left behind when they died. It's like having to put together an enormous jigsaw puzzle without knowing the final picture or even if you have all the pieces. But each piece can add more knowledge to our collective understanding of the way people lived in the past—provided we interpret it correctly.

From listening to secular authorities today, it's easy to get the impression that the more scientific and archeological discoveries we make, the less credible the Bible becomes. The truth, however, is just the opposite: The more we uncover about the history and peoples of the Middle East, the more the accounts of the Bible are substantiated.

Finds like the Dead Sea Scrolls proved that later copies of the Bible were just as accurate as those very early manuscripts. Inscriptions on tombs have verified the existence of people mentioned in the Bible (sometimes people who are only referenced in the Bible). Documents written on clay and papyrus have revealed details about ancient legal practices, business contracts, and societal arrangements that corroborate details of biblical stories, clear up misunderstandings caused by an incomplete knowledge of life in ancient times, and even verify that the Bible uses proper terminology for things or people.

Scores of archeological discoveries have affirmed references and stories from every major portion of the Bible, capturing the attention of even the secular media. An article from the October 25, 1999, issue of U.S. News and World Report said, "In extraordinary ways, modern archaeology has affirmed the historical core of the Old and New Testaments—corroborating key points of the stories of Israel's patriarchs, the Exodus, the Davidic monarchy, and the life and times of Jesus."

The Rose Book of Bible Charts, Maps, and Timelines provides an excellent summary of the top archaeological discoveries pertaining to events from both the Old and New Testaments. Also, check out the Biblical Archeology Society's website at www.biblicalarcheology.org for news of the latest discoveries and stories about what it's like to work on an archeological dig.

It is important to understand that while biblical archeology can help us verify historical facts about life in Bible times, it is still a forensic search—like a detective trying to reconstruct a crime scene, we can only make educated guesses about what the evidence shows. Likewise, the basic truths of the Christian faith aren't material things and so can't be directly verified by archeological discoveries. While archeology can confirm the historical reliability of the biblical account, adding strength to the credibility of the Bible, believing in Jesus as Savior remains a personal decision.

The Four Evangelists

The major writers of the New Testament recorded the same events but with divergent details, indicating that they are independent eyewitnesses. These same writers cited more than thirty historical figures whose existence has been confirmed by ancient non-Christian writers and/or archaeological discoveries. This early, independent eyewitness testimony within one generation of the events of Jesus' life provides ample evidence that the New Testament events cannot be considered merely legendary.

Now it's time to for you to do some digging on your own. Pick at least one of the following assignments and complete it before moving on in the study.

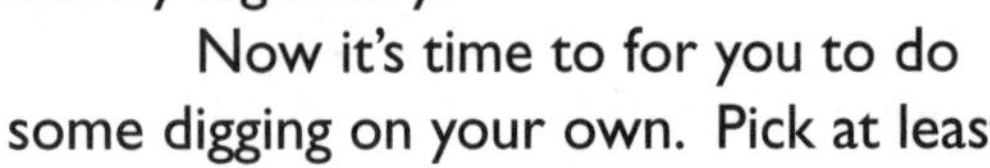

Assignment 1: List at least five verses that substantiate the Resurrection and provide the following evidence for each:

a. Who was/were the eyewitness(es)?
b. What did they witness? Provide facts.
c. What was the setting (the place, time, situation, etc.)?
d. What other specific details did the writers record that prove they were eyewitnesses?

Assignment 2: Interview a non-Christian friend. Ask him about his religious beliefs and if he believes the New Testament tells the truth. If not, why does he doubt it? Afterwards, write a two- to three-page letter to that person responding to his objections and explaining the evidence that convinces you that the New Testament is true. If you feel it is appropriate, use the letter to open further dialogue with your friend. Make sure to remember throughout that you are an ambassador for Christ.

Assignment 3: Find five significant archaeological discoveries related to the New Testament. Write a paragraph briefly describing each find and why it is significant to establishing the truth of the Bible.

Assignment 4: Go to www.Crossexamined.org and click on "Resources and Links" to find links to several Christian apologetics sites. Browse these sites for articles, videos, and podcasts and pick two that deal with the reliability of the New Testament documents. After reading/listening to them, write a one- to two-page paper summarizing their main arguments.

TOOK

WHAT DO I DO NOW?

Have you ever gone on vacation and then returned to tell your friends about it? Perhaps there were things you saw and did that your friends found hard to believe. How could you prove to them you saw the things you saw? You might have shown them pictures. But if you didn't have a camera, you would have to convince your friends in some other way of what you saw and experienced. You might have called upon your brother, sister, or a friend who was with you to confirm your story. If so, your stories would have to contain enough of the same details so the people who doubted you would be convinced.

This scenario is similar to what you have seen in this chapter—multiple people documenting the same historical events with such detail and accuracy that it leaves little doubt that they were eyewitnesses. But the New Testament eyewitnesses were not explaining their vacations. They were describing the facts and events surrounding the life, death, and resurrection of Jesus Christ. Your vacation may have been fun, but it won't have the same kind of eternal effect on your life or the lives of others as the resurrection of Jesus will. The testimony of the New Testament writers is the most important eyewitness testimony in history.

Because the spread of Christianity is based on sound eyewitness testimony, you can tell others the same story those witnesses told 2,000 years ago. This is your challenge—to use the facts at your disposal to support the story of the New Testament. You can help others you know understand that the New Testament is not just a collection of moral tales or fables but, rather, a real-life record of world-changing events accurately captured by faithful eyewitnesses.

THINKING ABOUT WHAT YOU LEARNED

Answer the following questions to sum up what you have learned in this chapter.

A. ***Why is it significant that the New Testament writers record the same basic events with diverging details?***

B. How does the fact that the New Testament writers referenced important historical figures of their day add credibility to the Bible?

C. Name four facts that make it nearly impossible to believe that the New Testament was a fictionalized account (see IDHEF, pages 271–272).

DON'T MAKE THE SAME MYTH-TAKE!

Many people today think the Bible is just a book of myths, perhaps with good moral teachings, but myths nonetheless. However, as we have seen, there are too many verifiable eyewitness details from multiple sources in the New Testament documents for them to be merely myths. But could they be invented stories with a lot of good historical data? Not likely. In the first century, there was no such genre of literature as the historical novel. These people were writing history, not fiction. Besides, most of these men died for what they believed, and even the most dedicated authors don't die for a novel!

CHAPTER 11

TOP TEN REASONS WE KNOW THE NEW TESTAMENT WRITERS TOLD THE TRUTH

BEFORE STARTING THIS CHAPTER

- Read chapter 11 of *I Don't Have Enough Faith to Be an Atheist* (IDHEF), pages 275–297.

ROAD MAP OF THE "TWELVE POINTS THAT PROVE CHRISTIANITY IS TRUE"

This chapter covers the following points:

The New Testament is historically reliable, as evidenced by
a) early testimony,
b) eyewitness testimony,
c) authentic testimony, and
d) eyewitnesses who were not deceived.

KEY TOPICS

After completing this chapter, you should be able to:

- Describe why the New Testament writers included:
    a. Embarrassing details about themselves.
    b. Embarrassing details about Jesus.
    c. Difficult sayings of Jesus.
    d. Elements of Jesus' life that contradicted the Jewish expectations of the Messiah.
- Explain why the New Testament writers distinguished Jesus' words from their own words.
- Discuss the significance of divergent details in eyewitness testimony.
- Discuss why the New Testament writers challenged others to verify their facts.
- Explain the importance of how the New Testament writers described miracles.
- Explain the significance of the New Testament writers abandoning their sacred beliefs and practice.
- Discuss the apologetic difference between New Testament martyrs and martyrs from other religions.

KEY TERMS

Write the definitions for these words found in your reading:

Sanhedrin

Pharisees

Martyr

JUSTIN MARTYR

A second-century Christian apologist, Justin earned his name by refusing to deny his faith in the face of death. Given the choice to sacrifice to pagan gods or be scourged and beheaded, Justin chose to remain true to his Christian faith and was killed. The writings he left behind would impact the thinking of later church fathers Tertullian and Irenaeus and remain inspiring today.

Justin was born in AD 103 to a pagan family in the Roman town of Flavia Neapolis in Palestine. Highly intelligent, Justin studied several different branches of philosophy including Stoicism and the teachings of Plato, though he felt something was lacking in the worldly schools of thought. Then, in an encounter with an elderly Christian man on a seashore in Ephesus, Justin learned of Jesus and the principles of Christianity. He was drawn by stories of Christians refusing to give up their faith under torture and threats of death. Here was the

QUESTIONS THAT GRAB YOUR MIND

Through our investigations in the last chapter, we learned that the New Testament contains verifiable eyewitness testimony. But how do we know the authors of the New Testament didn't embellish the stories of miracles? Consider these questions:

1. Have you ever lied to make yourself look good or to get out of trouble? Haven't we all?
2. Have you ever lied to make yourself look bad or to get into trouble? Of course not! Who would do that?

Do people invent or embellish stories that will get them beaten, tortured, and killed? When trying to deceive people, do they provide obvious ways in which their lies can be exposed? Do they invent impossible standards and then subject themselves to them? Do they willingly suffer persecution and death because of their lies when they could save themselves by simply admitting they're not true?

knowledge he had been searching for—a verifiable faith so secure that people were willing to die rather than deny it.

He converted to Christianity and began writing apologetic treatises, using examples from Christian scriptures and pagan philosophy to intellectually prove the truth of the gospel message. Though nearly a dozen works are attributed to Justin by historians of the day, only three have survived. His *First Apology* and *Second Apology* defended Christianity to pagan friends and important Roman figures. His *Dialogue with Trypho*, a debate between Justin and an influential Jew named Trypho, sought to prove that Jesus' teachings fulfilled the Old Testament rather than supplanting it.

In his writings, Justin sought to show, first, that the execution of Christians merely for their beliefs was immoral for they had broken no laws; and second, that the common accusations against Christians (such as atheism, sorcery, and even cannibalism) were wrong. He outlined the basic tenets of Christianity and gave an overview of its practices, such as baptism and the Lord's Supper, to show that Christians were moral and productive citizens. Justin also wrote that Jesus and Christianity were the fulfillment of fragments of truth that had been available since the beginning of the world.

In AD 165, Justin and six other men were arrested and brought to trial for their beliefs. When given the choice between renouncing Christianity and offering sacrifices to pagan gods or being tortured and killed, Justin answered simply that anyone would be foolish to exchange truth for a lie. He told the judge that he welcomed suffering for Christ because that meant he would be able to claim a greater reward in heaven. Justin and his companions were beheaded. The court's record of the proceedings have been preserved.

Your investigations in this chapter will help you discover that the stories in the New Testament are accurate and written without embellishment. You'll see that the authors had everything to lose and nothing to gain by sticking to their testimony when threatened with imprisonment and death.

1. ***When people tell you something embarrassing about themselves, does it make you believe them more or less? Why?***

SO WHAT?

In this chapter you are going to have the opportunity to look at the New Testament documents from a new perspective—one that is the opposite of today's secular claims. Many people today think that the authors of the New Testament were biased individuals who invented, exaggerated, or embellished stories for their own benefit. Yet nothing could be further from the truth. The New Testament writers accurately recorded and promulgated what they saw despite the fact that it cost them dearly to do so. As you'll see, they never would have invented what they wrote. Armed with this truth, you'll be a better and more confident ambassador for Jesus.

FACTS IN THIS CHAPTER

As you begin your study of this chapter, remember that we already know the New Testament documents were written within fifteen to forty years after the life of Jesus and include multiple eyewitness testimonies of His life, death, and resurrection. But did the eyewitnesses embellish or exaggerate their stories? This chapter will show they did not. It will provide the top ten reasons we know the New Testament writers told the truth.

EMBARRASSING DETAILS

One of the questions the book asks is if people ever lie to make themselves look bad. This question relates to "the principle of embarrassment," which is one of the tests historians use to assess whether a historical document is telling the truth. It states that if a statement of fact is embarrassing to the author(s), it's probably true. After all, who is going to lie to make himself look bad? People will usually weave a tale that makes them look appealing—smart, kind, brave, caring, or loyal—and save the negative attributes for when they describe their enemies. They are far less likely to admit their own faults, confess their sins, and reveal their worst mistakes.

But the New Testament is filled with embarrassing details! The New Testament writers often depict themselves and the other apostles as dim-witted, bumbling, doubting cowards who ran away at the first sign of trouble. In fact, the women who stayed to witness the crucifixion and returned to visit the tomb are shown as being bolder than Christ's closest disciples. Why would the apostles say all this if they were inventing a story? Wouldn't they have turned it around, depicting themselves as bravely following Jesus to the cross, if the story were a collective work of fiction? It appears that they had a greater desire to tell the truth than to make themselves look good!

The Denial of Peter by Caravaggio

2. ***Describe two of the embarrassing details the New Testament writers revealed about themselves and explain why it isn't likely that they would have made them up.***

   Detail 1:

   Detail 2:

3. ***Describe two of the potentially embarrassing details the New Testament writers revealed about Jesus and explain why it isn't likely that they would have made them up.***

   Detail 1:

   Detail 2:

DIFFICULT SAYINGS

Curcifixion of Christ by Zurbarán

Most countries, corporations, and religious groups depict their leaders in the best possible light, claiming that they are bright, courageous, caring, and representative of everything that is good and wholesome. They are connected to all the right people and the latest trends. Their followers accentuate and exaggerate the positives and downplay the negatives. Often it's nothing but spin—good public relations and marketing strategy.

But the New Testament writers were different. They were honest—brutally honest. Instead of preventing anything from being written that would make people think less of Jesus or damage their cause, they included embarrassing accusations and mischaracterizations that painted Jesus in a negative way.

Furthermore, the Jesus story is far from what a Jewish person would make up about the promised Messiah. The last thing the Jews were expecting was a sacrificial Messiah who would allow Himself to be killed by their oppressors. They expected a Messiah who would conquer their oppressors. Consequently, the death-and-resurrection story is not something Jews would make up, especially in light of the fact that the Jews believed that anyone hung on a tree was under God's curse (Deuteronomy 21:23).

4. ***If you were a writer making up the New Testament story to get people to follow you and Jesus, what would you have written regarding:***

   Your intelligence?

   Your bravery?

   Who discovered the empty tomb?

Your faith in the resurrected Christ?

What other people thought of Jesus?

5. What did the New Testament writers actually say about these things?

Their intelligence?

Their bravery?

Who discovered the empty tomb?

Their faith in the resurrected Christ?

What other people thought of Jesus?

DEMANDING SAYINGS

It would have been easy for the New Testament writers to record only the comforting, encouraging, and uplifting things that Jesus said, so that everyone would love Him. That strategy might have increased His following and certainly would have made it easier to do what He asked. But the New Testament writers also recorded some of Jesus' extremely difficult commands and even stories in which He condemned people for their actions. Because those commands and condemnations impacted the writers themselves, is it more likely that they invented these difficult sayings or that Jesus really said those things?

6. ***Summarize two of Jesus' commands from the Sermon on the Mount. Why is it unlikely that the authors would have included these kinds of commands unless they were true?***

   Command 1:

   Command 2:

THE WRITERS' WORDS VERSUS JESUS' WORDS

Many of the New Testament epistles were written to counteract significant controversy in the early church. Paul wrote I Corinthians to confront sexual immorality in the church at Corinth. He wrote Galatians to address legalism in the church in the province of Galatia. There were heresies creeping into the church at Colossae, so Paul wrote Colossians. Although it might have been easier to solve these controversies by simply making up quotes from Jesus, Paul didn't do that. In fact, all the New Testament writers were very careful to distinguish Jesus' words from their own, so that what they said was never mistaken for something Jesus had said. Why would they be so careful if they were inventing Christianity? And why would they work so hard to combat theological controversies if they were merely maintaining an invention?

7. ***What evidence do we have that Paul did not invent sayings of Jesus? Why is that significant?***

RESURRECTION EVENTS THE WRITERS WOULD NEVER HAVE INVENTED

In their description of Jesus' resurrection, the New Testament writers again depicted events that made them look bad and gave others the credit for things the apostles should have handled. If the account of Jesus' burial were fictional, wouldn't the disciples have taken credit for claiming and burying Jesus' body, rather than giving Joseph of Arimathea, a member of the Sanhedrin, the credit for laying Jesus to rest? Wouldn't they have crafted the story of finding the empty tomb with themselves in the role of faithful followers, waiting outside for Jesus to appear, instead of giving women (invisible members of society of that time) credit for having more faith and devotion than His closest companions?

8. ***If the New Testament writers were making up the Resurrection story, why would they NOT say:***

The body was in a Jewish Tomb?

The disciples ran away?

The women were the first witnesses?

Many priests were converted (Acts 6:7)?

REFERENCES TO HISTORICAL PEOPLE

More than thirty characters in the New Testament have been confirmed as historical by either archaeology or non-Christian sources. Some of these figures were very significant in Jesus' life, including John the Baptist, Pilate, and Caiaphas.

9. How does the fact that the writers referenced real historical people confirm the truth of the New Testament?

10. What is the Caiaphas Ossuary? Why is it significant? (Refer to your answer on page 182.)

DIVERGENT DETAILS: PROBLEM OR PROOF?

Within the gospel accounts, some of the details differ. Skeptics point to these divergent details as proof that the New Testament writers were inconsistent, saying they discredit the entire New Testament.

However, differences in similar eyewitness testimonies are not necessarily contradictions. When there are multiple witnesses to an event—a car accident, for example—it is unlikely that two people will see and report exactly the same details. Why? Perhaps because each individual witnessed the accident from a different angle based on his or her location. Perhaps because each was focused on a different part of the accident or simply described what he or she saw in a unique way. These types of testimonies are complementary and help to complete the details of the overall accident.

This is common in eyewitness testimony. For example, some survivors of the *Titanic* disaster said that the ship went down whole, while others said it broke in two before it sank. But all agreed on the central fact that the *Titanic* sank.

If two witnesses gave exactly the same word-for-word testimony, a judge would suspect collusion—that they had rehearsed their stories beforehand in order to hide the truth. The fact is that independent eyewitnesses rarely describe all the same details, and they never use exactly the same words.

Apply this to the burial and resurrection of Jesus. The New Testament writers agree on the central facts but provide different details because of their unique focus and perspective. (And even if there are seemingly irresolvable contradictions between those details, the central fact that there was an actual resurrection is not invalidated.)

11. How would you respond to a friend who claimed that the New Testament documents cannot be trusted because they don't agree on all the details?

CHALLENGE TO VERIFY

After making many seemingly outlandish claims, especially those having to do with miraculous events, the New Testament writers encouraged their readers to check out for themselves the truth of the facts presented. This provides another layer of authenticity. For at the time when people would be most suspicious of the apostles' claims, there were eyewitnesses still living who could confirm or deny the truth of what the apostles were saying. Far from trying to hide the truth (if in fact the Jesus story was made up), the writers invited outsiders to try and disprove what they had written. This is a very stupid move to make if the apostles knew their story to be a lie, but a very compelling proof for their veracity.

NEW TESTAMENT WRITERS AND MIRACLES

When a person wants to make a story more significant, dramatic, or appealing, he or she might embellish it with extravagant details. This could have easily been the case with the resurrection of Jesus, but the evidence points to the opposite conclusion—that the New Testament writers described the events they witnessed with an almost bland detachment.

12. Geisler and Turek point out the Gospel writers' restraint in their descriptions of miraculous events, especially the resurrection itself. Why is this significant? What does it say about the trustworthiness of the Gospels?

WHY WOULD THE WRITERS ABANDON THEIR BELIEFS?

When Jesus began His ministry in the first century, the Jews already had a nearly two-thousand-year-old relationship with the God of the universe. They were His chosen people, with a rich tradition of religious practices. Yet after the alleged resurrection of Jesus, thousands of pious Jews changed their theology almost overnight, abandoning long-held religious practices and instituting new ones. Not only that, but they also held to their new theology and practices despite suffering persecution and death for their stand. Why would they do this if Jesus had remained in the grave?

Only an impact event could explain why the apostles abandoned Judaism for Christianity. What's an impact event? It's something that impacts you so greatly that it can change your life and way of thinking forever.

Most of us have experienced impact events. For example, what did you do on October 23, 2011? You probably have no idea. So why can you remember where you were and what you were doing ten years earlier on September 11, 2001? (This is assuming you're old enough to remember; if not, ask your parents what they were doing that day.) It's because on September 11, 2001, there was an impact event—an event that had a tremendous emotional impact on all of us who witnessed it. The details of that experience are forever seared into your mind. You might not remember what you had for breakfast yesterday, but you will never forget what you were doing on 9/11.

If the events recorded in the New Testament documents really happened—healings, a man walking on water, the feeding of five thousand, assassinations, intense persecutions, resurrections of the dead—don't you think these would qualify as impact events? Do you suppose eyewitnesses would have had any trouble remembering them? If you saw someone rise from the dead, wouldn't you remember it?

13. List three religious practices the Jewish believers changed after the Resurrection (see IDHEF, pages 290–293).

NEW TESTAMENT MARTYRS

A martyr is someone who believes strongly enough that his cause is right that he chooses to die for it. There have been religious martyrs throughout history. So how do Christian martyrs differ from martyrs of other religions? Why do we think the New Testament martyrs prove Christianity is true, but that martyrs from other faiths do not prove their religion is true? The key difference is that the New Testament martyrs were eyewitnesses to a miraculous yet historically verifiable event—the Resurrection. Other martyrs have no such evidence to back up their claims.

Curcifixion of St. Andrew by Fugel

14. People might die for a lie they think is the truth, but no one will die for a lie they know is a lie. How does that statement explain the central difference between martyrs of other religions and the martyrs of the New Testament?

LOOK

YOU DO THE DIGGING

In this chapter, you learned ten reasons to believe that the New Testament writers faithfully and accurately recorded what they saw without exaggeration or embellishment. These ten reasons add to the evidence presented in previous chapters to show that the New Testament established an accurate and early account of the facts about the life, death, and resurrection of Jesus.

The New Testament writers recorded embarrassing facts about themselves and Jesus. They were not afraid to include the demanding sayings of Jesus, even though this could have caused their readers to decide not to follow Jesus. The New Testament writers also resisted putting their own words into Jesus' mouth. They included events related to the Resurrection that would not have been invented, and they cited more than thirty historically confirmed people in their record. Their testimony included divergent details (a hallmark of eyewitness testimony), and their miracle stories were not exaggerated or embellished. They even challenged others to check out their facts.

MUHAMMAD

Muhammad is known today as the author of the Quran and the most important figure in Islam. Muslims consider him to be the last and most important prophet of Allah, sent to restore the world to the original monotheistic religion taught by Abraham. Born in AD 570, Muhammad was orphaned at a young age and taken in first by his grandfather, then his uncle, and trained as a merchant. Muhammad's reputation for honesty and integrity helped the business grow and attracted the attention of his employer, the widow Khadijah, who asked him to marry her.

When he was forty years old, Muhammad reported to his wife that, while meditating alone in a cave, he had received a revelation from Allah. Although Muhammad was distressed by the experience, Khadijah consoled him and convinced him that the vision was real and that it came from the same god who spoke to Moses. Three years later in Mecca, Muhammad began publically preaching that Allah is one god—with no equal, human or divine—and that he expects complete surrender and obedience. Muhammad also said that he had been appointed Allah's prophet, the last in a line of great men like Abraham, Moses, and Jesus.

Muhammad's teachings were met with hostility, for the polytheistic Arabian tribes around him didn't want to give up their gods. His ideas also threatened their economic system of trade—polytheism brought business to Mecca. As more people were converted by Muhammad's teachings, the leaders began to see him as a threat rather than just a nuisance. The Meccan leaders began persecuting Muhammad and his followers, who fled to Medina in 622. This exodus is known as the Hijra, and marks the starting date of the Islamic calendar.

Once settled in Medina, Muhammad made peace between the warring tribes in the region and began converting them to his side, using their men to raid caravans from Mecca. Soon, war broke out between the polytheistic Arabian tribes of Mecca and Muhammad's Islamic forces in Medina. The first major battle occurred at Badr and was a triumph for the Muslims. The Meccans gathered more men and attacked a few weeks later at Uhud, this time defeating the Muslims. Over the next three years, Muhammad made alliances with nearby tribes while also working to sabotage Meccan alliances. In 627, Meccan forces besieged Medina, but Muhammad's fortifications held. Failing to conquer Medina weakened Mecca's prestige, but also resulted in the signing of a treaty that lasted two years.

In 630, war broke out again. Muhammad marched against Mecca with a force of nearly 10,000 men and conquered it. Once in charge, Muhammad declared amnesty for most of the inhabitants, provided they converted to Islam. Then he set about stabilizing the region, spreading Islam to the nearby tribes and making them swear loyalty to him. Less than two years later, Muhammad fell ill and died. His family finalized the Quran, which held his religious revelations, and compiled the Hadith, which contained his instructions for living. Islam continued to spread over the next few centuries, and today is the second-largest religion in the world.

The New Testament Jews didn't need a new religion—they already believed they were God's chosen people—so why would they invent one? That the followers of a Jewish carpenter were able not only to change their religious beliefs, but be willing to suffer persecution and die for this new faith is strong evidence that Jesus actually did rise from the dead.

Now it's time to for you to do some digging on your own. Pick at least one of the following assignments and complete it before moving on in the study.

Assignment 1: Interview a non-Christian friend about her thoughts on the New Testament, asking why she doesn't believe the New Testament documents are true. Use your clarifying questions to get the discussion going. If you feel it is appropriate, follow up by offering some of the evidence you studied in this chapter for her to consider. After the discussion, write a two- to three-page summary of the conversation, emphasizing her objections and how she responded to your questions and evidence.

Assignment 2: Write a one- to two-page paper citing at least ten details or events from the New Testament that would be embarrassing to the writers and thus unlikely to be invented.

Assignment 3: Go to www.Crossexamined.org and read the article "Gospel Contradictions? Why They Don't Exist—A Little Experiment to Teach Skeptics about New Testament Accuracy." Then summarize the article's main points and explain how the article shows that divergent eyewitness details do not invalidate the fact that there really was a plane crash.

Assignment 4: Read two articles from www.Answering-Islam.org, and then summarize their arguments. In a one- to two-page paper, discuss how these arguments relate to proofs for the truth of Christianity.

TOOK

WHAT DO I DO NOW?

You'll have the opportunity to share what you learned in this chapter with people around you who are looking for the truth. Although your words can have a strong influence on people, it is even more vital that your lifestyle backs up what you say. The New Testament writers not only recorded the truth but lived it by suffering persecution and death for what they said they saw. Their words and actions lined up!

As you talk with people about the truths you've learned, be aware that they will be watching to see if you live as if you really believe them yourself. You might be mocked or ostracized when you share these truths, but your life will be a lasting testimony for Jesus. Even as the New Testament writers had to sacrifice for what they believed, you may be called on to do the same.

THINKING ABOUT WHAT YOU LEARNED

Answer the following questions to sum up what you have learned in this chapter.

A. *Summarize why each of the ten reasons we studied in this chapter helps confirm that the New Testament writers were telling the truth. How could you use these details to answer friends' questions about the truth of Christianity?*

Reason 1:

Reason 2:

Reason 3:

Reason 4:

Reason 5:

Reason 6:

Reason 7:

Reason 8:

Reason 9:

Reason 10:

B. Chapter 11 ended with a brief discussion of the history of Islam. Answer the following questions, using what you've learned about the New Testament.

a. *If New Testament martyrs validate the truth of Christianity, why don't today's Muslim martyrs validate the truth of Islam?*

b. *Although Muhammad himself claimed not to do miracles, why are there miracles attributed to him? Why don't they prove the truth of Islam?*

c. *What was the difference in how Christianity and Islam spread in their early years?*

d. *When did the crusades begin? What were they a response to?*

A MORE LIKELY STORY

If humans invented the Resurrection story, we think it would go more like this:

> Jesus came to save the world, and he needed our help. That's why we were there for him every step of the way. When he was in need, we prayed with him. When he wept, we wept with him. When he fell, we carried his cross. The gates of hell could not prevent us from seeing his mission through!
>
> So when that turncoat Judas betrayed Jesus to the Romans (we had always suspected Judas), and they began to nail Jesus to the cross, we laughed at them. "He's God! The grave will never hold him! You think you're solving a problem, but you're really creating a much bigger one!"
>
> Although we assured the women that everything would turn out all right, they couldn't handle the crucifixion. Squeamish and afraid, they ran to their homes and hid behind locked doors. But we men stood steadfast at the foot of the cross, praying for hours until the very end. When Jesus finally took his last breath and the Roman centurion confessed that Jesus was God, Peter blasted him. "That's what we told you before you nailed him up there!" (Through this whole thing, the Romans and the Jews just wouldn't listen!)
>
> Never doubting that Jesus would rise on the third day, Peter announced to the centurion, "We'll bury him and be back on Sunday. Now go tell Pilate to put some of your 'elite' Roman guards at the tomb to see if you can prevent him from rising from the dead!" We all laughed and began to dream about Sunday.
>
> That Sunday morning, we marched down to the tomb and tossed aside those elite Roman guards. Then the stone (the one that took eleven of us to roll into place) rolled away by itself. Jesus emerged from the tomb and said, "I knew you'd come! My mission is accomplished." He praised Peter for his brave leadership and congratulated us on our great faith. Then we went home and told the women the good news.

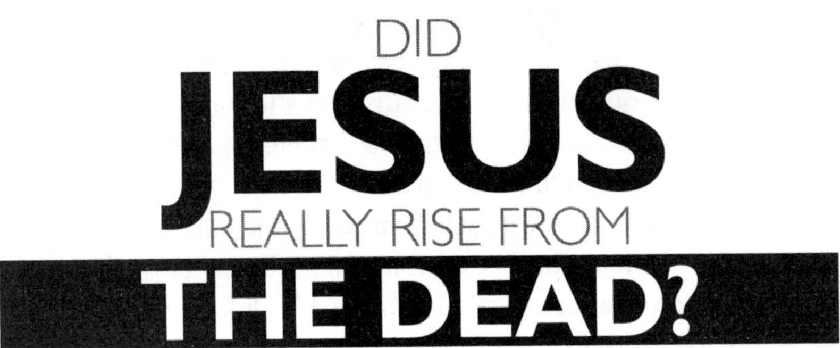

BEFORE STARTING THIS CHAPTER

- Read chapter 12 of *I Don't Have Enough Faith to Be an Atheist* (IDHEF), pages 299–324.

ROAD MAP OF THE "TWELVE POINTS THAT PROVE CHRISTIANITY IS TRUE"

This chapter covers the following points:

The New Testament is historically reliable, as evidenced by
a) early testimony,
b) eyewitness testimony,
c) authentic testimony, and
d) eyewitnesses who were not deceived.

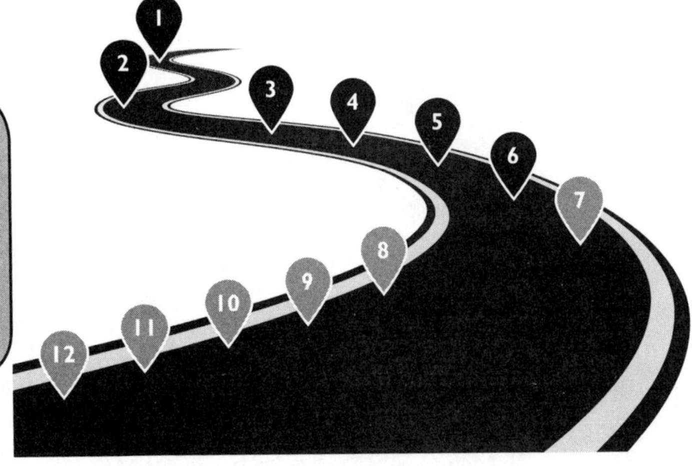

KEY TOPICS

After completing this chapter, you should be able to:

- Name several historical facts that all scholars agree on concerning Jesus and Christianity.
- Describe and refute alternative theories to the Resurrection often given by skeptics.
- Explain how context supports the Resurrection.
- Refute skeptics' objections regarding extraordinary evidence and self-canceling miracles.

HOOK

QUESTIONS THAT GRAB YOUR MIND

If you could get an honest answer to just one question in life, what would it be? There are many important questions in life, but only a few really matter for all eternity. At the top of the list are *Does God exist?* and *Did He raise Jesus from the dead?*

We have seen that the evidence for God's existence is quite strong. According to good reason and what we observe in the universe around us, we live in a theistic universe where miracles are possible. But did the resurrection miracle really happen? Did Jesus really rise from the dead? Christianity rests on the historical claim that He did.

The evidence thus far shows us that the New Testament writers did not lie, create a legend, or embellish the truth. Since their sincerity is not at question—they told us what they *thought* was the truth—is it possible they were deceived about the Resurrection? That's what we'll investigate in this chapter.

Mosiac of Alexander the Great from the fourth century.

ALEXANDER THE GREAT

Known and studied throughout history, Alexander the Great is considered one of the greatest military commanders of all time. At the height of his power, Alexander's empire stretched from Greece and Egypt in the west to the Himalayas in the east.

Alexander was born in 356 BC the favorite son of Philip II, king of the city-state of Macedon in northern ancient Greece. He was raised in the manner of aristocratic Macedonian youths, taught to read, play the lyre, ride, fight, and hunt. Alexander was educated by the famed philosopher Aristotle for three years until the age of sixteen, when Alexander joined his father Philip on military campaigns throughout Greece. His father was seeking to unite the city-states of Greece under his rule, a goal he accomplished before being assassinated by his own bodyguard in 336 BC

At the age of twenty, Alexander was

1. ***C. S. Lewis wrote, "Christianity, if false, is of no importance, and if true, of infinite importance. The only thing it cannot be is moderately important." Do you agree or disagree with that statement? Why?***

appointed his father's successor. Ambitious and competitive, with a thirst for glory, Alexander had already proven to be a capable commander and strategist. After reestablishing control over Greece, Alexander secured his northern borders and then marched into Asia Minor. The Persian Empire was his next target, and in a campaign that lasted ten years, Alexander slowly conquered Persia. He besieged Tyre, a biblical city on an island, and eventually captured it by building a causeway of rubble from the mainland. Then he marched south into Egypt, taking control of it and proclaiming himself Pharaoh. He also founded the city of Alexandria, which became a center of culture and learning. Leaving Egypt, Alexander headed into Mesopotamia, where he finally defeated the Persian king, Darius III, and proclaimed himself the new Persian ruler. It seemed that no nation could stand against him.

In 326 BC, Alexander moved southeast to invade India, but was stopped when his men refused to go any further. Weary of battle, they rebelled, insisting on returning home to see their families. Given no choice, Alexander reversed course, arriving back in Persia two years later. This proved to be the farthest Alexander's empire would extend.

While in Babylon, Alexander—then just thirty-two and never defeated in battle—fell ill and died a few days later. After a struggle over his remains, his body was eventually laid to rest in Alexandria in Egypt. The suddenness of his death threw the empire into chaos. Although Alexander's wife Roxane was pregnant, the young heir wouldn't be able to rule for many years. His closest generals tried to hold the empire together, but none had Alexander's charisma or ambition. The empire split apart.

Despite his relatively short reign, Alexander had a tremendous impact on the known world. He was responsible for bringing Greek culture and thought to Asia Minor, a process later known as Hellenization. He founded no fewer than twenty cities that bore his name. His military tactics would be studied throughout history and continue to be taught in military academies around the world. Eventually the life and legacy of Alexander the Great took on the sheen of folklore and legend.

SO WHAT?

What's so important about the Resurrection? What if Jesus did not rise from the dead? Is it really that big of a deal?

It is a *huge* deal. Christianity is based on the fact that Jesus rose from the dead. As the apostle Paul wrote in his first letter to the church at Corinth, "If Christ has not been raised, your faith is futile; you are still in your sins. Then those also who have fallen asleep in Christ are lost. If only for this life we have hope in Christ, we are of all people most to be pitied" (1 Corinthians 15:17–19).

If Jesus remained in the tomb, then Christianity is an irrelevant deception and we don't have forgiveness for our sins. A holy and just God must punish sin, or He wouldn't be holy and just. Without Jesus' sacrificial payment for our sins, we would be separated from God for all eternity. That's what hell is—separation from God.

So the question "Did Jesus really rise from the dead?" is actually the most important question of all. Our eternity depends on the answer.

FACTS IN THIS CHAPTER

So it's clear that the New Testament writers didn't write legends, outright lies, or exaggerated truth. But were they deceived? Unable to cast doubt on the writers' sincerity, skeptics claim that perhaps the disciples *thought* they saw a resurrected Jesus but were mistaken.

In this chapter we'll look at several alternative theories to the Resurrection put forth by skeptics, such as the hallucination theory, the swoon theory, and the stolen body theory. But possible theories are just that—they are possibilities. Just because something *could* have happened doesn't mean it *did!* It's one thing to offer an alternative theory to the Resurrection; it is quite another to provide evidence that the alternative theory is true. We will see that the possibilities put forth by skeptics not only have no evidence to support them, but there's evidence to believe that these theories are absurd.

Additionally, in our study of this chapter we will focus on the importance of context. Should we believe all miracle claims, or are the miracle claims in the New Testament more believable because of the surrounding circumstances? We will also examine the demand for extraordinary evidence and address the question of self-canceling miracles from other religions.

FACTS ABOUT JESUS AND CHRISTIANITY

The resurrection of Jesus is central to the Scriptures and Christianity. If it is not true, then Jesus was a fraud and the rest of the Bible is irrelevant. That's why for Christians it's encouraging to note that Bible scholars across the board agree on a number of historical facts relating to Christianity.

2. ***Of the twelve agreed-upon facts about the Resurrection (see IDHEF, pages 299–300), summarize the three you think are the most important to showing Christianity is true. What do these facts mean for Christianity? How could you use them in a discussion with a friend?***

3. ***All the evidence we've studied points to the conclusion that the New Testament writers were careful historians and trustworthy witnesses. Why then do people continue to look for alternate explanations?***

When considering the truth of the New Testament accounts of Jesus' life, death, and resurrection, there are only four possibilities: 1) The stories are legend; 2) the stories were outright lies; 3) the stories were embellishments; or 4) the stories are all historically accurate. As discussed on pages 300–301, the best explanation of the evidence seems to be number four—that the stories about Jesus and His resurrection are historically true. Unwilling to accept this conclusion, skeptics have one last out: Perhaps the disciples were sincere but deceived. The burden of proof is on the skeptics to show that this was the case. They have come up with several theories to explain why the disciples only thought Jesus had risen from the dead.

The Resurrection of Christ by Seghers.

HALLUCINATION THEORY

One theory frequently offered by skeptics is that the disciples were hallucinating—they wanted Jesus back so badly that they created a shared illusion that He had risen from the dead. But this is scientifically implausible. Even if several members of a group were hallucinating, they wouldn't have the same hallucination. Just like people don't have group dreams, they don't share group hallucinations either. This theory also doesn't explain the fact that the risen Jesus was seen and even touched by hundreds of people over a period of forty days (1 Corinthians 15:6). Nor does it explain why the Jews and Romans didn't simply produce the body of Jesus and squash Christianity before it got started.

WRONG TOMB THEORY

Another explanation skeptics give for the disciples' belief that Jesus had risen is that on Sunday morning they all went to the wrong tomb. Finding it empty, they declared that Jesus had risen and went about proclaiming His power. But this theory also has fatal flaws. The disciples weren't the only ones who would have had to visit the wrong tomb—the Jewish leaders and their Roman guards would also have had to be mistaken about where Jesus' body had been placed (or else they could have marched the disciples to the right tomb and showed them the corpse). This theory also doesn't explain how hundreds of people afterward saw Jesus alive and well.

Other tombs near the traditional tomb of Christ.

SWOON THEORY

A third theory is that Jesus didn't really die—instead He fainted from His mistreatment, was mistakenly assumed to be dead, and was entombed, only to revive later. This theory demonstrates a lack of understanding of how brutal the process of crucifixion was. Even modern doctors believe that Jesus died, especially once the soldiers thrust a spear into His side. It also assumes that the professional executioners made a mistake in pronouncing Him dead, Joseph of Arimathea mistakenly embalmed an unconscious man, and the disciples thought nothing was amiss when a battered and broken Jesus appeared to them Sunday morning.

STOLEN BODY THEORY

This is the earliest of the alternate theories as to what happened to Jesus, since it is the story the Jewish leaders circulated as soon as they found the tomb empty. But even then, they had trouble proving it was the truth, for it meant that the disciples knowingly perpetrated a hoax and then went to their graves calling it the truth.

The transport of Christ to the sepulcher by Ciseri.

Crucifixion by Tintoretto.

SUBSTITUTE THEORY

Another far-fetched theory is that it was not actually Jesus who was crucified and died, but that someone took His place on the cross. However, this idea (offered by many Muslims today) doesn't match the eyewitness accounts and historical sources. It also means that those closest to Jesus, such as John and Jesus' own mother, who watched Him die, were just as deceived as the Roman executioners and the Jewish leaders standing at the foot of the cross. And what happened to the body of the substitute? Couldn't that have been produced by Jesus' enemies as proof that He didn't die and therefore wasn't resurrected?

When all is said and done, there is no alternate theory plausible enough to explain away all of the evidence supporting the New Testament account. Therefore, we must choose the explanation that requires the least amount of faith to believe: that Jesus died on the cross for our sins, was buried, and rose again the third day.

4. *How does a theory differ from evidence? What makes a theory credible?*

5. Fill in the chart below, summarizing the five alternate theories discussed here and listing facts that refute each theory.

ALTERNATE THEORY	WHAT THE THEORY CLAIMS	THE FACTS THAT REFUTE IT

6. ***Why is it implausible that the resurrection story was copied from pagan resurrection myths? (See IDHEF, pages 311–312.)***

DOES THE CONTEXT SUPPORT THE RESURRECTION?

Remember the illustration about the importance of context in chapter 5? A man has just slashed open the stomach of a helpless woman. Without context, that scenario sounds like a killer was at work. But add the fact that the man is a doctor trying to save the life of the woman's baby by performing an emergency caesarian section, and the man becomes a hero rather than a murderer. When you know the context of the facts, the way you interpret the evidence can change dramatically.

Now let's turn our attention to Jesus' resurrection. What is the context in which the Resurrection is reported to have occurred? Many of the skeptics do not take the overall context of the supporting evidence into consideration, due to their theological presupposition that God does not intervene in the universe. Instead of fairly evaluating the evidence, they wrongly presuppose that miracles do not occur and, therefore, there must be another explanation for Jesus' resurrection (however implausible such an explanation might be).

Turek and Geisler provide four points of context for the resurrection: 1) that since we live in a theistic universe, miracles are possible; 2) that ancient documents predicted miracles; 3) that historically confirmed witnesses say they saw miracles happen and confirmed their claims with their blood; and 4) that the basic storyline of the New Testament has been confirmed using external sources. Based on this context, it is more reasonable to believe that the miracle of the Resurrection actually took place than to believe it did not.

7. ***Briefly explain why the first three points of context for the miracle of the resurrection help us conclude that it actually happened.***

   Miracles are possible in a theistic universe.

Ancient documents predicted miracles.

Eyewitnesses saw miracles happen.

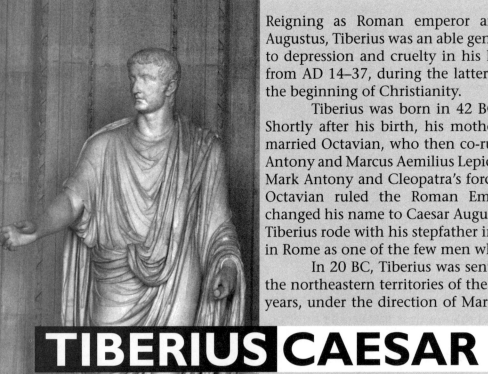

Photo: Jastrow.

TIBERIUS CAESAR

Reigning as Roman emperor after the death of Caesar Augustus, Tiberius was an able general in his prime but prone to depression and cruelty in his later years. He ruled Rome from AD 14–37, during the latter half of Jesus' lifetime and the beginning of Christianity.

Tiberius was born in 42 BC into an aristocratic line. Shortly after his birth, his mother divorced his father and married Octavian, who then co-ruled the empire with Mark Antony and Marcus Aemilius Lepidus. Following the defeat of Mark Antony and Cleopatra's forces at the Battle of Actium, Octavian ruled the Roman Empire unopposed, and he changed his name to Caesar Augustus. At the age of thirteen, Tiberius rode with his stepfather in the triumphal procession in Rome as one of the few men who could succeed him.

In 20 BC, Tiberius was sent on military campaigns to the northeastern territories of the empire. Over the next few years, under the direction of Marcus Agrippa (a close friend and advisor of Augustus), Tiberius became an able military commander and administrator, learning when to use force and when to use diplomacy. Tiberius married Agrippa's daughter Vipsania and continued to campaign, strengthening Rome's northern frontier. Tiberius's son Drusus was born in 13 BC, the same year Tiberius was honored for his success by being appointed consul of Rome, a high political position.

A year later, Marcus Agrippa died. At Caesar's request, Tiberius divorced his wife Vipsania, whom he loved, and

EXTRAORDINARY EVIDENCE AND SELF-CANCELING MIRACLES

The skeptics' last line of defense against miracles is to doubt that they can be proven at all. They do this by suggesting that extraordinary claims—like those for miracles—require extraordinary evidence. Although that sounds good on the surface, they run into problems when they try to define extraordinary.

If they define *extraordinary* as "evidence beyond the natural," then the skeptic is saying that a miracle, like the Resurrection, can only be confirmed by another miracle. This is an impossible standard of proof. They would then need another miracle to confirm that one, ad infinitum.

If they say *extraordinary* means "repeatable evidence," then no historical event could be verified today, because historical events have already happened and cannot be repeated. They don't require repeatable evidence for the Big Bang, spontaneous generation, or macroevolution, but they believe those things occurred.

If they define *extraordinary* to mean "more evidence than is usually required," then the New Testament fits the bill nicely. We have more eyewitness documentation, with more external historical confirmation than any other historical event. So even when skeptics set the

married Julia, Augustus's own daughter and Agrippa's widow. The two hated each other, and Julia took every opportunity to humiliate Tiberius. Tiberius slowly began to slide into depression, throwing himself into his military missions.

Six years later, Tiberius returned to Rome, where Augustus made him the second-most powerful man in Rome. However, Tiberius announced his intention of withdrawing from politics and military life altogether, content to let power pass to his stepsons, who were being groomed to rule. Yet by AD 4, both of his stepsons were dead, and Augustus called Tiberius back to Rome. He formally adopted Tiberius as his son, declared him his heir, and gave him unprecedented power. Tiberius set off again on a campaign into Germania that lasted two years.

Ten years later, Augustus died, and Tiberius became the reluctant emperor of Rome, though deferring most of the honors the Senate tried to bestow on him. Rather than embarking on costly campaigns of conquest, he chose to strengthen the existing empire by building additional bases of power, using diplomacy as well as military threats, and generally refraining from getting drawn into petty squabbles between competing frontier tyrants. The result was a stronger, more consolidated empire.

In AD 22, Tiberius shared his authority with his son Drusus and began withdrawing from politics. When Drusus died a year later under mysterious circumstances, Tiberius fell into depression and increasing paranoia. In AD 26, he retired from Rome altogether and went to live on the island of Capri, and leaving the government in the hands of Lucius Sejanus, prefect of the Praetorian Guard. In a series of purges, Sejanus began removing those capable of opposing his power. He then plotted to overthrow Tiberius, but his treachery was discovered and he was tried and executed.

Luke introduces the adult ministry of Jesus by saying that it was the "fifteenth year of the reign of Tiberius Caesar"(Luke 3:1) when Jesus was baptized. That was AD 29. Tiberius died eight years later in AD 37 while in self-imposed exile, leaving Rome to his grand-nephew Caligula. Though remembered as one of Rome's greatest generals, history has also painted Tiberius as one of its weakest emperors.

standard of proof at a nearly impossible level, the New Testament is able to pass. And, after all, most skeptics certainly aren't so strict about the evidence for any other event in history, especially something like spontaneous generation.

A second objection, introduced by David Hume, states that miracles cannot be used as evidence for any religion because they are based on poor testimony and are found in every religion. According to this line of thinking, miracle claims are self-canceling. Yet this objection relies on a faulty generalization—lumping all religions into the same category, regardless of the hard evidence we have separating Christianity from the rest. It also doesn't allow for the fact that we live in a theistic universe. (To be fair, the most compelling scientific evidence for this was found after Hume's death.) Finally, the miracles reported in the New Testament show clear evidence of God's power and moral character and were even predicted years or centuries beforehand, setting them apart from any other religion's miracle claims.

8. ***Why is God careful not to overwhelm humans with miraculous displays of His power? (See IDHEF, page 322.)***

9. ***How do the miracles claims of other religions compare to the miracles described in the New Testament? (See IDHEF, page 323.)***

LOOK

YOU DO THE DIGGING

Based on the evidence supporting the miraculous events reported in the New Testament, the most logical conclusion is that Jesus was the Son of God, who came to earth to pay the price for our sins in order to reconcile us to a holy God. Now it's time to for you to do some digging on your own. Pick at least one of the following assignments and complete it before moving on in the workbook.

Assignment 1: Read the article at www.GaryHabermas.com titled "Explaining Away Jesus' Resurrection: The Recent Revival of Hallucination Theories." In one to two pages, summarize Dr. Habermas's critique of the hallucination hypothesis and explain how you could use his information in a discussion with skeptical friends.

Assignment 2: Go to www.reasonablefaith.org and read the article titled "The Resurrection of Jesus" by Dr. William Lane Craig. Summarize the main points of the article in outline form.

Assignment 3: Go to the "Games" section at www.GaryHabermas.com and play the Resurrection game until you can make it through all eight levels, recording what you get wrong at each stage. If you need help with answers, read *The Case for the Resurrection of Jesus* by Gary Habermas and Michael Licona.

Assignment 4: Interview a non-Christian friend to find out his thoughts about the resurrection of Jesus. Ask him why he doesn't believe in the resurrection and diplomatically offer some evidence in return. Don't forget to use the three questions from chapter 6. Afterward, summarize your conversation in one to two pages, highlighting tactics that worked as well as points you need to study further.

TOOK

WHAT DO I DO NOW?

The central point of the Scriptures is the resurrection of Jesus. Without that event, Christianity and the entire New Testament are false and irrelevant. Many skeptics claim that the New Testament writers were deceived, that perhaps the apostles honestly thought that Jesus had risen from the dead but were mistaken. Unfortunately for the skeptics, this theory falls short in the believability department.

We have seen that the major alternative theories regarding the Resurrection all fail. The burden of proof must lie with the skeptics. Skeptics have not met that burden because they have provided no evidence, just possible theories. To believe their theories, we would have to believe in absurdities and improbabilities (like everyone sharing the same hallucination or the authorities never thinking to produce Jesus' dead body). Accepting such alternative theories would require more faith than simply believing in the Resurrection.

Moreover, we have seen that the context in which the Resurrection is said to have occurred supports it. We live in a theistic universe were miracles are possible; the Old Testament texts say that miracles are to be expected; and eyewitness testimony confirms that miracles actually did occur. Objections regarding extraordinary evidence and self-cancelling miracles are faulty and do not affect the conclusion that Jesus rose from the dead.

As you share what you have learned in this chapter, remember that you have more than a theory, an idea, or a hypothesis on your side. You have positive eyewitness testimony and corroborating circumstantial evidence that Jesus really did rise from the dead. It's up to you to take that message—which impacts everyone for all eternity—to those around you.

THINKING ABOUT WHAT YOU LEARNED

Answer the following questions to sum up what you have learned in this chapter.

A. Using I Corinthians 15:12–20, briefly explain why Jesus' resurrection is so central to Christianity.

B. Briefly explain why . . .

The New Testament story is not a legend (see IDHEF, page 300).

The New Testament story is not a lie.

The New Testament story is not an embellishment.

MAKE YOUR STAND ON THE RESURRECTION!

Dr. William Lane Craig states, "The significance of the resurrection of Jesus lies in the fact that it is not just any old Joe Blow who has been raised from the dead, but Jesus of Nazareth, whose crucifixion was instigated by the Jewish leadership because of his blasphemous claims to divine authority. If this man has been raised from the dead, then the God whom he allegedly blasphemed has clearly vindicated his claims. Thus, in an age of religious relativism and pluralism, the resurrection of Jesus constitutes a solid rock on which Christians can take their stand for God's decisive self-revelation in Jesus."

Will you take your stand on the resurrection of Jesus? The resurrection changes lives forever. You can be someone God uses to bring about that change in the lives of many. You just need to love people and look for opportunities to articulate the facts you've learned with gentleness and respect (1 Peter 3:15). Will you?

CHAPTER 13

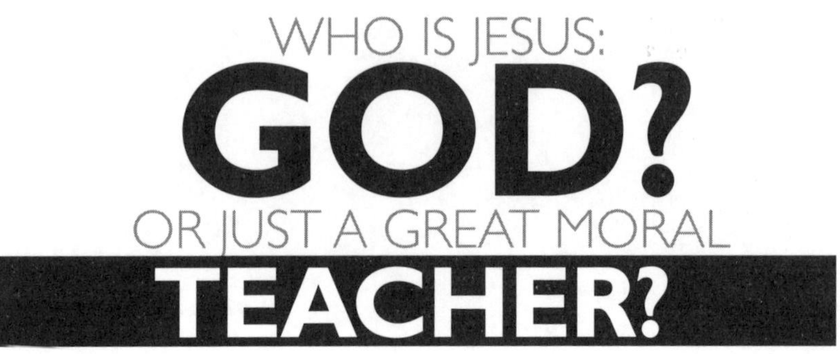

WHO IS JESUS:
GOD?
OR JUST A GREAT MORAL
TEACHER?

BEFORE STARTING THIS CHAPTER

- Read chapter 13 of *I Don't Have Enough Faith to Be an Atheist* (IDHEF), pages 327–354.

ROAD MAP OF THE "TWELVE POINTS THAT PROVE CHRISTIANITY IS TRUE"

This chapter covers points 7–12:

7 8 9 10 11 12 The New Testament says Jesus claimed to be God, which was miraculously confirmed by fulfilled prophecies, miraculous deeds, and His resurrection. *Therefore, Jesus is God,* and whatever He teaches is true. Since Jesus taught that the Bible is the Word of God, it must be true and anything opposed to the Bible is false.

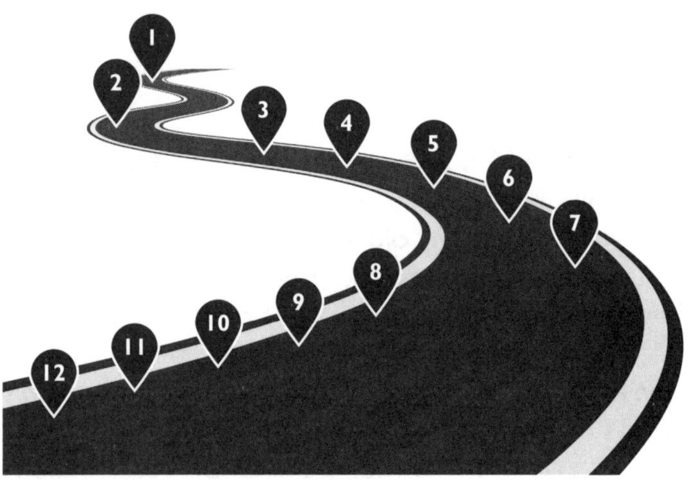

KEY TOPICS

After completing this chapter, you should be able to:

- Describe the importance of the Great Isaiah Scroll and Isaiah 52:13–53:12.
- List three reasons why the Suffering Servant in Isaiah 52–53 is not Israel.
- Explain what is meant by "the box top" to prophecy.
- Discuss two New Testament verses in which Jesus directly claimed to be God.
- Discuss three New Testament verses in which Jesus indirectly claimed to be God.
- Discuss two New Testament verses that affirm Jesus' deity through His actions.
- Name three proofs that Jesus is God.
- Describe and refute objections to the deity of Jesus.

KEY TERMS

Write the definitions for these words and phrases found in your reading:

Essenes

Septuagint

Trinity

QUESTIONS THAT GRAB YOUR MIND

Who are the people you admire and want to imitate? Athletes? Actors? Musicians? Businessmen? Scientists? War heroes? Generally people we admire have done something that sets them apart from others. But as we have seen, no one in history stands apart more than Jesus.

Just who was Jesus Christ? Did He claim to be God? Was He God? If He was God, then why didn't He know things such as when He is coming back? And how could God die? Was Jesus just a good teacher—if He lived at all?

In this chapter, we will look at who Jesus claimed to be. We'll examine His identity and address questions about His deity. Was He God or just a good person? If He wasn't God, then that presents some real problems for Christians. But if He is God, then the problem lies with those who do not have a personal relationship with Jesus.

A careful look at the evidence will show not only that Jesus was God, but also that He was the predicted Messiah and the resurrected Lord whose perfect life and sacrifice enables sinners to be reconciled to God. This is a very important chapter. Study it well.

*1. **Why does it matter whether or not Jesus really was God?***

SO WHAT?

Many people today claim that all paths lead to God. But what do they mean by "God"? Are they talking about Jesus, Allah, Krishna, a cult leader, or someone else? Which one is really God? The stakes couldn't be higher. If Jesus is God, then whatever He taught is true. If Jesus is not God, then He wasn't even a good man—he was a liar or a lunatic.

BOOK

FACTS IN THIS CHAPTER

In the last few chapters, we have established that the writings of the New Testament are accurate. An easy way to remember much of the evidence for the New Testament is to use alliteration. Consider seven lines of evidence that begin with the letter "E."

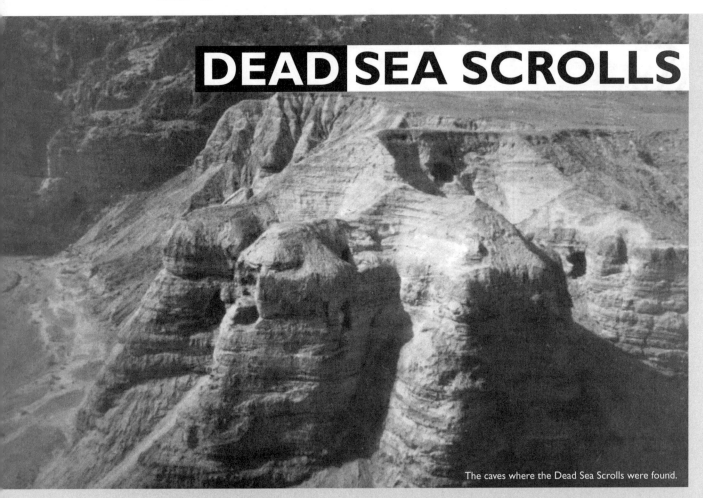

DEAD SEA SCROLLS

The caves where the Dead Sea Scrolls were found.

One of the greatest archeological finds in history was discovered by a young Bedouin shepherd in 1947. While searching for a lost animal in the hills along the northwest shore of the Dead Sea in Israel, Muhammed edh-Dhib and his cousin stumbled on a cave containing a number of ancient scrolls. Muhammed took several home with him. He kept the scrolls hanging on a tent pole while he figured out what to do with them, periodically taking them out to show people. Eventually, the Bedouin took the scrolls to Bethlehem to find a buyer.

We've seen that the New Testament writers have given us testimony that is:

- Early
- Eyewitness
- Embarrassing
- Excruciating (meaning they suffered and died for it)

We also have testimony from secular historians and archaeology that we will call:

- Extrabiblical
- Enemy

As news of the discovery spread, historians and antiquities dealers began to take notice. Four of the scrolls found their way to Mar Samuel of the Syrian Orthodox Church. Hearing of the discovery, archeologist Dr. John Trever met with Samuel and photographed the scrolls. These photos proved invaluable to later scholars, as the ink on the scrolls quickly deteriorated after they were removed from their linen wrappings. The scrolls were eventually moved to the Shrine of the Book at the Israel Museum in Jerusalem where they remain today, carefully preserved.

The discovery of the scrolls prompted archeologists to examine the site around the original cave, thereafter known as Cave 1. Located near the ruins of an old Jewish settlement called Khirbet Qumran, Cave 1 yielded seven scrolls altogether, including the famous Great Isaiah Scroll (nearly twenty-four feet long). Over the next few years, archeologists found eleven caves in total and collected nearly a thousand scrolls or fragments.

The scrolls included portions of every book of the Old Testament except Esther, along with manuscripts of apocryphal books (religious writings not included in the canon) and manuals detailing the rules and practices of the Jewish sect that lived at Khirbet Qumran. In all, thirty-nine copies of the book of Psalms were discovered, along with multiple copies of the books of the Torah (Genesis through Deuteronomy). Other finds included the Copper Scroll, which contained a list of locations where treasure had been buried, and the Temple Scroll, which was the longest scroll found—nearly twenty-seven feet long.

Traditionally, Khirbet Qumran was thought to be the home of a group of Essenes, a Jewish sect that believed in holding all property communally and maintaining a pure lifestyle (similar to medieval monks). Archeologists believe it is likely that the Essenes at Qumran copied and hid the scrolls before being attacked by the Romans during the First Jewish-Roman War (A.D. 66–73).

The discovery of the Dead Sea Scrolls—some of them dating back to 100 BC—proved how accurately the Bible documents had been transcribed over time. The scrolls are the oldest known surviving copies of the biblical documents yet still contain essentially the same message as the books we have in our Bibles today.

In 2011, high-resolution digital scans of the most famous of the Dead Sea Scrolls, including the Great Isaiah Scroll and the Temple Scroll, were released online through the Israel Museum at Jerusalem. Check out their website www.english.imjnet.org.il and click the "Digital Dead Sea Scrolls" link to get your own glimpse of biblical history!

Now we will look at testimony from the Old Testament that we'll call:

- Expected testimony (because the arrival of the Messiah was predicted in the Old Testament, we should expect testimony of His arrival)

Old Testament prophecy will help us answer the question of Jesus' identity and deity and back up the already strong evidence for the truth of the New Testament. We'll also investigate Jesus' own direct and indirect claims to be God and answer common objections to His deity. We'll also learn about the Trinity and how a proper understanding of the Trinity helps us answer difficult theological questions.

So prepare to dig in and learn not just the facts, but also the eternal impact of knowing beyond any reasonable doubt that Jesus Christ is the Messiah, the Savior of the world.

THE GREAT ISAIAH SCROLL

The Great Isaiah Scroll found near the Dead Sea is the oldest complete biblical manuscript discovered so far, dating to around 100 BC It also contains the clearest and most complete prophecy about the coming Messiah, the Suffering Servant. Understanding this powerful prophecy will help us see that Jesus was expected long before He arrived.

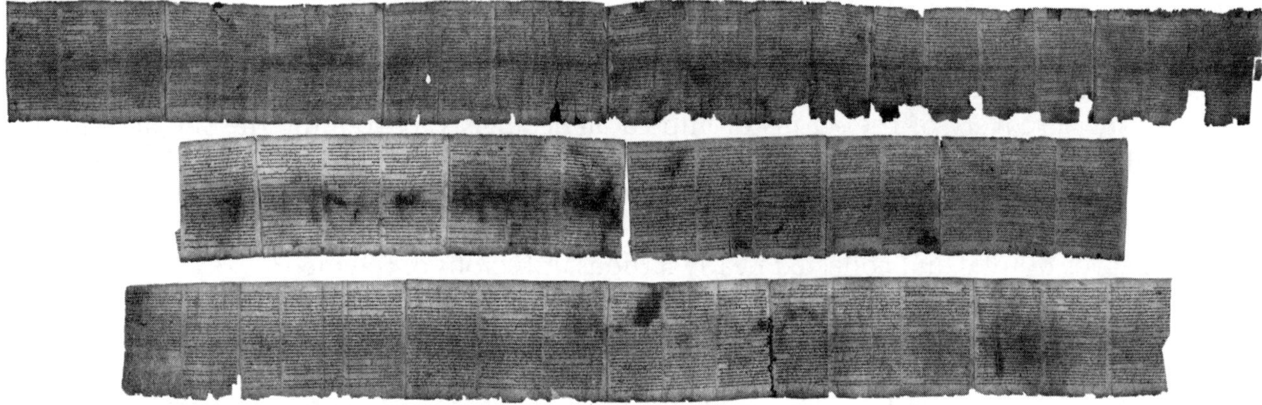

The Great Isaiah Scroll.

2. ***Read Isaiah 52:13–53:12 and list at least ten characteristics of the Suffering Servant.***

3. ***Why is the Great Isaiah Scroll so important to the whole of Scripture and to people who put their trust in Jesus?***

WHY CAN'T THE SUFFERING SERVANT BE ISRAEL?

Traditionally, the most prominent Jewish interpretation of Isaiah 53 was that it predicted the coming Messiah. It was only about a thousand years ago, after contact with Christians claiming that Jesus fulfilled these prophecies about the Messiah, that the interpretation was applied to the nation of Israel. But in order to make this interpretation work, the meaning of the passage needs to be stretched and changed.

4. ***List three reasons why the Suffering Servant in Isaiah 52–53 cannot be Israel (see IDHEF, pages 333–334).***

Not only are there problems with interpreting the Suffering Servant in Isaiah 53 as the nation of Israel instead of Jesus, but there are also other Old Testament Messianic passages that have been fulfilled by Him as well. As far back as Genesis, a Savior is predicted that will return mankind to the kind of harmonious relationship with God that Adam and Eve enjoyed during the initial days in the Garden of Eden.

The textbook refers to these as bull's-eye passages, since each narrows the field of candidates to a single man—Jesus Christ.

5. ***Summarize the nine prophecies listed on pages 334–336. How could you use these in a discussion with a non-Christian friend?***

THE BOX TOP TO PROPHECY

Hindsight, people say, is 20/20. Some skeptics believe that because we know what happened to Jesus historically, Christians read back that knowledge of Jesus into some Old Testament prophecies that may or may not have anything to do with Him. They point to Psalm 22 as an example.

Some Christian scholars recognize that this psalm, written by King David, predicts the way in which Jesus would be crucified. Although other interpretations have been offered for this passage, the details clearly parallel what happened to Jesus at the crucifixion. The simplest explanation, then, is that this psalm predicted Jesus' death.

Although it may be true that the meaning of certain messianic prophecies became clear only after Jesus' life, death, and resurrection, that doesn't make those prophecies any less true, less applicable to Jesus, or less amazing. Jesus' life serves as the box top for many pieces of the prophetic puzzle found throughout the Old Testament.

6. ***Why do the authors believe that Psalm 22 is referring to Jesus' crucifixion? List several of their reasons (see IDHEF, page 339).***

DIRECT CLAIMS OF JESUS THAT PROVE HE IS GOD

We have seen from our study that Jesus is the only person who met the predicted qualifications of the Messiah. Because the Messiah had to be God, there must be evidence to show that Jesus was God. Did He claim to be God, either directly or indirectly? Did He prove He was God by the things He did? The answer to both questions is yes!

Let's look at the direct claims Jesus made regarding His deity—the very words out of Jesus' mouth with which He proclaimed Himself to be God. Consider Jesus' response to Caiaphas, found in Mark 14:61–64, as well as His response to the Pharisees reported in John 8:56–59. If Jesus was not claiming equality with God, then why did the Jewish leaders have Him killed?

7. ***Why is Jesus' reference to Himself as the Son of Man important?***

8. ***What is the significance of Jesus calling Himself "I Am"?***

INDIRECT CLAIMS OF JESUS THAT PROVE HE IS GOD

Jesus not only directly claimed to be God, but made several other statements that clearly implied He was God. In addition, Jesus declared His deity within parables.

When Jehovah's Witnesses come to your door, they will tell you that Jesus never claimed to be God. When they do, ask them this question: If Jesus never claimed to be God, then why did they kill Him? For telling people to love their neighbors? The truth is that Jesus was killed *precisely* because He claimed to be God. Such a claim was considered blasphemy to the Jews and sedition to the Romans (to whom Caesar was a god). Review pages 342–344 of the book to look at the claims Jesus made regarding His deity and how they refer back to the Old Testament.

9. Summarize four instances in which Jesus linked Himself to God that stand out the most to you. How would you use these in a discussion with a secular friend?

ACTIONS OF JESUS THAT PROVE HE IS GOD

Jesus not only claimed to be God, but He also acted like God by forgiving sins, claiming authority in heaven and earth, giving His followers a new commandment, requesting that they pray in His name, and accepting worship. Jesus' actions could only be accomplished and proclaimed acceptable if He were truly God. Otherwise, He was guilty of blasphemy and deceit and cannot be considered a good moral teacher.

10. How did the following New Testament writers and figures state or imply that Jesus was God?

John

Paul

Peter

Matthew

The writer of Hebrews

Demons

11. There are four possibilities regarding the identity of Jesus: legend, liar, lunatic, or Lord (see IDHEF, pages 346–347). Why are the first three implausible?

Resurrection by Czechowicz.

THREE PROOFS THAT JESUS IS GOD

Jesus not only claimed to be God, but He also acted like God and proved it in ways no other man could have. First, He fulfilled many messianic prophecies written by ancient prophets hundreds of years before His birth. The odds of an ordinary man fulfilling even a handful of these prophecies are highly improbable. Yet Jesus fulfilled seventy-one Old Testament prophecies to the letter. Second, He lived a sinless life and performed miraculous deeds as proof that what He claimed about Himself and taught about the New Covenant was true. Those closest to Him agreed that He was sinless—can you say that about the people you are closest to? Even His enemies agreed that there was no fault to be found in Him (Luke 23:14). Third, Jesus predicted not only the time and circumstances of His own death, but also that He would rise again—and He accomplished it. Talk about putting your money where your mouth is! There is no one else in history like Jesus, God in human flesh.

OBJECTIONS TO JESUS' DEITY

As usual, skeptics put forth creative objections in order to try to disprove the deity of Jesus. You need to be aware that if skeptics can disprove the deity of Jesus, then the rest of the beliefs of Christians are basically without foundation. If Jesus is not God, then He is just another man, and a Christian's faith is no longer in the God of the universe.

The objections discussed here are fairly common, so it is a good idea to study up on the answers.

First, some skeptics claim that if Jesus had been God, He would have been more open about His deity, communicating it clearly instead of veiling it in parables and cryptic Old Testament references. Yet Jesus came to earth as a humble servant, not a lofty king. In fact, He narrowly avoided trouble with crowds of people who wanted to proclaim Him their political ruler and lead them into war with Rome. His mission was to help people understand the New Covenant that He was instituting, a process that would take time and subtlety, one that would have been hindered by too overt a proclamation of His deity.

Second, some skeptics claim there were times when Jesus indirectly denied His deity when questioned. They reason that if He truly were God, He wouldn't have backed away from proclaiming His deity when someone else brought up the subject. Take the story of the rich young ruler, for example (Mark 10:17–27). Skeptics claim that Jesus' response to being called good—that "no one is good but God"—deflected the implication of deity away from Himself. Yet looked at in the greater context of the passage, it is clear that Jesus was asking the rich young ruler to think about his own intellectual position—if he really meant to say that Jesus was God. Instead of turning down the honor of being linked with God, Jesus indirectly affirmed His deity.

Third, some skeptics claim that because the concept of the Trinity—three Persons in one divine nature—puts Jesus as subordinate to God the Father, Jesus cannot truly be God. But this confuses the functions that the three Persons of the Trinity fulfill with their essence. In essence, Jesus is fully God, yet He has unique responsibilities that the other members of the Trinity do not share. While on earth, Jesus also had two natures: a divine one, perfect and all-knowing, and a human one that got tired and hungry and had limited knowledge. Although the concept of the Trinity may be difficult to wrap your mind around, that doesn't mean it is illogical or unreasonable.

12. ***The Trinity is three Persons in one divine nature. Jesus is one Person who has two natures—human and divine. Geisler and Turek use a triangle and circle to illustrate this. They say whenever you ask a question about Jesus, you really have to ask two questions. What are the two questions?***

An early copy of Rashi's commentary on the Talmud.

RASHI

Rashi was a medieval French Jewish scholar known today throughout Judaism as the author of the definitive commentaries on the Tanach (the Hebrew Bible) and the Talmud (rabbinical writings on Jewish law, customs, and history). In fact, his commentary on the Talmud has been included in every printed edition of the Talmud since the 1500s. His full name was Rabbi Shlomo Itzhaki, from which the acronym Rashi was created.

Rashi was born an only child in Troyes, France, in 1040. His father, a rabbi, began Rashi's religious studies at the age of five. At the age of seventeen, Rashi left Troyes to study the Talmud under a prominent rabbi in Worms in what is now Germany, then moved to nearby Mainz after the rabbi's death to continue his studies. By all accounts, Rashi was a serious student who took copious notes on interpretations of the religious scriptures, trying to distill their meaning into the clearest presentation.

At the age of twenty-five, fully versed in the teachings of both the Tanach and the Talmud, Rashi returned to Troyes to join the rabbinic leadership there. He was responsible for answering questions about Jewish law, or halakha. Because he thought the Jewish scriptures were difficult to understand, especially for young children, he also began compiling and editing his notes in order to create an easy-to-understand commentary on the scriptures. Five years later, Rashi opened his own yeshiva, or school, to teach the truths about the Tanach and Talmud that he had learned. For the remainder of his life, Rashi taught and wrote, supporting himself as his father had—by making wine.

Though Rashi had no sons, he did have three daughters who worked with him as he compiled his commentaries and responded to questions about Jewish law and theology. They all married yeshiva scholars, who carried on Rashi's legacy of scholarship. Rashi also worked to determine the correct text of the Talmud, which had been copied and recopied by hand many times, slowly allowing errors to creep in. With access to many different copies of the Talmud in the busy trade city of Troyes, Rashi was able to compare manuscripts to better determine what the original texts had said.

Near the end of his life, Rashi devoted all his time to finishing his commentaries, relying on the help of his daughters and sons-in-law. He died in 1105 and was buried in the city of Troyes under what is now a large square, where a monument stands commemorating Rashi and his contribution to Jewish scholarship. Even today, his commentaries are eagerly studied by young yeshiva students and experienced rabbis alike, and remain popular for their clarity and simplicity.

13. How could Jesus be God if He didn't know when He was coming back?

14. Why wasn't Jesus more overt in His claims to be God?

15. The New Testament writers claim to be eyewitnesses several times. Paul even does so before King Agrippa, claiming that "the King is familiar with these things, and I can speak freely to him. I am convinced that none of this has escaped his notice, because it was not done in a corner." If this exchange is historically accurate as recorded in Acts 26, why is this strong evidence that the Resurrection actually happened?

16. How would you respond if someone said to you, "The Bible is just a religious book—you can't trust its view of historical events"? (Don't forget to start with the three questions!)

LOOK

YOU DO THE DIGGING

It is not uncommon to hear someone say that Jesus was a good man or a great moral teacher. But if Jesus is not God, as He claimed, then how can we trust anything else He said? Did He really fulfill all the Old Testament prophecies concerning the Messiah? If He isn't the Messiah, then by what authority should we accept His teachings? And why should we base our lives and future on the Bible at all?

We've seen that Jesus directly and indirectly claimed to be God and proved it by His actions, something the writers of the New Testament epistles confirmed. His actions were those of God, because no mere moral teacher could perform miracles like Jesus did. He also fulfilled numerous prophesies, including predicting and accomplishing His own resurrection. And by the admission of even His enemies, He lived a sinless life.

Now it's time to for you to do some digging on your own. Pick at least one of the following assignments and complete it before moving on in the study.

Assignment 1: Dr. Michael Brown is perhaps the leading Messianic Jewish apologist. He's written several volumes answering Jewish objections to Jesus being the Messiah. Visit realmessiah.com and read Dr. Brown's defense of Jesus as the Messiah, particularly his defense of Jesus as the Suffering Servant from Isaiah 52–53. Summarize the Jewish objections to Isaiah 53 and Dr. Brown's responses in a one- to two-page paper.

Assignment 2: Interview a Jewish friend. Ask why she does not believe Jesus is the Messiah. Find out how she came to that conclusion and offer some responses to her objections. Summarize your conversation and what you learned in one page.

Assignment 3: Go to YouTube and watch the five-minute video "Did Jesus Claim to Be God?" by Lee Strobel. Then go to CrossExamined.org and click on the "Resources and Links" tab. Read the article "Did Jesus Claim to Be God?" and summarize the points from the video and article in outline form.

Assignment 4: Pages 350–352 of the book include a discussion of the Trinity and Jesus' deity. One of the points discussed is that Jesus had two distinct natures—human and divine. Write a two-page paper explaining what these two natures are and how they were demonstrated in Jesus' life and events in the Old Testament. Include supporting scriptures. For help, watch the eight-minute video "A Jewish Christian Explains the Holy Trinity" by Dr. Michael Brown on YouTube or check out the resources at www.CrossExamined.org to find more information on the Trinity.

TOOK

WHAT DO I DO NOW?

This chapter has provided evidence that Jesus is God. Many people around you are searching desperately for the answer you have found. Some are so hungry for that truth that they have made up their own gods, combining philosophy, religion, opinion, and personal preference and experience to come up with a god that suits their needs. Unfortunately, these made-up gods have no power to forgive sins, answer prayer, or offer eternal life. You now have the ability to make an articulate case that Christianity is true. Now is your opportunity to tactfully present that case to others. There is one God whose coming was predicted, who worked miracles, and who was sinless. And He is the one they should get to know personally.

THINKING ABOUT WHAT YOU LEARNED

Answer the following questions to sum up what you have learned in this chapter.

A. Briefly explain three ways Jesus proved He was God and give a Scripture reference to support each (see IDHEF, page 348).

B. Summarize how you would explain the Trinity to a friend, especially Jesus' fully divine and fully human natures (see IDHEF, pages 350–352).

C. Briefly explain three of the theological problems the concept of the Trinity solves (see IDHEF, page 353).

DON'T WIN ARGUMENTS AND LOSE SOULS!

In today's politically correct culture, the name of Jesus is the only religious name that anyone dares to mock or take in vain. Jesus is a touchy subject for many people, so you may encounter serious resistance or even ridicule if you begin sharing your renewed understanding about Jesus' being God. This propensity may increase as you come into contact with people from other nations and religions, each of which comes with its own particular view of who God is. You will need to be sensitive to understand *what* others believe about God, *why* they chose to believe that, and *how* they came to believe in their god. Learn to ask questions and listen carefully before offering evidence. Jesus doesn't want you to win arguments and lose people. Provide evidence for Christianity, but do so with gentleness and respect.

CHAPTER 14

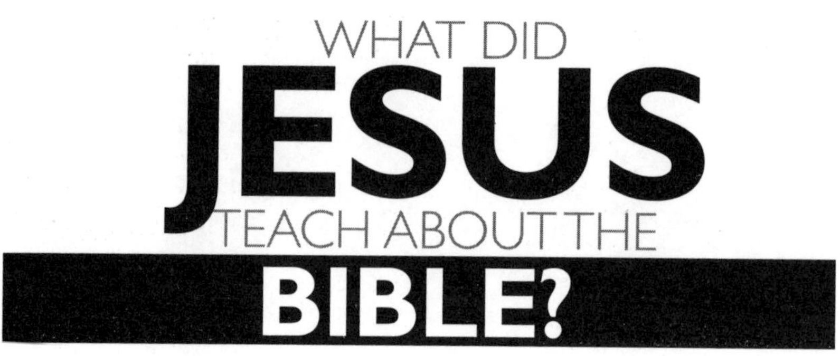

BEFORE STARTING THIS CHAPTER

- Read chapter 14 of *I Don't Have Enough Faith to Be an Atheist* (IDHEF), pages 355–376.
- Read appendix 2 and appendix 3, pages 402–411.

ROAD MAP OF THE "TWELVE POINTS THAT PROVE CHRISTIANITY IS TRUE"

This chapter covers points 7–12:

7 8 9 10 11 12 The New Testament says Jesus claimed to be God, which was miraculously confirmed by fulfilled prophecies, miraculous deeds, and His resurrection. Therefore, Jesus is God, and whatever He teaches is true. Since Jesus taught that *the Bible is the Word of God*, it must be true and anything opposed to the Bible is false.

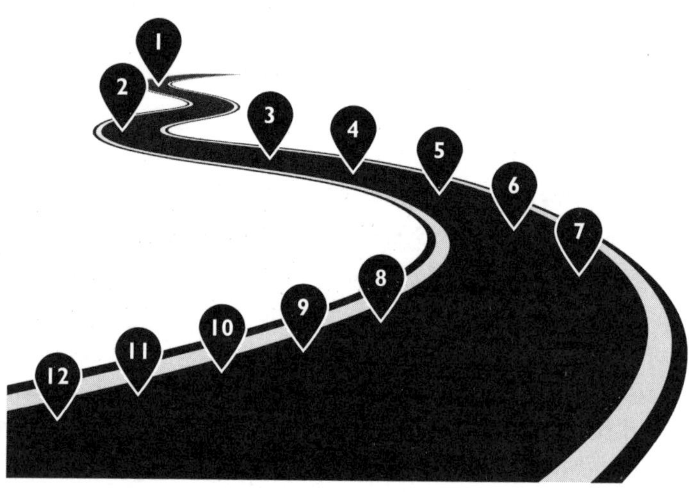

KEY TOPICS

After completing this chapter, you should be able to:

- List and explain the seven ways Jesus taught that the Old Testament was the Word of God.
- Refute the Accommodation Theory and the Human Limitations Argument.
- Describe how 1 John 4:6; 1 Corinthians 2:10, 13; Galatians 1:11–12; and 1 Thessalonians 2:13 support the inspiration of the New Testament.
- Explain how miracles support that the New Testament was inspired.
- Explain the significance of Luke 4:14–21 regarding who Jesus was.
- Discuss what the canon is and how we know who wrote the gospels.
- Defend the inerrancy of the Bible.

KEY TERMS

Write the definitions for these words and phrases found in your reading:

Infallible

Inerrant

Canon

Council of Hippo

HOOK

QUESTIONS THAT GRAB YOUR MIND

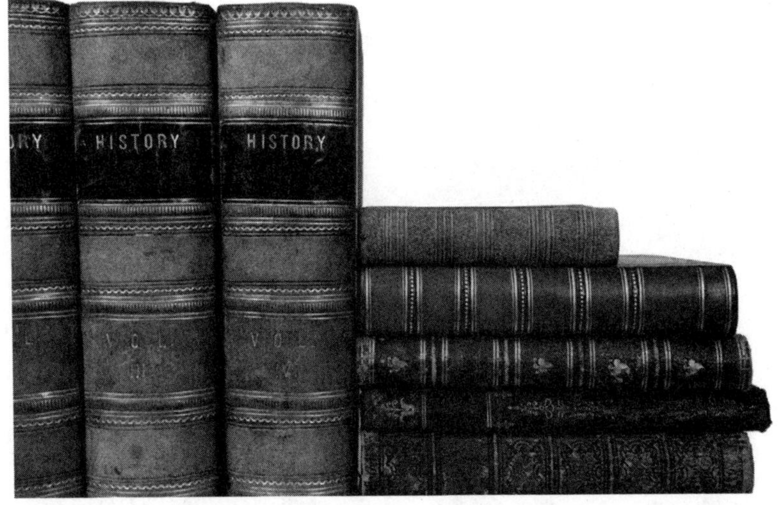

How do you know if the history books you study in school are accurate? Are you sure they don't contain errors? What proof do you have that the authors are credible and knowledgeable enough to write on the subject of history?

None of us have observed events that happened 1,000 years ago or even 100 years ago. Yet we believe they happened. Most of what we know we take on authority. But as we have seen throughout the study, we don't take the New Testament on blind faith—there is good evidence that the New Testament is trustworthy. We have already seen that we have historically reliable accounts of the life, death, and resurrection of Jesus. If Jesus really is God, then whatever He teaches must be true. If He teaches that certain writings are the Word of God, then we can believe Him.

1. Many people claim that their book(s) of religious teachings speaks the truth. How is knowing and believing Jesus taught that the Bible is the Word of God different from what other religions believe about their holy books?

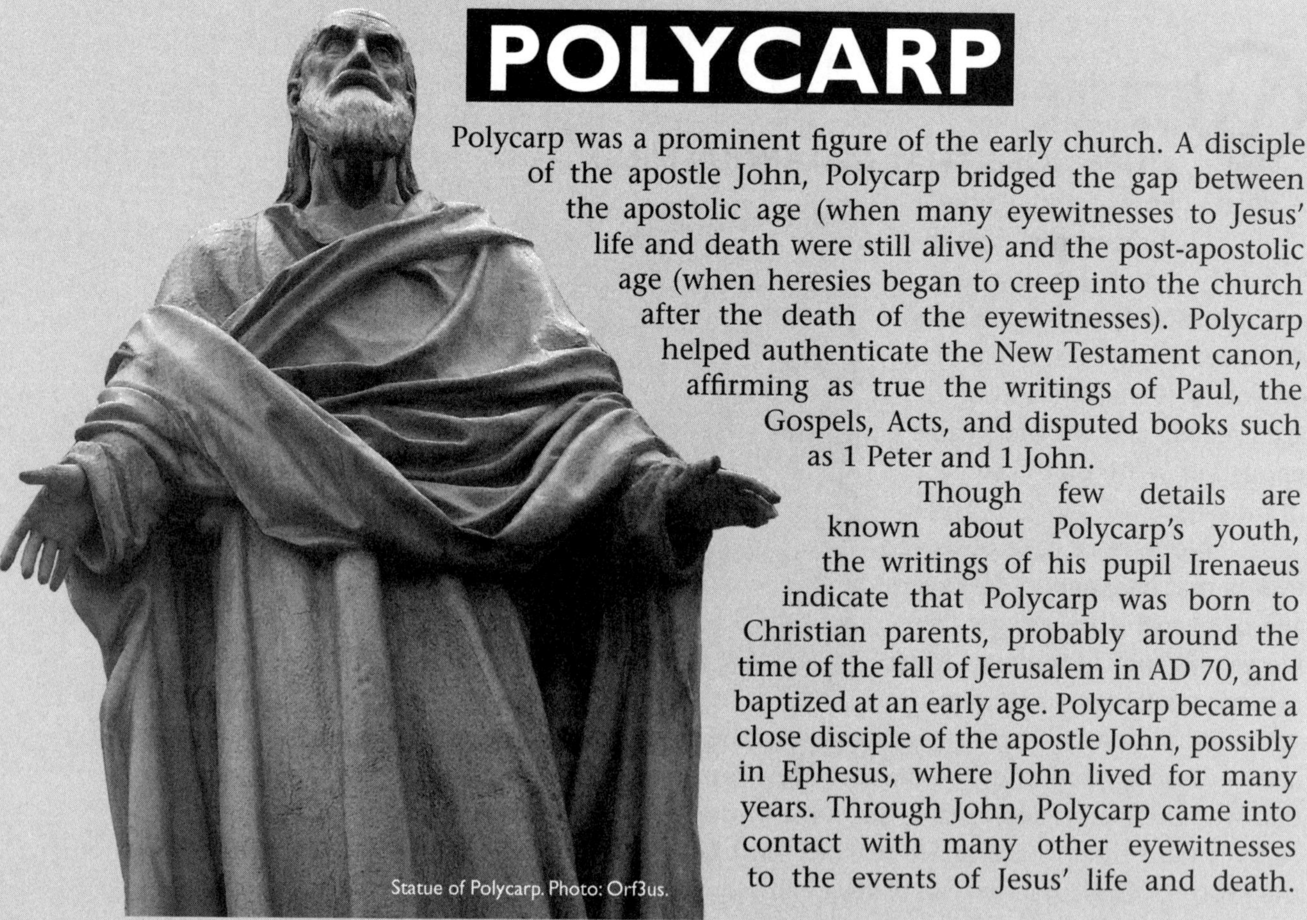

Statue of Polycarp. Photo: Orf3us.

POLYCARP

Polycarp was a prominent figure of the early church. A disciple of the apostle John, Polycarp bridged the gap between the apostolic age (when many eyewitnesses to Jesus' life and death were still alive) and the post-apostolic age (when heresies began to creep into the church after the death of the eyewitnesses). Polycarp helped authenticate the New Testament canon, affirming as true the writings of Paul, the Gospels, Acts, and disputed books such as 1 Peter and 1 John.

Though few details are known about Polycarp's youth, the writings of his pupil Irenaeus indicate that Polycarp was born to Christian parents, probably around the time of the fall of Jerusalem in AD 70, and baptized at an early age. Polycarp became a close disciple of the apostle John, possibly in Ephesus, where John lived for many years. Through John, Polycarp came into contact with many other eyewitnesses to the events of Jesus' life and death.

SO WHAT?

Everyone has some kind of religious perspective or commitment (even atheists), and every religion has a core set of teachings or doctrines its adherents follow. But is there verifiable evidence that those doctrines are true?

We have evidence that the doctrines expressed in the Bible are true. Jesus not only believed that the Bible was the Word of God, He authenticated it. By the historically reliable New Testament documents and corroborating data from non-Christian sources, we see that Jesus really is God. Therefore, because whatever God teaches must be true, we can believe Jesus when He taught that the Bible is God's Word. This makes the Bible much more than just a good book or collection of religious stories. It is the only book that is confirmed by God Himself as containing the truth. Since Jesus is God and He taught that the Bible is the Word of God, then all other gods and religious teachings of man are false if they do not line up with the Bible!

Irenaeus also states that John appointed the young Polycarp as bishop to the church at Smyrna, a position Polycarp held until his death.

His long life—stretching nearly ninety years—enabled him to verify which teachings of the second century church were correct and which had strayed into error. The only major writing of his that has survived is the Letter to the Philippians, in which he cites or alludes to a full two-thirds of the books of the New Testament. Polycarp also took a strong stand against heresies such as Gnosticism (which claimed that Jesus was not God but attained divinity through special knowledge, which he taught to the disciples) and Marcionism (which taught that the merciful God taught by Jesus was not the same as the wrathful God of the Old Testament).

Toward the end of his life, Polycarp traveled to Rome to visit with Anicetus, the leader of the Christian church there and a predecessor of Clement of Rome. A dispute had arisen between the Asiatic and Roman churches over the proper celebration of Easter. Although the two leaders weren't able to agree on exact details or dates, they parted on good terms, satisfied that neither side was falling into heresy. Shortly after his return, however, Polycarp and the church at Smyrna were subjected to a time of severe persecution. Several members of the church were arrested and killed, while others went into hiding. Eventually, Polycarp—then an old man—was arrested and brought before the governor. He was told that he must renounce Jesus and worship the Roman emperor or he would be killed. Polycarp answered calmly, "Eighty and six years have I served him, and in nothing hath he wronged me; and how, then, can I blaspheme my King, who saved me?"

Polycarp was burned at the stake, a martyr for the sake of Christianity. According to the *Martyrdom of Polycarp*, an early Christian writing, Polycarp was stabbed to death when the flames failed to touch him. But it's his witness in the face of death that has inspired Christians throughout history.

BOOK

FACTS IN THIS CHAPTER

This chapter brings the case we've been seen building from the first chapter to a conclusion—showing that the Bible is the Word of God. So let's investigate how we know what should be included in the Bible and investigate the question of possible errors.

JESUS AFFIRMS THE OLD TESTAMENT AS THE WORD OF GOD

There are seven ways Jesus taught that the Old Testament was the Word of God. (His confirmation doesn't apply to any other writings in the world.) But Jesus didn't just say the Old Testament was the Word of God—He lived accordingly, fulfilling the law for us and sacrificing His life in place of ours.

First, the fact that Jesus frequently quoted from the Old Testament as an absolutely trustworthy source shows that it is divinely authoritative. Second, Jesus claimed that not even the smallest pen stroke in the Old Testament would be lost, demonstrating the imperishability of the Scriptures. Third, Jesus stated outright in several instances that the Old Testament was infallible, or never wrong. Fourth, Jesus affirmed that although people err, the Bible remains inerrant. Fifth, Jesus upheld the historical reliability of the Old Testament, specifically citing as true some of the stories that modern historians have the hardest time with (such as those of Noah and Jonah). Sixth, Jesus upheld the scientific accuracy of the Old Testament, saying that if the Bible wasn't correct about the physical world we can see, how could it be correct about the spiritual world we cannot see? Seventh, Jesus taught that the Old Testament had ultimate supremacy over other religious writings, especially the traditions of the Jews.

2. ***For each point above, supply a corroborating verse and explain how it supports the point (see IDHEF, pages 357–359).***

Point 1:

Point 2:

Point 3:

Point 4:

Point 5:

Point 6:

Point 7:

OBJECTION 1: JESUS WAS MERELY ACCOMMODATING JEWISH BELIEFS

Unable to argue with Jesus' support of the Old Testament as the trustworthy Word of God, skeptics try to discredit Jesus by saying that He was wrong or didn't really mean what He said. The first objection is that, in saying the Old Testament was true, Jesus was just accommodating the preexisting beliefs of the Jews—in other words, playing to the crowd so that they would understand and follow Him.

But this is clearly not true. Jesus was careful to maintain the highest standards of truth, and many times that character trait put Him at odds with the Jewish leadership. After all, if He was confirming everything they believed in and agreed with, why would the Jewish leaders have Him killed?

OBJECTION 2: JESUS WAS LIMITED BY HIS HUMAN NATURE

A second argument skeptics like to put forth is that Jesus had a human nature and therefore was limited by human frailties. They reason that since He was human, there were things He didn't know and could therefore have made mistakes in His teaching, no matter how sincere

He may have been at the time. But that confuses not knowing with misunderstanding. In His human nature, Jesus may not have known all things, but what He did know He knew correctly. Moreover, Jesus stated that He only taught the things that God the Father gave Him to teach, so the standard for everything Jesus said while in human form was God's own standard of perfection. To accuse Jesus of succumbing to human limitations and propagating error is to accuse God of allowing it.

3. ***How you would answer someone who said, "Jesus was all about love. He wasn't all that concerned about theology"?***

4. ***How would you answer someone who said, "Jesus was just a man, so He could have made mistakes"?***

SUPPORT FOR THE INSPIRATION OF THE NEW TESTAMENT

Jesus not only taught that the Old Testament was the Word of God, but also that the New Testament would come through His apostles. He said that the Holy Spirit (which He would send to Earth after He left) would remind them of His words and teachings so that they could record the truth for future generations. Listen to what Jesus said to the apostles in John 14:25–26:

> "All this I have spoken while still with you. But the Counselor, the Holy Spirit, whom the Father will send in my name, will teach you all things and will remind you of everything I have said to you."

The apostles subsequently claimed that they wrote the New Testament documents under the inspiration of the Holy Spirit (yet without losing their own unique perspective and style).

5. Look up the following verses and summarize what each says about the inspiration of the New Testament.

1 John 4:6

1 Corinthians 2:10, 13

Galatians 1:11–12

1 Thessalonians 2:13

MIRACLES SUPPORT THAT THE NEW TESTAMENT WAS INSPIRED

Although the apostles and other eyewitnesses of their day affirmed that the New Testament documents were divinely inspired, adding weight and significance to their writing, it is easy for anyone to claim that they have received a message from God. In fact, you can turn on the television today and find people who claim to have received special revelation from God that affects your life. So how can we know for certain when God has actually spoken?

St Paul Healing the Cripple at Lystra by Dujardin.

The apostles not only claimed to have received their message from God, but they proved it by performing verifiable miraculous signs—a supernatural seal of approval from God on their words and teachings. In several places in the New Testament, the writers backed up their claims of divine inspiration by referring to the signs and wonders they and other apostles had done. Hebrews 2:3–4 says, "God also testified to it [the truth of the message] by signs, wonders, and various miracles, and gifts of the Holy Spirit distributed according to his will." Paul claimed to have done miracles in the presence of the local church (2 Corinthians 12:12), and he wrote that the risen Jesus appeared to more than 500 people (1 Corinthians 15:3–8). Because it would have been simple for the people in Corinth and elsewhere to verify whether such miracles had indeed occurred, it would have been foolish for the apostles to point to signs unless they had happened.

6. ***How would you respond to a friend who said that by using miracles described in the Bible to verify the Bible's message, you're using circular reasoning?***

7. ***When did the apostles' ability to do miracles end? How is this evidence that the ability to work miracles belonged to God and not the apostles? (See IDHEF, page 366.)***

8. ***Explain the significance of Jesus' actions in Luke 4:14–21.***

THE CANON OF SCRIPTURE

It's clear that Jesus promised to leave His apostles with a message, inspired by the Holy Spirit whom He would send. It's also clear that the apostles claimed to have received the message, which they verified by performing miracles. But how do we know that the inspired message from the apostles made it into the Bible we have today, with nothing lost and nothing extraneous added? Wasn't the canon—the list of books to be included in the New Testament—put together by fallible men a few generations after Jesus' death?

While it is true that the official list of New Testament books was compiled at the Council of Hippo in AD 393, the church leaders didn't determine what would be included; they discovered what God had inspired. They relied on the testimony of the earliest Christian generation—men such as Polycarp—to determine which epistles and Gospels had been written by the apostles. But long before the Council of Hippo, the early church knew which documents were authentic and showed it by quoting from them, giving them the same weight and importance they gave to the Old Testament scriptures. There was a clear chain of provenance for the church fathers to follow, authenticating the twenty-seven books included in the New Testament as the inspired Word of God.

9. ***Because Jesus said the apostles would be guided into "all truth," what two basic questions did the early Christians need to answer to determine which writings should be considered part of the New Testament canon? (See IDHEF, page 368.)***

10. ***Why did it take so long to officially settle the canon? (See IDHEF, page 370.)***

THE INERRANCY OF THE BIBLE

Is it possible that the Bible contains error? The book provides the following argument:

1. God cannot err.
2. The Bible is the Word of God.
3. Therefore, the Bible cannot err.

In order to prove the conclusion false, we would have to prove that either premise one or two was false. We know that since God is the unchanging standard of truth, He cannot err. (If the being we call God could err, then there would have to be an unchanging standard of truth beyond Him, making that higher being the real God.) So the first premise must be true. And if we deny that the Bible is the Word of God, then we are disagreeing with Jesus, whom, as we have seen, proved beyond a reasonable doubt that He is God. So the second premise must also be true, making the conclusion—that the Bible cannot err—true as well.

Therefore, if we think we have found an error in the Bible, it's more likely that we are in error. Often critics of the Bible will point to seeming problems and claim that nothing the Bible says can be trusted. But most often the "problems" they highlight are simple misunderstandings based on their own faulty assumptions.

NICODEMUS & THE PHARISEES

A prominent Pharisee and a member of the Sanhedrin, the Jewish ruling council, Nicodemus is mentioned three times in the Gospel of John. The first time, he comes by night to speak with Jesus, whom he honors as a great teacher from God (John 3). His second appearance is when he speaks on Jesus' behalf before the Sanhedrin (John 7:51). Lastly, he provides spices and ointments for Jesus' burial, in quantities grand enough for the burial of a king (John 19:39–41).

These three instances sketch a picture of a wealthy and influential Jew, well versed in the Hebrew Scriptures, who came to believe that Jesus is the Son of God. (For why else would he risk the wrath of both the Jews and Romans to honor Jesus in death?) In addition to his high political rank, Nicodemus was a teacher of Israel, meaning that he was

First, some critics assume that divergent accounts of events in the Gospels mean that the accounts contradict each other. This is not the case. Indeed, divergent details offer a fuller view of the event and provide evidence that the authors really were eyewitnesses and didn't get together to create an elaborate hoax.

Second, many critics fail to look at the full context of a passage and draw conclusions based on a fragment of the message. Anyone's words, if taken out of context, can be twisted into something false or something that contradicts the original message.

Third, some critics assume that everything the Bible talks about has God's stamp of approval. This, they say, validates polygamy and murder as just as acceptable to God as self-sacrifice and nobility. But this isn't the case. The Bible clearly distinguishes between commandments and history, and even these unflattering elements are proofs for the authenticity of the Bible.

Fourth, some critics forget that the Bible was written by humans and will thus have human characteristics. Each author brought his own unique style and perspective to the writing, which remained even though every word was inspired by God.

If you are interested in further study of the fallacies of the critics' reasoning, read Dr. Geisler's book *The Big Book of Bible Difficulties*, co-authored with Tom Howe.

known as an authority on the interpretation and application of Scripture. Yet it was difficult for him to understand and believe the things Jesus told him.

As a Pharisee, Nicodemus would have devoted his life to the study of the Scriptures, becoming intimately familiar with both the written law and the oral tradition of the Jews. The Pharisees, though primarily of the middle class, were the most prominent religious party in Israel at that time and dominated the ruling council. They also dictated to the Jewish people the proper habits of worship, prayer, and sacrifice that would please and glorify God. The Pharisees were careful to avoid contact with anything unclean, both impure things and outsiders, separating themselves from anything deemed unholy. They believed it was their duty to keep themselves and the nation of Israel pure, teaching that the way to please God was to obey all of His commands and laws.

Being a member of the Sanhedrin meant that Nicodemus was considered one of the seventy most important men in Israel, even at a time when Palestine was ruled by the Romans. The Sanhedrin was presided over by the high priest, and its members were made up of both Pharisees and Sadducees (a rival party to the Pharisees that was more conservative and aristocratic, but had less influence among the Jewish people). Although the Sanhedrin had the power to try and judge its own people for certain crimes, the Romans had decreed that they did not have the authority to condemn someone to death. So when the Sanhedrin wanted to have Jesus killed, they were forced to take him to the Roman courts for a death sentence to be passed legally.

It is amazing that someone with as much political and religious influence as Nicodemus would risk his career and social standing to ally himself with a poor teacher from Galilee, the backwoods of Israel. Yet he did, growing from a timid seeker who came to Jesus under cover of night into a bold follower of Jesus who helped prepare His body for burial with all the honors due the King of the Jews.

11. If errors are ever found in the New Testament documents, will this necessarily disprove the Resurrection or Christianity? Why or why not?

12. In light of the evidence for God, Jesus, and the Bible, who has to have more faith—the Christian or the non-Christian? Why?

YOU DO THE DIGGING

Jesus never referred to the Bible as a mere book with good teachings that might be comforting or helpful, or even as a book that had good stories in it. Instead, Jesus taught that the entire Bible was the Word of God—not just some of it, but all of it—and that it has ultimate supremacy over any teaching of man. He quoted the Old Testament as authoritative on matters of life. He promised that the Holy Spirit would guide the apostles to write the New Testament. And he scolded religious leaders for nullifying the Word of God by their tradition. Today we need to be careful that we don't allow our own religious traditions and opinions to overrule the written Word of God.

Now it's time to for you to do some digging on your own. Pick at least one of the following assignments and complete it before moving on in the study:

Assignment 1: We know the Old Testament is reliable because of the testimony of Jesus. But the reliability of the Old Testament can be established by other means as well. Research five significant archeological discoveries that affirm the Old Testament. List each discovery and describe how it affirms the historical accuracy of the Old Testament.

Assignment 2: Research the canon of the New Testament and write a two- to three-page paper detailing your findings. Define what the word canon means and list the process the early church fathers went through to discover which books are in the canon.

Assignment 3: Are we sure we have the entire Bible? Could there be other books lost to time? Go to STR.org and search for the January/February 2011 edition of Solid Ground titled "No Lost Books." Summarize the main points in a one- to two-page paper. (You may need to register to access the material.)

Assignment 4: Read the introduction of the book *The Big Book of Bible Difficulties* by Norman Geisler and Tom Howe (formerly titled *When Critics Ask*). Outline the seventeen errors critics make when they say there are problems in the Bible and provide examples for each.

TOOK

WHAT DO I DO NOW?

It might be tempting to tell your non-Christian friends, "Jesus said the Bible was the Word of God and that settles it!" But that could easily cause people to reject you and the faith you are an ambassador for. Think about what it took to help you come to faith in Jesus and belief in the Bible.

As you complete your study of this chapter, think about how your life should reflect not just the evidence that the Bible is the Word of God, but also how Jesus wants people to engage in a personal relationship with Him and accept the free gift of eternal salvation. How can you use the information you've gained from this chapter with non-Christian friends in a way that will bring them closer to the message of the gospel?

THINKING ABOUT WHAT YOU LEARNED

Answer the following questions to sum up what you have learned in this chapter.

How would you respond to a skeptical friend who said that the Christian doctrine of the inerrancy of the Bible isn't falsifiable? (See IDHEF, page 373.)

B. What unique fact sets Christianity apart from any other religion? (See IDHEF, page 374.)

C. From earlier chapters, you know that all nontheistic religions are false because they don't properly explain the universe we live in. Now explain how we can know which of the three theistic religions contains truth (see IDHEF, page 376).

Judaism

Islam

Christianity

GET READY!

I Don't Have Enough Faith to Be an Atheist is only the start of your preparation as a Christian apologist. Since God is an infinite being, we will never completely comprehend Him, His creation, and His purpose for the universe and our lives. God is the only perpetual novelty—you will never become bored with God because there will always be more to explore and learn. There are many books and websites where you can go to continue your study and become a strong ambassador for God. A good place to start is www.CrossExamined.org, which will link you to other sites and resources. Are you prepared to be an ambassador for the Creator of the universe? If you will boldly show the world why you believe in God, Jesus, and the Bible, you will reap rewards now and in eternity.

CONCLUSION

THE JUDGE, THE SERVANT KING, AND THE BOX TOP

BEFORE STARTING THIS CHAPTER

- Read the conclusion of *I Don't Have Enough Faith to Be an Atheist*, pages 377–388.

KEY TOPICS

After completing this chapter, you should be able to:

- Explain and support the importance of God's justice.
- Describe why Jesus' perfect life and crucifixion provides the way for sinners to be reconciled to God.
- List and answer (with supporting scriptures) the five most consequential questions in life.
- Understand the destiny of all mankind and how anyone can experience peace and eternal life with God through Jesus Christ

QUESTIONS THAT GRAB YOUR MIND

Where are most people looking for fulfillment in life? What are their most important questions about life? Where will they find the answers?

Though people come from different cultures and lifestyles and have differing desires, they all seem to ask the same basic questions about what life is all about and what happens when it's over. Just look around. There is abundant evidence that human beings are struggling to answer these questions. Some people are walking pharmacies, using drugs (both prescription and illegal) to ease the symptoms of frustration, confusion, and depression because they can't figure life out. Others devote their lives to work, thinking money and success will make them happy. Others pursue entertainment and pleasure to take their minds off their problems. Some turn to mysticism or the occult, looking for hidden information that can help them know how they are supposed to live.

TV "reality" shows portray the mixed-up lives of people trying to deal with the complexities of everyday life. Self-help titles line the shelves of bookstores and libraries, all purporting to hold the solutions to life's problems. Following sports teams provides people with artificial victories, while watching action movies gives them a sense of adventure. While there is nothing necessarily wrong with cheering on your favorite team, some people put so much time and energy into them because they grasp no real meaning to life beyond them.

The bottom line is that people are searching for meaning in all the wrong places. Nothing the world has to offer will satisfy the void left in their souls by a broken relationship with God. As we've seen throughout this study, only Christianity offers real truth, so only through the teachings of the Bible can people learn what the truth is and how to apply it to their lives. Treating symptoms won't cure the disease. Only by accepting Jesus' sacrifice on the cross and becoming reconciled to God can sin and the symptoms of hopelessness be healed. Can you help them? What can you do to change their hopelessness into fulfillment? Let's find out.

1. ***Why do people invent their own gods rather than turning to the one true God for answers?***

2. ***What would you say to someone who told you, "I believe I am going to heaven because I'm a good person"?***

SO WHAT?

If the Bible is true and you have already accepted the sacrifice Jesus made for you, then you have become an ambassador for the God of the universe. God is working through you to reach others for Him. You need to take all the scientific, logical, and historical evidence provided in this book and use it to let people know that there is a God behind the universe and that He loves them. There can be no higher calling. What you do every day has ultimate meaning, now and into eternity.

FACTS IN THIS CHAPTER

This chapter brings to a conclusion your study of the evidence for God in the universe by providing us with a perspective on God that helps us see His holiness, justice, and love for all people. He has done this so people everywhere can know Him personally and eternally. We now know that the Bible is the "box top" to life and that it provides the answers to the five most consequential questions in life. But that doesn't mean everyone is going to accept those answers. People have a choice. So whom will you serve—God or yourself?

GOD AS JUDGE

There exists a dilemma between God's justice and His love. Think of a set of scales, like the ones Lady Justice carries. For centuries, scales had two containers, one on either side, connected by a horizontal arm and balanced on a vertical stand. Items of value (such as gold nuggets) were placed on one side, and then weights were placed on the other until the two sides balanced. Then a payment was made based on the weight of the valued object.

Now imagine that you could weigh God's love and justice, putting love on one side and justice on the other. Which side would weigh more? Is God's justice greater than His love, or is His love greater than His justice?

The answer is neither. God is infinite in every attribute, including justice and love. In fact, the attributes are coexistent and alone are incomplete—love without justice will not punish sin, and justice without love will not offer forgiveness. The results of one without the other would be devastating.

When an infinitely just God judges sinful human beings, there arises a kind of dilemma between His justice and His love. He must punish sin due to His justice, but He also wants to forgive sin due to His love. His solution? He chose to save mankind from the consequences of sin by punishing a sinless substitute who voluntarily took our punishment for us. And so God remains just, in that our sin has been properly punished, yet He showed His love and mercy by paying the price for our sins Himself.

3. Why can't good works cancel out bad works?

4. In light of God's infinite justice and infinite love, why must Jesus be the only way to eternal salvation? Why is John 14:6 not just an arbitrary claim?

RECONCILIATION BECAUSE OF JESUS' PERFECT LIFE AND CRUCIFIXION

The only way God could satisfy His justice and love was to send His Son to take our punishment. So Jesus, the second Person of the Trinity, voluntarily gave up His divine place and took on human form to reach us. As Philippians 2:7 says, "He made himself nothing, taking the very nature of a servant." It was God's infinite love that sent Jesus to take on the role of a humble human servant and to endure an agonizingly painful death so that God's infinite justice could be satisfied. Here's how it works:

a. God loved His sinful creations, but needed payment for their sins in order to satisfy His just nature.
b. So He offered up His only Son—a flawless substitute—as the payment that would satisfy His requirement for justice.
c. Accepting that payment enables us to be reconciled to God.
d. We are not just forgiven, but we are also given Jesus' righteousness in the eyes of God. His righteousness is imputed to us. So when God looks at us, He sees Jesus' perfection, not our sins and struggles.

That's the effortless beauty of the gospel. There is nothing we can do to earn salvation—we can only accept the gift of salvation, freely offered, and become reconciled to God.

5. ***Show from Philippians 2:5–8 how Jesus' humility gave us the offer of salvation without negating our ability to accept it.***

6. ***What is the moral of the story of the Servant King?***

THE FIVE MOST CONSEQUENTIAL QUESTIONS

In the introduction to the book, we discussed the five most consequential questions in life. You learned that the answers to each of these questions depend on the existence of truth and God, the possibility of miracles, and the historical reliability of the New Testament documents (and ultimately the entire Bible). Because the evidence shows that truth exists (points 1 and 2), a Being outside of our universe exists (point 3), miracles are possible in a theistic universe (points 4 and 5), and the Bible is historically true and theologically reliable (points 6–12), then we know that the answers to the five most consequential questions in life are discoverable and can be found in the Bible.

7. ***For each question below, provide the answer and include a supporting scripture.***

   a. Where did we come from?

b. Who are we?

c. Why are we here?

d. How should we live?

e. Where are we going?

WHY HELL IS LOVING AND NECESSARY

The following is adapted from a brief article by Frank Turek written for the book *Is God a Human Invention?* by Sean McDowell and Jonathan Morrow.

> I have often doubted the existence of hell. The concept of eternal punishment bothers me. But upon reflection, hell, like many other Christian doctrines, seems not only fair, but also necessary. How so? Let me ask you a couple of questions: Have you ever been abused, exploited, or dissed? Have you ever been mistreated, lied to, or victimized in any way?
>
> We all have to some degree. It feels horrible enough, but how much worse do you feel when the culprits get away with it—when the guilty escape justice? I don't know about you, but that makes my blood boil. I want justice! In fact, I demand it.
>
> If there is no afterlife, then there is no ultimate justice. People who have committed some of most horrific acts in history go to their grave without ever getting punished for their deeds. After murdering at least six million people, Hitler died in the comforting arms of his mistress and experienced nothing else.

After murdering more than twice that many, Stalin died in bed after shaking his fist one last time at God. And millions of unknown murderers, rapists, and child abusers throughout history never got their just deserts during their lives on earth.

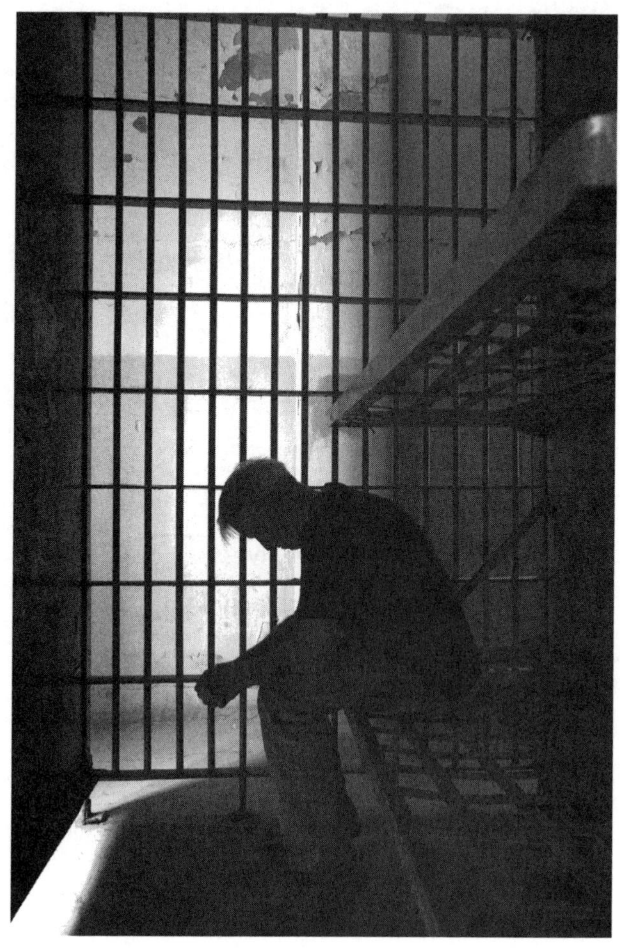

If there is a God—and there is much convincing evidence that there is—then hell is necessary for people like this. But what about your average non-believers? Why hell for them?

I have debated atheist Christopher Hitchens a couple of times. Sadly, Hitchens died in December 2011. I can tell you he wasn't a Hitler or a Stalin. He was a sinner just like you and me. But Hitchens admitted that he didn't want to go to heaven even if it exists. Why not? Because heaven would be "hell" to him. He didn't want to be in God's presence here on earth, so why would he want to be with God in eternity? He wanted to be separated from God, and separation from God is ultimately what hell is.

God gives us the free will to reject Him and His offer of forgiveness. Free will means even God can't force us to love Him. Love, by definition, must be freely given; it cannot be coerced. So God doesn't send people to hell—people send themselves there. (A loving God certainly will not force people into heaven against their will.) He respects our choices and separates Himself forever from those who don't want Him.

But why forever? First, it wouldn't be right of God to annihilate unbelievers. Hitchens is made in the image of God just like all of us. God cannot annihilate His own image. That would be an attack on Himself. So He quarantines those who reject Him. Second, a crime can take only seconds to commit, but the punishment is typically much longer (especially a crime against an eternal being). Third, it may be that those in hell go on sinning in the next life, thereby continuing their rebellion against an eternal God. Finally, since God is perfectly just, everyone will receive the perfect degree of punishment in hell or reward in heaven.

So despite my doubts, since God is just and loving, hell is necessary. In fact, hell is the main reason Jesus came (Mark 10:45). If there is no hell, what is He saving us from? If there is no hell, an innocent Jesus died a brutal death for nothing. Guess I ought to start doubting my doubts and let everyone know about what Jesus has done! How about you?

8. ***Why won't God just annihilate unbelievers after death? On the flip side, why can't God just save everybody?***

9. ***Why is free will a vital part of God's plan? Why must every person be given the chance to either accept God or reject Him?***

10. ***How would you answer a friend who said that God is evil for sending people to hell?***

YOU DO THE DIGGING

This last chapter presents a loving God who must judge sin. He has been reaching out to people since Adam and Eve's fall in the Garden of Eden. His ultimate act of love was to send His Son Jesus to suffer and die in payment of our sin. This is a powerful message—especially in a culture that sees God as a killjoy—and is one you should be ready to share with the people you meet at school, work, sports, etc.

Despite the fact that you have all this evidence now—and hopefully can articulate it in a loving and persuasive way—don't expect everyone to immediately accept Jesus as their Savior. Why? Because some will cling to their own beliefs in spite of the evidence. Others simply don't want to submit to God for a variety of reasons. (Christopher Hitchens, for example, seemed mad at God. That's why at our debates I summarized Christopher's attitude in one sentence: "There is no God, and I hate Him!") Your job is to be faithful to share the good news and then leave the results to God.

Now it's time for you to do some digging on your own. Pick at least one of the following assignments and complete it before moving on in the study:

Assignment 1: Research the other two major theistic religions—Islam and Judaism—and make a chart that compares the following:

a. Their background/history
b. Their major figures and scriptures
c. Their views of:
   Sin
   Heaven
   Hell
   Jesus
   Salvation
   Eternity (or final destiny)

Assignment 2: Go to www.CrossExamined.org and watch one of Frank Turek's debates with Christopher Hitchens. List the arguments made by each debater. What did you think were the strong and weak arguments in the debate? Do you think Hitchens's resistance to God is intellectual or a matter of personal choice? Why?

Assignment 3: The textbook ends by pointing out that people will still have doubts and questions. In fact, doubts can be good because they compel a person to look for answers. However, they can also be difficult to overcome for some. Go to www.GaryHabermas.com and look up articles on doubt. Summarize the points in outline form. How might you help yourself or others overcome doubts and questions?

WHAT DO I DO NOW?

Your study of this book is nearly finished, but your work has just begun. We hope you have learned a great deal through examining the evidence presented here. Now you have the privilege to go out and share this wonderful news with the people God brings your way. Remember to be a compassionate ambassador for God, always sharing the truth in love!

THINKING ABOUT WHAT YOU LEARNED

Answer the following questions to sum up what you have learned in this study:

A. When it comes to Jesus, what's the difference between belief that He is the Savior and belief in Him as savior. Do you believe in Him or just that He existed?

B. Do you still have doubts about Christianity? Are they intellectual, emotional, or volitional? In light of the evidence, is it more reasonable to doubt the Bible or to doubt your doubts? Do you have to have all the answers right now?

C. What are three specific, tangible things you can do after finishing this study to continue your apologetics training?

D. Do you know people who need to accept Jesus as Savior? Choose four or five and write their names below. Commit to pray for them every day for a month, asking that God would prepare their hearts to hear the kind of evidence you've been studying. Also pray for opportunities to share your newfound knowledge with them. When you get such an opportunity, remember to be tactful—the best way to witness is through your lifestyle, showing every day that what you believe changes the way you live. If you encounter resistance, ask these two questions:

1. "If I ask you an important spiritual question, will you give me a brutally honest answer?" (Most people will say yes.) Then ask . . .

2. "If Christianity were true, would you become a Christian?" The answer will reveal how much of the person's objection is intellectual and how much is emotional or moral.

It can be easy when you finish a course to put your notes away and forget about what you have learned. The knowledge and information you have obtained through this course will prove invaluable over your lifetime. You must continue to deepen your knowledge of apologetics and grow in your relationship with Jesus and the knowledge of His Word to become a truly mature Christian.

MAKE AN ETERNAL DIFFERENCE!
In the end, there are only two kinds of people: those who accept Jesus and those who reject Him. Dr. Tony Evans advises those who reject Jesus to enjoy life now, because this is the only heaven they're ever going to experience. He also comforts those who have accepted Jesus by telling them to hang in there, because this is the only hell they're ever going to experience!

A loving God will not force anyone into heaven against his or her will. Those who don't want God now will not want Him in eternity either. However, your love for people can create opportunities to reach those people who presently seem unreachable. Some of your friends may mock you, but if you love them, they may call on you when they are faced with a crisis because they know you are a person of spiritual depth. Your prayers and friendship will have won you the opportunity to make an eternal difference. You can't prepare then, so start praying and preparing now.

APPENDIX I

IF GOD, WHY EVIL?

1. How does the objection from evil backfire on the atheist?

2. What is the ultimate source of evil?

3. ***Good can come out of evil (Genesis 50:20). What can we learn from suffering?***

4. ***We have finite knowledge and a temporal perspective, but God has infinite knowledge and an eternal perspective. How should this knowledge affect how we look at a specific situation when we can't see a good reason for evil?***

5. ***How would you answer a friend who asked why bad things happen to good people?***

6. ***According to the Bible, what will God ultimately do about evil?***

APPENDIX 2

ISN'T THAT JUST YOUR INTERPRETATION?

1. How would you respond to a friend who said, "That is just your interpretation"?

2. How would you respond to a friend who said, "Christianity is too exclusive"?

3. ***How would you respond to a friend who said "Christians are so intolerant—you think you have the only truth"?***

4. ***The most popular Bible verse in America fifty years ago was John 3:16. Now most people, even those who do not believe the Bible, are very familiar with Matthew 7:1, which says, "Judge not!" How is that verse taken out of context? And why is it self-defeating to claim that a person shouldn't judge others?***

5. ***Why is Christianity the only major worldview that secures human rights and champions religious freedom?***

6. ***Christians are not called to be tolerant so much as they are called to be loving. What's the difference? Is it ever right to be intolerant?***

APPENDIX 3

WHY THE JESUS SEMINAR DOESN'T SPEAK FOR JESUS

1. The Wrong Group: Who are the members of the Jesus Seminar?

2. The Wrong Motive: What's their motive?

3. The Wrong Procedure: How do they determine whether Jesus really said what's in the gospels?

4. The Wrong Books: Which books do they cite as authoritative over the Gospels of Matthew and Mark?

5. ***The Wrong Assumptions:* *Which clearly wrong assumptions do they make?***

6. ***The Wrong Dates:* *What dates do they give to the Gospels? How do we know those dates are too late? Why do they want the dates of the gospels to be late?***

GLOSSARY

Absolute truth—*Something that is true for all people, at all times, and in all places. Absolute truth is objective and unchanging.*

A.D.—*An abbreviation used indicate the period of history after Jesus' birth. The abbreviation stands for anno domini, a Latin phrase meaning "in the year of our Lord." It is equivalent to the Jewish abbreviation C.E., which stands for the "common era."*

Agnostic—*Someone who is unsure whether or not God exists or believes the truth of His existence cannot be known.*

Anomaly—*A rare, unexplained natural occurrence. Unlike a miracle, an anomaly is not connected with a truth claim and does not necessarily have a moral or theological meaning.*

Anthropic Constants—*Precise interdependent environmental conditions or factors about the universe that permit life to exist on Earth. The word anthropic comes from the Greek word for "mankind."*

Anthropic Principle—*A scientific principle that states the universe is extremely fine-tuned and designed specifically to support human life on Earth.*

Apologist—*Someone who shows how logic, reason, and evidence support or contradict a particular belief.*

Apostle—*A term for one of the followers of Jesus who witnessed Him after His resurrection. The word is derived from the Greek word apostolos, meaning "one who is sent forth as a messenger."*

Atheist—*Someone who does not believe any type of god exists.*

B.C.—*An abbreviation used to indicate the period of history before Jesus' birth. The abbreviation stands for "before Christ." It is equivalent to the Jewish abbreviation B.C.E, which stands for "before the common era."*

Big Bang Theory—*The scientific theory that the entire universe (space-time and matter) exploded into existence out of nothing.*

Canon—*A Latin word meaning "measuring rod" or "standard." In Christianity, it is the collection of inspired books, written and confirmed as authentic by the apostles, that make up the New Testament. Also refers to inspired Old Testament books*

Cosmic background radiation—*Remnant heat from the Big Bang explosion in the form of microwave radiation that has been subsequently stretched and cooled as the universe expanded.*

Cosmological Argument—*The argument that states that because the universe had a beginning, it must have had a cause.*

Council of Hippo—*The universal church council held in A.D. 393 in the Algerian city of Hippo. The council officially confirmed the canon of the New Testament.*

Creeds—*Compact declarations of belief that could easily be remembered in order to be passed along orally (e.g., 1 Corinthians 15:3–8).*

Deduction—*The logical process of lining up premises in an argument in order to arrive at a valid conclusion.*

DNA *(deoxyribonucleic acid)—The chemical that encodes instructions for building and replicating all living things.*

Early Church Fathers—*First-, second- and third-century figures in the Christian church who formulated doctrines and codified religious observances.*

Empiricism—*A theory that asserts that knowledge comes only or primarily through sense experience.*

Essenes—*A Jewish sect that existed in ancient Palestine from the second century B.C. to the first century after Christ's birth. The Essenes are traditionally thought to have been responsible for copying and preserving the Dead Sea Scrolls.*

First Law of Thermodynamics—*The scientific principle that states the total amount of energy in the universe is constant.*

Forensic—*A branch of science that focuses on explaining past events by observing evidence left behind.*

Fossil Record—*A paleontological term that refers to all the fossils that have been discovered, as well as to the information derived from them.*

General Revelation—*Things we can discover about God just from observing the universe around us (creation) or the Moral Law within us (conscience).*

Genetic Limits—*The limits to genetic change that appear to be built into biological creatures, allowing each kind to only make another of that kind, and calling into question the plausibility of macroevolution.*

Historical Reliability—*Describes a document or documents that have been confirmed to be telling the truth about past events.*

Induction—*The logical process of drawing general conclusions from specific observations (for example, the scientific method).*

Inerrancy—*The biblical principle that states the original manuscripts of the Bible are free of error.*

Infallibility—*The biblical principle that states the Bible's assertions are truthful and worthy of entire confidence (in contrast to fallible human words).*

Intelligent Design—*The scientific theory that says some features of the universe and life exhibit features that are positive evidence of having been designed.*

Irreducible Complexity—*A scientific idea that states many of the systems we observe in biological entities are composed of multiple interacting parts, where the removal of any part would cause the system to cease to function, which would preclude the system from being built gradually (as in Darwinian evolution).*

Kalam Cosmological Argument—*A philosophical argument for the beginning of time that states that because there cannot exist an infinite number of days before today, the universe must have had a beginning.*

Law of Causality—*The scientific law that states everything that had a beginning had a cause.*

Law of Entropy—*The scientific law that states without intervention, things tend to dissolve from order to disorder. This is also an aspect of the Second Law of Thermodynamics.*

Law of Non-contradiction—*A self-evident first principle of logic which states that contradictory claims cannot both be true at the same time and in the same sense.*

Law of the Excluded Middle—*A self-evident first principle of logic which states that something either is or is not—there is no middle alternative.*

Macroevolution—*The scientific theory that all life forms have descended from a common ancestor by natural processes without intelligent intervention. This has never been observed in nature.*

Manuscripts—*Handwritten copies of the original documents.*

Martyr—*A person who chooses to suffer death rather than renounce his/her religious principles.*

Materialism—*The philosophical theory that only physical things exist and that everything—including thought, feeling, mind, and will—can be explained in terms of matter and physical phenomena.*

Microevolution—*The change in gene frequency in a given population, normally in response to environmental pressures. It is adaptation within a species, rather than transformation into another species (macroevolution).*

Miracle—*A supernatural act of God, often used to confirm the words of God through a messenger of God.*

Molecular Isolation—*The scientific observation that the comparison of protein sequences in living organisms reveals distinct gaps between supposedly ancestral forms.*

Moral Law—*A philosophical argument for the existence of God which states that the existence of moral principles (basic, unchanging, objective principles of right behavior) shows that a moral Law-giver exists as well.*

Natural Selection—*A scientific theory which states that the individuals or groups best suited to their environment will survive; assumed by atheistic scientists to be a mechanism of evolution.*

Naturalism—*The philosophical idea that all phenomena can be explained in terms of natural causes and laws and thus excludes the possibility of the supernatural or spiritual.*

Panspermia—*A theory of the origin of life (originally suggested by evolutionist Fred Hoyle) which states that aliens seeded Earth with life from space. The word means "seeds everywhere."*

Pantheist—*Someone who believes that god is the universe—an impersonal god that exists in every part of the universe, including rocks, trees, you, and me.*

Pharisees—*A Jewish sect that emphasized strict interpretation and observance of the Mosaic law in both its oral and written form. The Pharisees were often rebuked by Jesus as legalists whose hearts were far from God.*

Pluralism—*The philosophical idea that all religions are equally acceptable and true, and that all religions lead to God in the end.*

Polytheist—*Someone who believes in many gods.*

Principle of Uniformity—*A scientific principle which states that causes in the past were like those in the present. For example, the principle of uniformity would require us to conclude that if something requires intelligence to come to be today, it must have required intelligence to come to be in the past.*

Prophecy—*An inspired utterance that is a revelation of divine will.*

Providence—*Events caused by God indirectly, employing natural causes or everyday circumstances.*

Psychosomatic—*Relating to the influence of the mind on the body, especially with respect to disease.*

Reductionism—*The philosophical theory that a complex idea or system can be completely reduced to its simpler parts or components. For example, some atheists believe life is nothing but chemicals.*

Relativism—*The philosophical notion that no ideas or beliefs are universally true; instead, all ideas are relative and dependent on the circumstances in which they are applied.*

Road Runner Tactic—*A method applying the law of non-contradiction to identify and refute self-defeating statements.*

Sanhedrin—*The judicial and ecclesiastical council of the ancient Jews, composed of seventy members and led by the high priest.*

Science—*Generally, a search for causes, usually by means of observation and repetition.*

Second Law of Thermodynamics—*The scientific principle that the universe is running out of usable energy and that nature as a whole is moving toward disorder rather than order.*

Self-defeating statement—*A statement that fails to meet its own standard and therefore cannot be true.*

Septuagint—*A Greek translation of the Hebrew Scriptures that dates from the third century B.C.*

Situational Ethics—*A relative system of ethics that evaluates acts in light of their context without appeal to moral absolutes.*

Skeptic—*Someone who doubts certain propositions or beliefs, typically religious beliefs.*

Special revelation—*Information we receive about God and Jesus that comes only from the Bible.*

Specified complexity—*An observable characteristic in living and non-living things that indicates design; something that has not only complexity, but also contains a specific message. For example, a group of random letters is complex but not specified. A sentence, such as "Take out the garbage, Son" is complex and specified and is positive evidence for an intelligent being.*

Spontaneous Generation—*The belief that life generated spontaneously from nonliving chemicals by natural laws without any intelligent intervention.*

Tanach—*The Hebrew Scriptures, a sacred book of Judaism consisting of the Torah, the Prophets, and the Writings.*

Teleological Argument—*An argument for the existence of God based on the evidence of order, purpose, and design in nature; from the Greek word telos, meaning "design."*

Theist—*Someone who believes in a personal God who created and sustains the universe but is not physically a part of the universe.*

Theories—*A set of statements or principles devised to explain a group of facts or phenomena, especially one that has been repeatedly tested or is widely accepted. Theories often can be used to make predictions about natural phenomena.*

Tolerance—*Treating those with different ideas respectfully and civilly. Unfortunately, some now believe that tolerance requires you to accept their ideas as true.*

Trinity—*The theological doctrine that God is one divine essence of three persons—the Father, Son, and Holy Spirit.*

Truth—*That which corresponds to its object or which describes an actual state of affairs.*

Volitional—*The act of willing, choosing, or resolving.*

ACKNOWLEDGMENTS

We are grateful for the hard work and helpful suggestions of the many who contributed in some way to this curriculum. Amanda Lewis, David Webb, Zan Tyler, Doug Powell, and the rest of the Apologia team led by Davis Carman, clarified the text, developed the layout, and added the outstanding biographies and graphics that make this work readable and attractive. Buff Winter, Stephanie Turek, Larry Blythe, and Christi Deason also offered helpful suggestions and corrections. Thanks to Dr. Norman Geisler for co-authoring the original *I Don't Have Enough Faith to Be an Atheist*, and to Southern Evangelical Seminary professors Dr. Tom Howe, Dr. Richard Howe, and Dr. Barry Leventhal who all have impacted this curriculum through their teachings in immeasurable ways.

ABOUT THE AUTHORS

Dr. Frank Turek is the award-winning author or coauthor of the books *I Don't Have Enough Faith to Be an Atheist*, *Legislating Morality*, and *Correct, Not Politically Correct*. As president of CrossExamined.org, Frank speaks to youth and adults at colleges, high schools, and churches, providing hard yet entertaining evidence for Christianity. He hosts the television series *I Don't Have Enough Faith to Be an Atheist* and the national radio program *CrossExamined with Frank Turek* and has appeared on many other programs including *The O'Reilly Factor*, *Hannity and Colmes*, *Politically Incorrect*, "The Bible Answer Man," and "Focus on the Family." A former aviator in the U.S. Navy, Frank holds a Doctorate in apologetics from Southern Evangelical Seminary.

Chuck Winter passed away shortly after completing this book. A gifted teacher and musician, Chuck helped plant several churches in North Carolina, South Carolina, and Florida. He is survived by his wife of thirty-six years and their three children.